StarLIT™ Literacy Intervention Toolkit Phonological Awareness

Teacher's Resource Guide

ETA 60314
ISBN 0-7406-3943-9

ETA/Cuisenaire • Vernon Hills, IL 60061-1862
800-445-5985 • www.etacuisenaire.com

Product Development Manager: Mary Watanabe
Consultant: Susan L. Hall, Ed.D.
Lead Editor: Carol Allison
Editorial Team: Barbara Wrobel and Samira Guyot
Production Manager: Jeanette Pletsch
Creative Services Manager: Barry Daniel Petersen
Graphic Designers: Elina Saksonova and Tiara Lynn Banovez

Printed in China.

05 06 07 08 09 10 11 12 13 14   10 9 8 7 6 5 4 3 2 1

Contents

StarLIT Literacy Intervention Toolkit for Phonological Awareness includes the following tools and manipulative materials:

	Quantity	Word Level	Syllable Level	Onset/Rime Level	Phoneme Isolation Level	Phoneme Segmentation and Blending Level	Phoneme Manipulation Level
Large Pocket Chart	1	●	●	●	●	●	●
Student Pocket Chart	6	●		●		●	
Segmenting, Blending, and Sorting Mat	6		●	●		●	●
Write 'N' Wipe Board	1						
Reading Rods® Picture Rods	52		●	●		●	
Reading Rods Phonological Awareness Pocket Chart Cards	52		●		●	●	●
Compound Word Picture Cards	24		●				
Rhyme Picture Cards	72			●		●	
Link 'N' Learn® Links	36	●				●	
SunSprouts® Wolf Puppet	1		●			●	●
Insects and Arachnids Learning Place® Game Cards	1 set		●		●	●	●
Fruits and Vegetables Learning Place Game Cards	1 set		●		●	●	●
Craft Sticks	10	●					
Frog Counters	36	●				●	●
Bear Counters	36	●					●
Bug Counters	36		●				●
Fruity Fun™ Counters	36		●			●	
Quiet Counters	36	●		●		●	●
Sorting Bowls	6	●				●	
Mystery Bag	1		●		●	●	●
Game Spinner	1	●	●			●	
Blank Cards	6	●		●			
StoryBlossoms® small books, *Eeny Meeny Miney Mouse* and *Fred Told Me*	2			●			●

The Reading Rods® teaching method is covered by U.S. Patent No. 6,685,477. Other U.S. and foreign patents pending.

Introduction

The StarLIT™ Literacy Intervention Toolkit for Phonological Awareness from ETA/Cuisenaire® offers intensive, explicit, systematic, and supportive intervention instruction in the six levels of phonological awareness. StarLIT uses existing assessment data to guide teachers in knowing where to intervene, how to get started, and how to accelerate learning for at-risk students. A companion to a core language arts instruction program, StarLIT contains everything teachers need for small group instruction. Fresh, new scripted activities, convenient instructional tools, unique and colorful student manipulatives, and creative extensions move students through small, incremental steps toward success. Portable and ready-to-use, StarLIT allows teachers simply to open the toolkit and begin to "help all children shine!"™

Help All Children Shine

The StarLIT Literacy Intervention Toolkit for Phonological Awareness is ideal for all schools, including those that receive Reading First federal funding. Primarily intended for classroom teachers, this kit is designed for use with groups of kindergarten and grade one children who need intervention instruction because of their below-benchmark scores on early literacy screening instruments. It is valuable to classroom teachers, as well as Title I teachers, reading resource teachers, special education teachers, teachers of students who are English language learners, and instructional aides.

The Next Step of Instruction

Many teachers have administered early literacy assessments and therefore have assessment data that indicates which children may be at future risk for reading difficulties. Often teachers have organized children into small homogeneous groups to focus on specific phonological awareness skills.

StarLIT helps teachers determine the next step of instruction to target specific phonological skills and strategies. It offers sound, clear lesson plans to explicitly and systematically teach phonological awareness skills. Considering that intervention is not a child's first instruction, teachers need fresh, new activities with colorful and fun, hands-on materials for children who learn in a variety of ways. StarLIT has been specially designed to meet those needs. It provides teachers with ready-to-use materials and instructional tools to conduct short, engaging learning experiences to promote children's achievement.

For Small Group Intervention

StarLIT is designed for small group intervention instruction, not whole class or core reading instruction. Teachers often present some phonological awareness activities to the whole class, and some children master the skills from this instruction alone. For any child who does not make adequate progress with the whole class, small group instruction is recommended. The National Reading Panel Report suggests that instruction in phonological awareness is most effective when taught in small groups.

A Companion to Your Reading Program

The phonological awareness instruction in this toolkit is delivered in a focused and targeted manner. For this reason it is important to emphasize that StarLIT is not intended to constitute the entire reading curriculum for kindergarten or any other grade. It is intended to be a companion to a language arts core instructional program in which all the components of reading instruction are well taught in an integrated fashion.

StarLIT is an intervention program designed for use during small-group instruction for homogeneously grouped children who require special help in developing a sufficient level of phonological awareness. Therefore, children who receive this focused phonological awareness instruction are also receiving instruction in all the other essential components of reading in their core program, including the alphabetic principle, vocabulary, letter knowledge, and comprehension.

Sound Organization and Development

Activities in this kit are organized by phonological awareness skill and level of difficulty. There is a systematic and sequential development of skills from awareness of larger phonological units like words or syllables, to smaller units such as phonemes. Activity lesson plans are based on a format of presenting a lesson overview, modeling the activity, continuing the activity together, and allowing for independent work. Activity extensions and adaptations are included for each lesson.

Portable Resource

StarLIT is ideal for intervention teachers who find it difficult to assemble, create, organize, store, and carry all the materials they need for small group lessons. This complete and portable resource allows teachers to maximize teaching time. Instructional tools are built in to allow teachers to set up quickly and conduct lessons anywhere. Even the back of the case can be used as a pocket chart as the teacher models an activity. Materials for children's use are organized in closable pouches and pockets. All materials in this self-contained toolkit can be secured and compactly stored for later use.

Unique Advantages

Unique to the marketplace, StarLIT offers this expansive *Teacher's Resource Guide,* which includes engaging and developmentally appropriate activities, research-based background information, and adaptable sample lesson plans. By combining everything in one complete kit, teachers are free to dedicate their time to teaching and working with children.

Advantages of StarLIT over activity and teacher resource books:

- Offers a systematic and sequential progression of phonological awareness skills
- Delivers information on reading research, phonological awareness background, and effective intervention strategies
- Contains 38 scripted, engaging activities that are pedagogically sound
- Provides ready-to-use teacher tools and materials for children
- Contains safe, colorful, and fun manipulatives for children
- Allows ease of storage and portability

Overview of Program Components

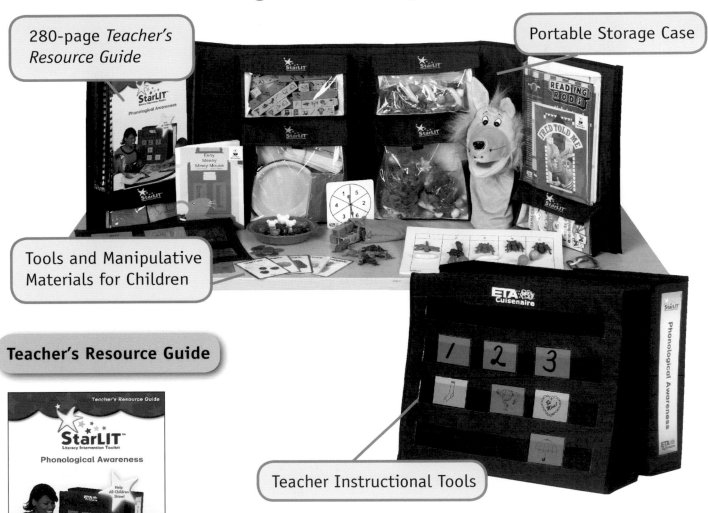

280-page *Teacher's Resource Guide*

Portable Storage Case

Tools and Manipulative Materials for Children

Teacher's Resource Guide

Teacher Instructional Tools

Introduction

The StarLIT *Teacher's Resource Guide* is organized in three sections. The first section contains the introduction, background information, and information on the phonological awareness continuum. Included in the background information is an overview of major research findings on effective phonological awareness instruction and a discussion about how intervention instruction is different from classroom core reading instruction.

Phonological Awareness Activities

The second section contains thirty-eight activities divided into six units, based on the level of phonological awareness. Four pages of instruction are included for each activity, including background for the teacher and scripted lesson pages for use with children. Activities follow a standard format, including the following sections:

List of Materials

Purpose

Model the Activity

Independent Activity

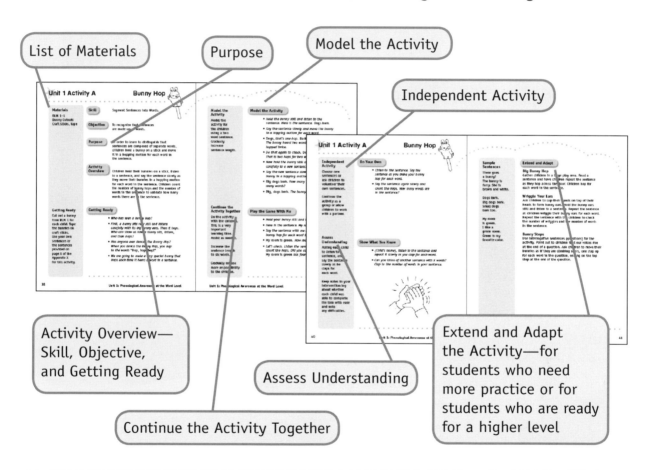

Activity Overview— Skill, Objective, and Getting Ready

Continue the Activity Together

Assess Understanding

Extend and Adapt the Activity—for students who need more practice or for students who are ready for a higher level

Lesson pages include scripted plans for the teacher organized under the following lesson areas:

- Getting Ready
- Model the Activity
- Play the Game with Me
- On Your Own
- Show What You Know

In addition, each plan concludes with specific suggestions for further independent work by children.

Sample Lesson Plans

The third section of the Teacher's Resource Guide contains Sample Lesson Plans. The purpose of including lesson plans is not to provide teachers with an exhaustive series of lessons. These lesson plans serve as samples for how teachers can think about designing their own lessons and provide models for teachers who wish to create additional activity lessons. StarLIT is an intervention toolkit, not a reading program. To vary instruction, teachers can adapt the materials in this kit to include many other materials from the classroom.

Carefully selected materials include a series of lesson plans for one week. Lesson plans from both an earlier and a later stage of development of phonological skills show how lessons change over time as children make progress in skill development.

Lesson Plan Format

Consistent lesson plan format includes:

- Stated instructional focus
- Area to record data that led to group placement
- Time allocation
- Activities to be taught
- Specificity about level of phonological awareness
- Specificity about the skill: for example, beginning, ending, or middle sounds

Appendices

Appendix I—Pronunciation of Phonemes
Appendix II—Minimal and Maximal Pairs
Appendix III—Syllables and Phonemes Chart
Appendix IV—Teacher's Notes

Phonological Awareness: A Critical Reading Skill

Phonological awareness is one of the major skill areas in early reading, and it is linked in critical ways to other language skills. In phonological awareness instruction, teachers focus childrens' attention on the separate and distinct units of sound in words. To become good readers and spellers, children need to have an awareness of each individual sound in a word and must be able to manipulate those sounds. The six stages of phonological awareness include:

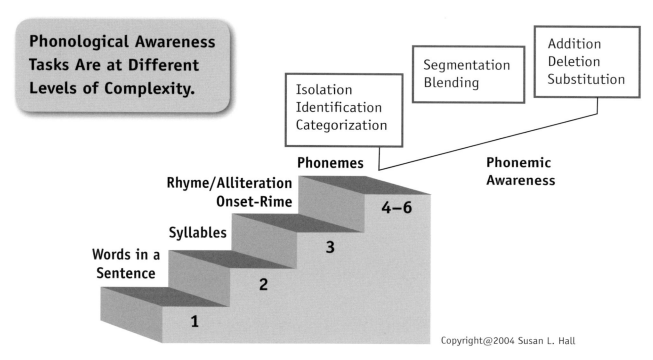

Phonological Awareness Tasks Are at Different Levels of Complexity.

Isolation
Identification
Categorization

Segmentation
Blending

Addition
Deletion
Substitution

Phonemes

Phonemic Awareness

Rhyme/Alliteration Onset-Rime

Syllables

Words in a Sentence

Copyright@2004 Susan L. Hall

1. Segmenting Sentences into Words
2. Segmenting Words into Syllables
3. Rhyme, Alliteration, and Onset and Rime
4. Phoneme Isolation, Identification, and Categorization
5. Phoneme Segmentation and Blending
6. Phoneme Addition, Deletion, and Substitution

The Link with Language Skills

Phonological awareness is linked with many other aspects of language development. Learning to isolate and manipulate the sounds in words is not an isolated language skill. Developing an awareness of the sounds in words is linked with childrens' oral language and vocabulary. There are reciprocal relationships between phonological awareness and many other language skills, including letter knowledge and vocabulary. In other words, children who have large oral vocabularies may have stronger levels of phonological awareness (Nagy and Scott, 2000). Developing more knowledge about letter names increases the growth of phonological awareness. Language skills reinforce one another.

Purpose of Phonological Awareness

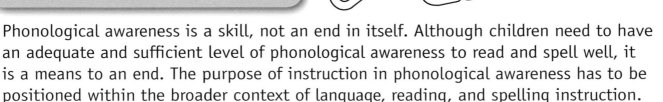

Phonological awareness is a skill, not an end in itself. Although children need to have an adequate and sufficient level of phonological awareness to read and spell well, it is a means to an end. The purpose of instruction in phonological awareness has to be positioned within the broader context of language, reading, and spelling instruction. It is one small but important component of language and reading development.

Integration of Language Skills

It is critical to keep in mind how the relationships between the different areas of reading impact instruction. In the course of instruction, teachers should take advantage of opportunities to integrate instruction in other skills into lessons that are primarily focused on developing phonological awareness. For example, if children are using the word *dragonfly* to segment syllables, the teacher can seize that moment to talk about dragonflies, provide some background knowledge about them, and make sure that all children have an opportunity to include this word in their oral language.

Feedback and Practice

Children who struggle with phonological awareness need explicit instruction followed by opportunities for feedback and the time to practice. One of the most important things struggling children need is immediate feedback and correction of their errors so that they can understand what they need to change and try it again right away. If a group is too large, it is impossible for a teacher to hear every child. Research suggests that small groups are better than one-to-one instruction for work in phonological awareness because it is helpful for children to listen to one another. Therefore, groups of three to five children are ideal for StarLIT.

Reading Research

Early Identification

One of the most significant insights of the past decade in the field of early reading is that promp identification of difficulties, coupled with effective intervention, can avert reading problems for many children. It is now possible for schools to accurately predict which children are at risk of later difficulties by screening all kindergarten through third grade children with effective early literacy assessment instruments (Torgesen, 2004).

Early Intervention

Equally important, research has demonstrated that by providing small group intervention instruction, many children can be caught up to benchmark standards and will read at grade level before the end of third grade. Another important finding is that the earlier the intervention is provided, the better. According to the National Institute of Child Health and Human Development, one of the National Institutes of Health, it takes four times as long to intervene in fourth grade as it does in late kindergarten (Lyons, 1994). This means that it may take two hours of instruction a day to improve a child's skills in fourth grade compared to 30 minutes of daily intervention in kindergarten.

National Reading Panel Report

The news about the effectiveness of early screening and intervention came on the heels of a decade of increasing attention to the importance of phonological awareness skills in early reading. This focus on phonological awareness was supported when the National Reading Panel (NRP) Report, which was published in 2000, described phonological awareness as one of several important topics in understanding the research about reading.

The panel's report discussed the converging evidence that children who receive instruction in phonological awareness will become better readers. The NRP not only recommended that reading instruction include phonological awareness but also stated that it is essential for children who struggle in early reading.

The focus of phonological awareness is broad. It includes identifying and manipulating larger parts of spoken language, such as words, syllables, and onsets and rimes—as well as phonemes. It also encompasses awareness of other aspects of sound, such as rhyme, alliteration, and intonation. Phonemic awareness is a subcategory of phonological awareness. The focus is narrow—identifying and manipulating the individual sounds in words. The following excerpt from the National Institute for Literacy's Report, <u>Put Reading First</u>, describes the important of phonemic awareness in learning to read.

Put Reading First: The Research Building Blocks for Teaching Children to Read

What does scientifically-based research tell us about phonemic awareness instruction?

Key findings from the scientific research on phonemic awareness instruction provide the following conclusions of particular interest and value to classroom teachers:

Phonemic awareness can be taught and learned.

Effective phonemic awareness instruction teaches children to notice, think about, and work with (manipulate) sounds in spoken language. Teachers use many activities to build phonemic awareness, including:

Phoneme isolation
Children recognize individual sounds in a word.

Phoneme identity
Children recognize the same sounds in different words.

Phoneme categorization
Children recognize the word in a set of three or four words that has the "odd" sound.

Phoneme blending
Children listen to a sequence of separately spoken phonemes, and then combine the phonemes to form a word. Then they write and read the word.

Phoneme segmentation
Children break a word into its separate sounds, saying each sound as they tap out or count it. Then they write and read the word.

Phoneme deletion
Children recognize the word that remains when a phoneme is removed from another word.

Phoneme addition
Children make a new word by adding a phoneme to an existing word.

Phoneme substitution
Children substitute one phoneme for another to make a new word.

Phonemic awareness instruction helps children learn to read.
Phonemic awareness instruction improves children's ability to read words. It also improves their reading comprehension. Phonemic awareness instruction aids reading comprehension primarily through its influence on word reading. For children to understand what they read, they must be able to read words rapidly and accurately. Rapid and accurate word reading frees children to focus their attention on the meaning of what they read. Of course, many other things, including the size of children's vocabulary and their world experiences, contribute to reading comprehension.

Phonemic awareness instruction helps children learn to spell.
Teaching phonemic awareness, particularly how to segment words into phonemes, helps children learn to spell. The explanation for this may be that children who have phonemic awareness understand that sounds and letters are related in a predictable way. Thus, they are able to relate the sounds to letters as they spell words.

B. B. Armbruster, F. Lehr, & J. Osborn, 2001.

Reading First Program

Following the NRP report, the U.S. Department of Education launched a major initiative to improve reading in some of the lowest performing schools in the country. This federal initiative, called the Reading First Program, requires schools to adopt practices that are based on the body of research about effective instruction in reading. This has come to be called Scientifically-Based Reading Research.

One of the requirements of Reading First is that funded schools must establish practices for periodic screening using a validated instrument. This screening data is used to identify which children are below benchmark standards and need intervention. Children with below-benchmark scores are placed in small intervention groups for additional help in developing skills that are below where they need to be to read well.

Data to Inform Instruction

One important component of the Reading First initiative and many other reform initiatives is a focus on using data to inform instruction. This focus, often referred to as data-driven instruction, has captured the attention of principals and district leaders. Many schools are working to implement new procedures whereby teachers learn how to interpret screening data to place children in a homogeneous group for additional help in a specific deficient skill area. Data also is used to determine what instructional techniques may help children make progress in meeting the critical milestones in early reading.

The Three-Tier Reading Model

Data is a cornerstone in systematizing the decisions to implement an approach to layers of special help that is sometimes referred to as the Three-Tier Reading Model. This model, described by the University of Texas Center for Reading and Language Arts in a publication by that name, is a framework for visualizing what tiers of instruction might look like in a school.

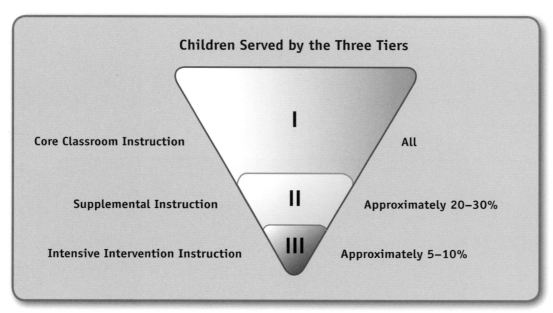

This material has been reproduced with the permission of the Vaughn Gross Center for Reading and Language Arts at the University of Texas at Austin, Copyright 2003.

Tier I is the core reading instruction that all children receive. This instruction typically is referred to as the language arts block. Many schools use a published reading curriculum, often called a basal, to support teachers in teaching this portion of the day.

Tier II is the first line of special help for children who are not making sufficient progress in developing the skills that are needed to learn to read. The instruction provided in Tier II is delivered in small groups of 3–5 children often for 30 minutes daily. This special help is intended to be in addition to the allocated time for the Tier I instruction rather than as a substitute for it.

Children who exhibit signs of difficulties in reading need more reading instruction time, not just instruction in a group of a different size. Often the instructional materials and strategies in Tier II are from a specialized intervention program, but at other times a teacher may reteach lessons from the core program or design her own lesson plans. Regardless of whether the instruction is from a published intervention program or teacher-designed lessons, it is critical to monitor the child's progress and study the data regularly. Some of the early literacy screening instruments provide alternate forms so that teachers can assess every one to three weeks and chart the scores.

Tier III is the third layer of instruction. It is the most intensive tier of instruction and is often delivered in smaller groups, with more systematic materials for more time daily. Some schools view Tier III as special education, but most experts in the field encourage schools to view Tier III as pre–special education. Collecting and analyzing data on the progress of these Tier III children is critical so that teachers will know if the instruction is effective before too much time passes. If the child is not making adequate progress, then the instruction must change. Teachers are encouraged to consider what elements of instruction to change to make instruction more effective.

The Preventive Model

Another topic that is receiving national attention in the area of reading achievement is the new federal procedures to identify children for special education services. In 2005, provisions of reauthorization of the Individuals with Disabilities Education Act (IDEA) go into effect. This act is the federal law that defines which children are eligible to receive special education services and outlines the qualification process. Embedded in this act is a vision that schools will institute practices for early identification and intervention.

IDEA embraces the Preventive Model because of the evidence that fewer children will be recommended for special education services if schools implement intensive early intervention practices. There will be fewer referrals for diagnostic testing because more children will be on-track with instruction provided in the regular education setting. Children whose scores do not improve, even with consistent and well-designed intervention instruction, become candidates for referral for further diagnostic testing. Because information about progress from the first levels of help is considered during the qualification process for whether a child is entitled to receive special education services, this approach is commonly referred to as the response-to-intervention model.

Elements of Effective Programs

Phonological awareness intervention is most effective when used within a school context where many of the elements of the Preventive Model are present. Ideally, the school will use a framework similar to the Three-Tier Model and the Response-to-Intervention approach.

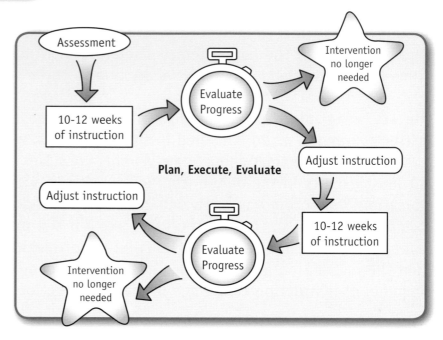

Adapted from The 3-Tier Reading Model, UTCRLA

These elements include:

- School-wide focus on improving reading achievement with a model for how to organize to achieve improvement

- An approach to reading instruction that includes tiers of instruction whereby children who are not making adequate progress toward critical milestones receive small-group focused instruction

- A process for screening all K–3 children with a validated early literacy assessment instrument

- Procedures to identify which children are at risk of later difficulties based on data from the screening instrument, other assessment data, and teacher observations

- A process for placing each child who is not achieving critical milestones in a small group setting

- Selection of the appropriate instructional focus for each intervention group

- Determination of the type of intervention instruction needed by each group

- Frequent data collection and analysis to monitor the progress of each group and each child receiving intervention instruction

Data-Driven Intervention Instruction

Children at Risk

In a number of important ways, intervention instruction is different from the instruction in reading that classroom teachers provide as part of the core curriculum during the language arts block. First, it is provided only to some of the children in a class. Children who score at or above benchmark on a research-based early literacy screening instrument do not receive this small-group intervention instruction because they don't need it. Intervention instruction is only provided to children whose data show that they are at risk of reading difficulties.

Focused Skill Instruction

Second, the instruction is focused on only one or two skills at a time rather than covering all five essential components of reading instruction. For example, children with deficits in phonological awareness may be grouped together to work on this skill. Instruction may start with the initial sound in the word and progress to working on identifying and manipulating the ending sound. Typically, children learn the beginning and ending sounds before the middle sound in the word. Awareness and isolation of the sounds can then be followed by instruction in segmenting all the sounds in the word. Eventually the group may work on manipulating sounds to change from one word to another.

Continued Core Reading Instruction

Because intervention instruction is focused on only one or two skills at a time, children should not miss instruction in the other essential components of the core reading program to attend their intervention group. Typical intervention time is quite short; this does not allow the teacher time to read a book aloud during every intervention lesson. Children need to be working on skills during the intervention session. However, all children also need that read-aloud time, so it should be done during core reading time with the whole class.

Targeted Instruction for Small Groups

Third, intervention instruction is delivered in small groups. It is critical that the group size is small enough so that the teacher can provide instruction that is targeted to meet the needs of each child in the group. Many researchers recommend group sizes of between three and five children. Smaller groups enable the child to respond to more questions in a lesson. When the child makes an error, the teacher can reteach and tailor a follow-up question to enable the child to practice the concept just taught. By giving the child another explanation and a chance to immediately apply the learning, it is more likely that the child will master the skill. Because the instruction is tailored, it is critical that the group size be small enough to enable the teacher to observe and respond to each error made.

Regular and Intensive Instruction

Fourth, the instruction is regular and intensive. Most intervention groups meet daily for 30 minutes, with the most intensive groups often meeting for two 30-minute sessions per day. This regular instruction is critical for making immediate progress. Intensity of instruction is also important. If the group is not making adequate progress, it may be necessary to intensify the instruction by altering the instructional techniques, reducing the size of the group, extending the time, changing the materials, or replacing the intervention teacher.

Scaffolding Instruction

Intensity of instruction can also be increased by providing more scaffolding. When children aren't mastering the concept, it often helps for the teacher to provide more modeling or more guided practice before the child is given an opportunity for independent practice. Sometimes the teacher breaks the task into more steps, makes each step more concrete through use of manipulative materials or graphic organizers, or allows children to practice the steps separately before combining them. Teachers also start by asking the child to choose between two options and then move to open-ended questions. During an effective intervention lesson, the teacher will be able to use some of these options to intensify instruction as much as needed for the children to master the concepts.

Flexible Grouping

Fifth, the groups are flexible. Children are moved out of these flexible groups as soon as progress-monitoring data shows that they have reached and maintained the benchmark level for a reasonable period of time. Often schools wait for a child to achieve benchmark for approximately a month before being removed from the group. Sometimes children are monitored for a few weeks after they exit the group to make sure that they remain at benchmark without the support of the small group instruction.

Progress Monitoring

This *Teacher's Resource Guide* presupposes that data-informed differentiated instruction will occur in small groups that are composed in order to teach specific deficient skills. Data is critical for making several decisions. Not only does the data inform decisions about which children need intervention and what skills they need, but it also is critical in deciding whether the child's progress is adequate. If there is no progress, or the rate of progress is minimal, then instruction must be intensified before too much time has elapsed. Therefore, continuous progress monitoring with an effective assessment instrument is critical.

Teachers and reading coaches need to monitor the progress of each child and each group. If the entire group is progressing too slowly, then the instruction has to be intensified. If the group is moving along well, but one child is not progressing as well as the rest of the group, then the teacher must move that child to another group. Teachers often keep charts for each child, and then they also plot all three to five children in a group on a single chart in order to compare the rate of progress of each child in the group. Progress monitoring is critical for deciding when to change instruction or the composition of the group.

The Phonological Awareness Continuum

Phonological awareness is a critical skill for early literacy. Phonological awareness is awareness of the sounds in our language. It is an umbrella term that includes awareness at both larger and smaller units of language. Phonological awareness includes awareness that sentences are composed of words and that words have smaller units, such as syllables, onsets, rimes, and phonemes.

Phonological awareness is the ability to distinguish and manipulate the smallest units in our language, which are speech sounds or phonemes. When, for example, children know that the word *cat* has three sounds (/k/ /a/ /t/), they are demonstrating phonological awareness. While awareness at the word or syllable level may develop earlier than awareness at the phoneme level, children need to be able to separate all the sounds in the word for reading and spelling.

Phonological awareness can be viewed along a continuum from largest to smallest unit, or from simple to more complex. Often this continuum is depicted as a stairway to show a progression from the bottom to the top step. There are multiple steps on this stairway, as follows:*

- Segmenting sentences to words—children walk one step for each word in a sentence.

- Segmenting words into syllables—children clap once for each syllable in their name

- Segmenting words into onset-rime, rhyming, or alliteration— children can manipulate the onset of the word (everything before the first vowel) separately from the rime (the first vowel and everything after it)

- Identifying and manipulating phonemes—children move a counter for each sound in the word

*Refer to the illustration on page 5.

The fourth step, phonemic awareness, can be broken into more components. Phonemic awareness is not only the last and most important step, it is also the most complex. Within phonemic awareness there are different levels of expertise. Below are three distinct levels within phonemic awareness:

- Working with one phoneme at a time—phoneme isolation, identification, and categorization
- Working with all the phonemes in the word—phoneme segmentation and blending
- Manipulating the phonemes in words—addition, deletion, and substitution

In line with this analysis of phonological awareness skills, the instructional activities in this toolkit have been divided into six units:

1. Words in a sentence
2. Syllables in a word
3. Onset-rime
4. Phonemic awareness—isolation, identification, and categorization
5. Phonemic awareness—segmentation and blending
6. Phonemic awareness—addition, deletion, and substitution

Characteristics of Effective Phonological Awareness Instruction

Instruction in phonological awareness should be engaging, short, and fun. Most teachers teach one or two skills at a time with strategies and activities that take 5–10 minutes each. It is preferable to integrate instruction throughout the day in short distributed practice spurts rather than to cluster it together and drag it on too long.

Most kindergarten teachers use transition times throughout the day, such as lining up to go to music or discussions around the calendar, to integrate a little phonological awareness. For example, instead of asking the boys to line up first, ask the children whose names begin with /s/ to line up first. While waiting for the calendar helper to walk up and find the correct numbers on the pocket chart for the date, ask children what sound is at the beginning of *Tuesday*.

Auditory Focused

Phonological instruction is auditory and without alphabet letters. The emphasis is on the sounds in words, not on the letters used to represent the sounds. Initially it is preferable to focus on the sounds without any letters. This prevents children from becoming distracted by the letter symbols rather than concentrating on hearing the sounds. Many times children are provided with counters to move to represent the distinct sounds in a word. This allows children to move something without having to use letters. Letters will be added later on.

Research has shown that phonological awareness continues to develop and is enhanced for many children by adding letters to the instruction. The goal is to develop initial awareness without letters and then add letters as soon as children demonstrate an adequate and sufficient level of phonological awareness to benefit from instruction in sound-letter correspondence.

Instructional Time and Sequence

For children in kindergarten it is possible to plan instruction that progresses sequentially along the phonological awareness continuum. Teachers can start by developing awareness of the words in a sentence, then syllables in a word, and then the onset and the rime. Once children have demonstrated that they know that these larger units exist, they can work up to phonemic awareness. Children begin with isolating the first sound in a word, then the last, and finally the middle vowel.

It is important to keep in mind that the larger phonological awareness units are only stepping stones to phonemic awareness, and the lower levels deserve less instructional time. Think of them as "warm ups" for getting ready to work at the phonemic level. Less time should be spent on the word and syllable level, for example, because the most important skill for reading and spelling is phoneme segmentation. Some researchers have begun to question the value of instruction in these lower levels. Until more research examines the degree to which word, syllable, and onset/rime awareness contributes to the development of phonemic awareness, it is best to dedicate only limited time to words, syllables, and onset-rimes and to focus the majority of instruction time on helping children develop phonemic awareness. Phoneme segmentation may be the most critical skill within phonemic awareness because children need to be able to separate all the sounds in words in order to map the sounds to print for reading and spelling.

Integrate Instruction to Accelerate Learning

While there may be time to teach the stages of the phonological awareness continuum when working with kindergarten children, there is an urgent need for children who are behind in first grade to catch up. The time that it takes to progress up the steps of phonological awareness cannot be afforded to these older children. First graders who are behind in phonological awareness and the alphabetic principle are way behind. Children should be able to segment all the sounds in a word by the end of kindergarten so that they can master associating sounds and letters during the first several months of first grade.

If a child is not at benchmark in both the alphabetic principle and phoneme segmentation by the middle of first grade, there is no time to go back to begin with early phonological awareness and progress up the phonological continuum before instructing in letter-sound associations. Instruction needs to be integrated—that is, skills need to be taught all together, in order for the child to progress as quickly as possible. At this point the learning curve needs to be accelerated.

Phonological Awareness and Learning a Second Language

Phonological awareness is the understanding that language is made up of words, syllables, rhymes, and sounds. The transfer of phonological awareness and literacy skills from one language to another often depends upon a child's native language proficiency. Studies have shown that, whenever possible, phonological awareness should be taught in the child's native language.

The amount of time needed to learn to speak and read in English is directly related to a child's native language and literacy skills. English language acquisition depends on the age of the child at the initial time of exposure to the second language, previous schooling in the first language, and the type of instruction provided in the second language. Children with a solid native language base often acquire new language structures more rapidly than younger children because they have already developed the cognitive processes to analyze and apply language rules. The degree and nature of differences between the native and second languages can also affect a child's development of phonological awareness in English.

Oral Language and Literacy Development

Many studies have shown that oral language development provides the foundation for phonological awareness and reading. Evidence suggests that output, or language produced by the English language learners themselves, is critical for language development. Producing language necessitates that children process more deeply than is required when listening or reading. Thus, instruction should include focus upon oral language development in the form of oral class participation, child-teacher dialogue, and peer-peer interaction.

Oral Language, Phonological Awareness, and Reading

Many English language learners come to school with less general background knowledge, less experience with school language, weaker vocabulary, and poorer phonological and print awareness skills than native English speakers. Because reading comprehension is built on a foundation of oral language and phonological awareness skills, special support is needed for these learners. To decode unknown words, a child needs to have strong phonological skills, including the ability to hear, distinguish, and blend individual sounds, as well as knowledge of letter names, and the ability to match sound with print. Good phonemic decoding skills help build accurate memory for spelling patterns, and strong word reading skills are essential for good reading comprehension.

Children with weaknesses in oral language and phonological skills require intense, explicit, and supportive instruction. Instruction must be explicit in that it leaves nothing to chance and makes no assumptions about skills and knowledge that children will acquire on their own. Learners must be given more intensive and supportive teaching and learning opportunities. They need more positive emotional support in the forms of encouragement, feedback, and positive reinforcement.

More cognitive support should be provided through scaffolded instruction. This may include careful sequencing to gradually build skills and teacher-child dialogue that directly shows the learner what kind of thinking process is needed in order to complete a task. The interaction between the teacher and child leads the learner to discover the information or strategies that are critical to accomplishing a task, rather than simply being told what to do.

The Learning Environment

Teachers who foster supportive and low-anxiety learning environments minimize the anxiety inherent in experimenting with a new language. Offer consistent praise, and set developmental goals for children. Teachers should acknowledge and accept that most ELLs go through a silent period and should resist pushing children to speak too soon.

In order to provide effective instruction to foster oral language development and phonological awareness, teachers should do the following.

- Provide children with multiple opportunities to experience oral language and language play in a comfortable environment.
- Use meaningful, predictable texts for read-alouds or shared reading.
- Speak clearly and slowly.
- Model all activities for ELLs and repeat directions as needed.
- Plan activities that encourage interaction and talk among children.
- Incorporate total physical response, a technique through which the child responds to language input with body motions.
- Scaffold instruction and provide support for children by spending adequate time doing the activities with them.
- Increase Wait Time, the time between asking a question and requiring a response, to 30 seconds to 1 minute to allow time for children to process language.
- Read aloud to children regularly to introduce phonological awareness in an authentic way and to practice listening for a specific purpose.
- Use children's literature in the forms of stories, songs, poems, and rhymes to provide quality models of how English should sound.
- Foster a level of adequate achievement in one stage of phonological awareness before introducing the child to the next stage.
- Keep the emphasis on informality, enjoyment, and fun with word play.

Phonological Awareness at the Word Level

Word awareness is the knowledge that words have meaning. Children with word awareness can discriminate individual words in a passage read to them. Beginning readers must have this skill before they can extract meaning from what they read.

A Word from the Experts

" One of the crucial understandings that beginning readers need to develop is the concept of a 'word' as a collection of sounds that together provide meaning. They also need to learn that words come in various lengths and that they can be organized into sentences that together give a message. The more students are exposed to playing with words, the sooner they will develop understandings around words. "

Karen Tankersley, *The Threads of Reading: Strategies for Literacy Development, 2003*

Unit 1 Objectives

In this unit children will—
- Gain an awareness that spoken language is composed of words
- Recognize that sentences are made up of separate words
- Build sentences by organizing words to create meaning
- Segment sentences into individual words
- Deconstruct sentences by removing words
- Generate sentences of a prescribed number of words

Skills Connection

Young children begin to recognize words as separate entities. The understanding that sentences are composed of separate words provides the underlying framework for reading readiness. Later on, young writers realize that there are spaces between the words in sentences. This knowledge can help children avoid the problem of running words together on the page.

English Language Learners

Choose books for read-alouds that focus on phonological awareness. Focus on short sections of the text and have children listen for particular features of language. Rereading favorite texts provides opportunities for children to experience the sounds of language and rhythm and rhyme. Word play provides meaningful and fun language experiences.

Home-School Connection

Dear Parent,

Please support your child as he/she learns about words in a sentence. Give your child a small paper cup, containing raisins, cereal, or small crackers. Say a sentence aloud and ask the child to repeat each word while taking a piece from the cup for each word and placing the pieces in a row on the table. Ask the child to repeat the sentence as he points to each piece.

On-the-Go Assessment for Word Awareness

As children line up for recess, ask each child to listen to a sentence and tap, clap, or snap for each word.

Unit 1 Word Level Chart of Manipulatives

Activity	A—Bunny Hop	B—Frog on a Lily Pad	C—How Long Is My Sentence?	D—Take Away a Word	E—Word Cards	F—Spin a Sentence
BLM 1-1 Bunny Cutouts	●					
Craft Sticks	●					
BLM 1-2, 1-3 Lily Pad Pathway		●				
Frog Counters		●				
Link 'N' Learn® Links			●			
Quiet Counters				●		
Large Pocket Chart					●	
Student Pocket Chart					●	
Blank Cards					●	
Game Spinner						●
Sorting Bowls						●
Bear Counters						●

Unit 1: Phonological Awareness at the Word Level

Notes

Materials

- BLM 1-1
  Bunny Cutouts
- Craft Sticks

Skill

Segment sentences into words

Objective

To recognize that sentences are made up of words

Purpose

To learn to distinguish that sentences are composed of separate words, children hold a bunny on a stick and move it in a hopping motion for each word in the sentence.

Activity Overview

Children hold their bunnies on a stick, listen to a sentence, and say the sentence slowly as they move their bunnies in a hopping motion for each word in the sentence. Children count the number of bunny hops to validate how many words there are in the sentence.

Getting Ready

Copy BLM 1-1 and cut out a bunny for each child. Tape the bunnies onto craft sticks. Use your own sentences or the sentences provided in Appendix IV for this activity.

Build Background

- *Who has seen a bunny hop?*
- *First, a bunny sits very still and listens carefully with its big bunny ears. Then it hops. Who can show us how a bunny sits, listens, and then hops?*
- *Has anyone ever danced the Bunny Hop? When you dance the Bunny Hop, you hop to the words "Hop, hop, hop!"*
- *We can make a very special bunny that hops each time it hears a word in a sentence.*

Model the Activity

Model the activity for children using a two-word sentence. Gradually increase sentence length.

Continue the Activity Together

Spend enough time doing the activity with children. This is a very important learning time.

Increase the sentence length to six words.

Gradually release more responsibility to children.

Watch Me Play

- *Here is how to play the game. Hold the bunny still and listen to the sentence:* <u>Dogs bark.</u>
- *I say the sentence slowly and move the bunny in a hopping motion for each word.*
- <u>Dogs</u>, *that's one hop.* <u>Bark</u>, *that's another hop. The bunny heard two words, so the bunny hopped twice.*
- *To check, I do that again.* <u>Dogs bark</u>: *Hop, hop. That is two hops for two words.*
- *Now I hold the bunny still again and listen carefully to a new sentence:* <u>Big dogs bark.</u>
- *I say the new sentence slowly and move the bunny in a hopping motion for each word:* <u>Big dogs bark.</u>
- *How many times did the bunny hop? How many words are in the sentence?*
- <u>Big dogs bark.</u> *The bunny hopped three times.*

Play the Game with Me

- *Let's move our bunnies to show the words in the sentence.*
- *Hold your bunny still and listen to the sentence.*
- *Here is the sentence:* <u>My room is green.</u>
- *Say the sentence with me and make your bunny hop for each word in the sentence:* <u>My room is green.</u>
- *How many hops? Let's check. Listen to the sentence again, and count the hops.*
- *Did you count four hops?* <u>My room is green</u> *has four words.*

Unit 1 Activity A

Bunny Hop

Independent Activity

Choose new sentences or ask children to volunteer their own sentences.

Continue the activity as a group or allow children to work with a partner.

Assess Understanding

Ask each child to listen to a sentence, and then say the sentence slowly as the child claps for each word.

Keep notes in your intervention log about whether each child was able to complete the task with ease and note any difficulties.

On Your Own

- *Listen to the sentence. Say the sentence by yourself as you make your bunny hop for each word.*

- *Say the sentence again slowly and count the hops. How many words are in the sentence?*

Show What You Know

- [Child's name], *listen to the sentence and repeat it slowly as you clap for each word.*

- *Can you think of another sentence with* [number] *words? Clap once for each word in your sentence.*

Sample Sentences

1. There goes a bunny!
2. The bunny is furry.
3. She is brown and white.

4. Dogs bark.
5. Big dogs bark.
6. Small dogs bark, too.

7. Is my room green?
8. Do you like green rooms?
9. Is green your favorite color?
10. What color is your room?

Extend and Adapt

Big Bunny Hop
Gather children in a large play area. Read a sentence and have children repeat the sentence as they hop across the floor. Children hop for each word in the sentence.

Wiggle Your Ears
Ask children to cup their hands on top of their heads to form bunny ears. Hold the bunny ears still and listen to a sentence. Repeat the sentence as children wiggle both bunny ears together for each word. Repeat the sentence with the children to check the number of wiggles and the number of words in the sentence.

Bunny Steps
Use interrogative sentences (questions) for this activity. Point out to children that our voices rise at the end of a question. Ask children to move their bunnies as if they are climbing stairs, one step up for each word in the question, ending on the top step at the end of the question.

Unit 1 Activity B

Frog on a Lily Pad

Notes

Materials

- BLM 1-2 and 1-3 Lily Pad Pathway
- Frog Counters

Skill

Segment sentences into words

Objective

To recognize that sentences are made up of words

Purpose

To learn to distinguish individual words in a sentence, children move counters for each word they hear in a sentence.

Activity Overview

Children move frogs along a pathway on the BLM according to the number of words in a sentence.

Getting Ready

Tape the two BLMs together to create a game board. Let each child choose a frog counter of a different color.

Talk to children about their past experiences with frogs.

Explain that frogs begin at Start and jump along the Lily Pad Pathway until they reach Home.

Build Background

- *Who has visited a frog pond? Sometimes frogs rest on lily pads. Sometimes frogs jump from one lily pad to another.*
- *For this game we use a game board and a frog counter. The round spaces on the game board are lily pads in a pond.*
- *Can you find the lily pad marked* <u>Start</u>? *Our frogs can jump on the Lily Pad Pathway to get home.*
- *Find Home on the gameboard.*
- *When there is danger, our frogs can jump into the pond. Look for the splashes where frogs jump in the water.*
- *Can you find the Rocky Road Shortcut?*
- *Whose frog can jump all the way home?*

Model the Activity

Place Frog Counters at Start. Model the activity for children.

Watch Me Play

- *Here is how to play the game. Place frog at Start.*
- *The frog sits quietly and listens to a sentence:* Frogs jump.
- *I listen to the sentence again and move the frog one lily pad for each word:* Frogs jump.
- *Listen again to hear how many lily pads the frog should jump.*
- *I say the sentence again slowly and point to the lily pads to check if the frog is on the right lily pad:* Frogs jump. *One, two.*
- *Did the frog jump correctly? If the frog jumped two lily pads, it can stay there.*
- *If the frog is not in the right place, it will have to wait a turn.*
- *I must watch out for splashes! When there is danger, a frog will jump into the pond and then the frog must go back to Start.*
- *Will the frog get to* Home?

Continue the Activity Together

Decide how to take turns. Play the game with children.

Explain to children that if a frog lands on a splash, the frog must return to Start.

If a frog lands on the Rocky Road Shortcut, the frog goes directly to Home.

Play the Game with Me

- *Let's play the game together. Listen to the sentence and think about the words we hear.*
- *Our frogs will jump one lily pad for each word.*
- *Listen to the sentence:* Some frogs are green.
- *Say the sentence with me and make your frog jump one lily pad for each word:* Some frogs are green.
- *How many lily pads did your frog jump? Let's check. Say the sentence and count the lily pads.*
- *Did you count four jumps?* Some frogs are green *has four words.*

Frog on a Lily Pad

Notes

Independent Activity

Choose new sentences or ask children to volunteer their own sentences.

On Your Own

- *Listen to the sentence.*
- *Say the sentence as you make your frog jump for each word.*
- *Say the sentence again and count the jumps.*
- *How many words are in the sentence?*

Assess Understanding

Monitor whether each child hears the individual words in sentence.

Children may enjoy listening to a short sentence and jumping like a frog for each word.

Keep notes in your intervention log about whether each child was able to complete the task and note any difficulties.

Show What You Know

- *[Child's name], yes or no, are there are [number] words in my sentence?*
- *Say the sentence aloud and show us how many times your frog jumps.*
- *Can you think of another sentence with [number] words?*
- *Show us how many times your frog jumps?*
- *Who has a new sentence for our frogs?*

Sample Sentences

1. Frogs jump.
2. Brown cattails grow.
3. Frogs eat flies.
4. Watch out for snakes!
5. I heard a splash!
6. That bullfrog is huge!
7. Frogs have long tongues.
8. Watch the turtles swim.
9. Do you like frogs?
10. Jump, frog, jump!

Extend and Adapt

Fabulous Jumping Frogs

If you have access to a large play area, you may wish to have children jump like frogs on the sidewalk or on a chalk-drawn pathway. Read a sentence and then have children repeat the sentence as they jump the correct number of jumps. Repeat to check that the number of jumps matches the number of words.

Incorporating Children's Books About Frogs

Obtain a copy of one of the *Frog and Toad* series of books by Arnold Lobel. Read the book aloud to children. Once in a while, stop reading and repeat a sentence from the story. Ask children to make their frogs jump on their desks, according to the number of words in the sentence that you read. Have them self-check as they say the sentence aloud.

Nonfiction Read-Aloud

Find a nonfiction book about frogs. Stopping periodically while reading, have children repeat a sentence and make their frogs jump. Engage in a dialogue about where frogs live, what they eat, and how they jump.

Unit 1 Activity C

How Long Is My Sentence?

Materials

- Link 'N' Learn® Links

Skill

Use words to build sentences

Objective

To recognize that sentences are made up of words

Purpose

To demonstrate an understanding that sentences are made up of words, children create chains of links

Activity Overview

Children listen to a sentence, count how many words are in the sentence, and join the appropriate number of Link 'N' Learn links to one another to represent the number of words they hear.

Getting Ready

This activity may require lots of modeling.

Use counters if children cannot manipulate the links easily.

Many children enjoy using blocks to build towers or other buildings. Discuss how constructing a building with blocks is like building sentences.

Build Background

- *Let's practice joining the Link 'N' Learn® Links together. The easiest way to join the links is by going through the gate. Match up the open areas and press both links.*

- *We can begin the game with ten links placed in a cup or bowl in front of us.*

- *Who likes to play with blocks? What kinds of structures do you like to build?*

- *Construction workers use bricks, blocks, or lumber to build all kinds of buildings. We use words to build sentences.*

- *For this activity, we can use links to show how words build sentences.*

StarLIT™ Literacy Intervention Toolkit

Model the Activity

Use the list of sentences in Appendix IV.

It is important for children to see the one-to-one correspondence between the number of links and the number of words in the sentence.

Continue the Activity Together

Continue the activity with children.

Increase the number of words in each sentence as children are ready.

Gradually release more responsibility to children.

Watch Me Play

- *Here is how to play the game. Listen to this sentence:* <u>They work.</u>

- *Think about how many words you hear in the sentence. I select one link for each word.*

- *I use the links to build a sentence chain.*

- *Place the chain of links on the table. I point to each link and repeat the sentence.*

- *There are two words in the sentence, so there are two links.*

- *I leave the sentence chain on the table and get ready to build another sentence.*

- *I listen to the next sentence and repeat the activity.* <u>They work hard.</u> *How many words?*

- <u>They work hard.</u> *How many links are needed?*

- *Now there are two sentence chains on the table.* <u>They work.</u> <u>They work hard.</u> *Which chain is longer?*

Play the Game with Me

- *Let's use the links to show the words in a sentence. Listen to this sentence:* <u>This is a sidewalk.</u>

- *How many words do we hear? How many links will we need to build the sentence chain?*

- *Let's take the correct number of links from the bowl and put them together.*

- *Lay the sentence chain on the table and point to each link as we say each word in the sentence.*

- *Let's continue the activity using another sentence:* <u>This is a long sidewalk.</u> *Now we have two sentence chains.*

- *Which sentence has more words?*

How Long Is My Sentence?

Independent Activity

Children may enjoy working in pairs. One partner can say a sentence as the other creates the chain of links. Both match the number of links with the number of words in the sentence.

Assess Understanding

Monitor whether each child can form a chain of links to represent a sentence of a given number of words.

Keep notes in your intervention log about whether each child was able to complete the task with ease and note any difficulties.

On Your Own

- *Think of a new sentence.*
- *Decide who is partner 1 and partner 2.*
- *Listen to a new sentence from partner 1. Think about how many words you hear.*
- *Choose the correct number of links and put them together in a chain.*
- *Say the sentence aloud as you point to each link.*
- *Place the chain on the table. Now listen to a new sentence from partner 2. Make a new chain.*
- *Compare the length of the chains.*

Show What You Know

- *Say a sentence aloud and show me a sentence chain for that sentence.*
- *Can you think of a sentence with [number] words?*
- *Create a chain of links for that sentence.*
- *Who can say a sentence for a sentence chain with 6 links?*

Sample Sentences

1. They work.
2. They work hard.
3. Mom goes to work every day.

4. This is a sidewalk.
5. This is a long sidewalk.
6. Ride your bike on the sidewalk.

7. Let's walk.
8. Let's walk to school.
9. I walk my dog.
10. He likes to take a walk.

Extend and Adapt

Linking Arms

You may wish to demonstrate this activity by having children pretend to be words in a sentence. Children can link elbows to represent the words in a sentence. Say a two-to-six word sentence. Ask how many children will be needed to show the number of words in the sentence. Have that number of children come up in front of the group and link elbows in a line. Ask another student to point to each child as the group slowly repeats each word in the sentence.

Back in the Bowl

Begin with an empty bowl. Say a sentence for the group and have children listen for the number of words. Repeat the sentence. Ask children to place a counter into their bowls for each word in the sentence. Then have children count the number of counters. Later, you may wish to chart the number of short and long sentences.

Take Away a Word

Notes

Materials

• Quiet Counters

Skill

Remove words to deconstruct sentences

Objective

To recognize that sentences are made up of words

Purpose

To have children use counters to represent a sentence and to use their memory to determine words that are deleted.

Activity Overview

Children recognize one-to-one correspondence between counters and individual words in a sentence. As each counter is removed, children rely on memory to determine which word is missing.

Getting Ready

Provide each child with 6 Quiet Counters.

Tell children that remembering words is important to learning to read later on. This activity will help them practice remembering words in a sentence.

Build Background

• *Let's pretend to be eating licorice rope candy. What happens to the licorice rope when we take a bite?* [The licorice gets smaller.]

• *What happens when we take another bite?* [With each bite the licorice rope gets smaller until it is all gone.]

• *Place the Quiet Counters in a row. Pretend that the row of counters is a sentence and that each counter is a word.*

• *What happens to the sentence if a counter is taken away?*

• *What happens if another counter is taken away?*

Model the Activity

Use the sentences listed in Appendix IV.

Demonstrate lining up the counters in left-to-right direction from children's perspective. Keep directionality of text in mind as you and children say the words and point to or move each counter.

Model the activity as needed.

Continue the Activity Together

Allowing enough time for children to do the activity is very important.

Slowly increase the length of the sentences.

Gradually release more responsibility to children.

Watch Me Play

- *Here is how to play the game. Look at the row of counters on the table.*
- *Listen to this sentence:* <u>You run fast.</u>
- *There are three words in the sentence. There are three counters in the row.*
- *Now I repeat the sentence slowly and touch one counter for each word.*
- *Now I say the sentence again and move one counter for each word:* <u>You run fast.</u> *There are three words, and there are three counters.*
- *I take away one of the counters and say the sentence.* <u>You run ___.</u> *What word is missing?*
- *The sentence was* <u>You run fast.</u> *The missing word is* <u>fast</u>.
- *I take away another counter and say the sentence.* <u>You ___ ___.</u>
- *What is missing?* [<u>run</u> and <u>fast</u>]
- *I take away another word and take away another counter. I say the sentence.* <u>___ ___ ___.</u>
- *The whole sentence is gone! What words are missing?*
- *I try to remember the missing words. The sentence was* <u>You run fast</u>.

Play the Game with Me

- *Let's listen to a new sentence:* <u>Some trucks are big.</u>
- *Place counters in a row to show each word in the sentence.*
- *Move one counter for each word as we say the sentence together.* <u>Some trucks are big.</u>
- *Take one counter away and say the sentence again.* <u>Some trucks are ___.</u>
- *Say the sentence and touch a counter for each word. Say the missing word.* [<u>big</u>]
- *Let's continue the game together.*

Unit 1 Activity D

Take Away a Word

Independent Activity

Children may continue to play as a group or may work together with a partner. Partners may take turns supplying sentences for one another.

Assess Understanding

Monitor whether each child understands that sentences can be deconstructed by removing words.

Have each child supply a short sentence and represent the words with counters. Remove a counter and ask the child to tell what word is missing.

Keep notes in your intervention log and note any difficulties.

On Your Own

- *Listen to a new sentence.*
- *Say the sentence and move the counters. Tell what word is missing.*
- *Take one counter away each time.*
- *Continue to play until all of the words and counters are gone.*
- *Then use a new sentence and play again.*

Show What You Know

- *[Child's name], show me what happens when you take away any one of the counters.*
- *How do you know what word is missing?*
- *How can you make a sentence longer?*

Sample Sentences

1. You run fast.
2. You can run fast.
3. You and I run fast.
4. You and I can run fast.

5. Some trucks are big.
6. I like red sports cars.
7. This bus takes us downtown.
8. The subway train was crowded.
9. Let's go to the airport.
10. We like to fly.

Extend and Adapt

Freight Train

Form a line of four to six chairs to represent the cars of a train. Have one child sit in each chair. Say a sentence aloud. Beginning with the first car, ask each child to say a word in the sentence. Then uncouple the caboose of the train. Ask children to say the sentence aloud once more, deleting the last word. Continue play until all of the train cars have left the train and no words remain in the sentence.

Back in the Garage

Provide each child with a small container that can be used as a garage and six counters to use as cars. Have children listen to a sentence, take "cars" from the "garage", and place them in a row in front of them. Children should say the sentence as they move a car for each word. Tell children to continue to remove one car from the row and place it back in the garage. Children should repeat the sentence and supply the missing word. Continue play until no words remain.

Word Cards

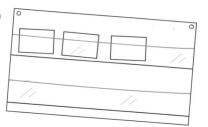

Notes

Materials

- Large Pocket Chart
- Student Pocket Charts
- Blank Cards

Skill

Segment sentences into words

Objective

To recognize that sentences are composed of words

Purpose

To learn to distinguish that sentences are composed of separate words, children place cards in pocket charts.

Activity Overview

Children listen to a sentence and place a card in the pocket chart for each word.

Getting Ready

Use the Large Pocket Chart and blank cards of the same color to demonstrate the activity.

Be sure that each child has a clear view of the pocket chart.

Build Background

- *Do you remember the nursery rhyme that says boys are made of ships and snails and puppy dog's tails? Who can tell us what a sentence is made of?*

- *A sentence is made of separate words.*

- *As we listen to a sentence, the words may sound like they are all connected, but there are actually little pauses between the words.*

- *We can use cards to show each word.*

- *For this activity, we put a card in the pocket chart to show each word in a sentence.*

StarLIT™ Literacy Intervention Toolkit

Model the Activity

Use the list of sentences in Appendix IV.

Demonstrate the one-to-one matching of blank cards with words in the sentence.

Remember to work in a left-to-right direction from *children's* perspective.

Watch Me Play

- *Here is how to play the game. Listen to the words in the sentence.* <u>Open the door.</u>
- *How many words do I hear? I choose one card for each word in the sentence.*
- *I repeat the words as I place the cards in the chart. (Left to right.)*
- <u>Open the door.</u> *There are three words in the sentence and three cards in the chart.*
- *I say the sentence again, as I point to each card.* <u>Open the door.</u>
- *Is there one card for each word? Does it match?*
- *I listen to a new sentence and repeat the activity.*
- *I make sure that there is one card in the pocket chart for each word in the sentence.*

Continue the Activity Together

Children use student Pocket Charts and blank cards.

Children place their cards from left-to-right in the chart.

Do the activity together until children feel confident.

Play the Game with Me

- *Let's use cards to show each word in a sentence.* <u>The door is open.</u> *How many words do we hear?*
- *Say the sentence with me as we as we place a card in the pocket chart for each word in the sentence.*
- *Place the cards from left to right in the chart.*
- <u>The door is open.</u> *How many cards are in the pocket chart?*
- *Let's repeat the sentence slowly as we point to each card.*
- *Do we have the correct number of cards in the pocket chart?*

Unit 1 Activity E

Word Cards

Notes

Independent Activity

Allow children to play the game independently.

On Your Own

- *Listen to the sentence and think about the words you hear.*

- *Say the words and place one blank card in the pocket chart for each word in the sentence.*

- *Remember to begin placing the cards on the left side.*

- *Repeat the words in the sentence as you point to each card.*

- *Is there a card for each word? How many words are in the sentence?*

Assess Understanding

Monitor whether each child hears the correct number of words in a sentence. You may ask the child to take a giant step for each word.

Keep notes in your intervention log about whether each child was able to complete the task with ease. Note any difficulties.

Show What You Know

- *[Child's name], say a sentence with four words. Show how many word cards should go in the pocket chart.*

- *Point to each card and say the words.*

- *Let's give [child's name] a thumbs up sign if we agree.*

Sample Sentences

1. I play.
2. He runs fast.
3. Come with me.
4. We can jump.
5. They play with us.
6. Let's go!
7. I like to run.
8. Children like to play.
9. Is the grass wet?
10. We have fun in the park.

Extend and Adapt

Word Kids

Substitute children for word cards. Say a sentence for the children and ask them to listen for the words they hear. Tell children that one child will stand up for each word. Have the children repeat the sentence, and ask how many children will need to stand. Have that number of children stand up in sentence order. Ask each child standing to say a word from the sentence.

Family Sentences

For a small group, you may wish to ask each child to think of a sentence with as many words as there are members in his family. Ask a child to tell the number of people in his family, say a sentence, and place that many cards in the chart. Then ask the other children to repeat the sentence as the child points to each card in the chart.

Group Sentences

Ask children to make up a sentence with as many words as there are children in the group. Then have children line up as the words in the sentence. Have each child in order say a word from the sentence to show how the number of children matches the number of words.

Unit 1 Activity F

Spin a Sentence

Materials

- Game Spinner
- Sorting Bowls
- Bear Counters

Skill

Segment sentences into words

Objective

To demonstrate an understanding of the number of individual words in a sentence

Purpose

To demonstrate an understanding of individual words in a sentence, children generate sentences of a prescribed number of words.

Activity Overview

Children generate sentences to show understanding of one-to-one correspondence between the number of counters and the number of words in sentences.

Getting Ready

Use the list of sentences in Appendix IV, or you may wish to use sentences and counters based on a seasonal theme or curriculum topic.

Use a removable sticker to cover the number 1 on the spinner.

Build Background

- *Let's have fun with Bear Counters. Place your 6 bears in the bowl.*

- *Spin for a number. If the spinner lands on the sticker, spin again.*

- *Take the number of counters from your bowl and place them in a row on the table.*

- *Use the counters to show the number of words in a sentence.*

Model the Activity

Encourage children to use the counters to support their thinking. Point out the one-to-one correspondence between the counters and the words in a sentence.

Model directionality of print. Place the first counter on the left and move in a left-to-right direction as you place counters for each word in the sentence.

Continue the Activity Together

Play the game with the children. This is a very important learning time.

To move play along, provide children with a topic for their sentences.

Encourage the group to validate each player's responses by giving a prescribed signal.

Watch Me Play

- *Here is how to play the game. I spin for a number.*
- *I take out the number of counters and place them in a row.*
- *Then I think of a sentence with the same number of words.*
- *Beginning with the counter on the left, I move a counter as I say each word in the sentence.*
- *I count to see if the number of counters and the number of words in the sentence match.*
- *Is the number of counters the same as the number of words in the sentence?*
- *Does the number of words match the number on the spinner?*

Play the Game with Me

- *Let's do this activity together. Spin for a number.*
- *Let's think of a sentence with the same number of words.*
- *Take that many counters from the bowl and place them in a row on the table.*
- *Beginning with the counter on the left, we move a counter as we say each word in the sentence aloud.*
- *Who can say the sentence aloud and count the words?*
- *Do we have one counter for each word in the sentence?*
- *Does the number of words match the number shown on the spinner?*

Spin a Sentence

Notes

Independent Activity

Children may work as a group or take turns with a partner.

Show What You Know

On Your Own

- *Spin for a number, choose counters, and place them in a row.*

- *Think of a sentence with that number of words.*

- *Say the sentence aloud and move one counter for each word in the sentence.*

- *Say the sentence aloud and count the words.*

- *Is there a counter for each word? Does the number of words match the number on the spinner?*

Assess Understanding

Monitor whether each child can complete the task with ease.

Keep notes in your intervention log.

Show What You Know

- [Child's name], *can you think of another sentence with* [number] *words?*

- *Place your counters in a row.*

- *Say each word in the sentence as you point to a counter.*

Sample Sentences

1. Apples grow.
2. Red apples grow.
3. I like to pick apples.
4. Apples taste great!
5. Do you like apples?

6. We visited the farm.
7. I rode in the wagon.
8. Hay is scratchy.
9. I picked a little pumpkin.
10. I like my little orange pumpkin.

Extend and Adapt

Bean Bag Toss

Draw a 6-block array on a large sheet of paper. Number the spaces 2–6 and label the extra block. Skip a turn. Have children take turns tossing a beanbag onto a numbered space on array. The child thinks of a sentence with that number of words. The child says the sentence aloud and he takes giant steps for each word in the sentence. The other children repeat the sentence and count the words to see if they match the number on the array. You may wish to vary the movements for this large motor activity.

Match the Sentence

Place a stack of playing cards with numbers 2–6 face down on the table. Taking turns, a player selects a card and makes up a sentence with that number of words. Then the card is placed face up on the table. The player says the sentence aloud as he points to the symbols on the card, for example, four of hearts: I am a boy. The other children repeat the sentence and count the words to verify the match. If the sentence matches the number, the player keeps the card. If it is not a match, the player returns the card to the stack. The player with the most cards at the end of play wins the game.

Phonological Awareness at the Syllable Level

Syllable awareness is the recognition that words are divided into parts, each part containing a separate vowel sound. A child with syllable awareness can identify *pen* as one syllable and *pencil* as two syllables. The awareness and manipulation of syllables is part of understanding how sounds fit together to form words and is essential to success in learning to read.

A Word from the Experts

In a study by Liberman (1974), a hypothesis was tested that children would master the skill of segmenting a spoken word into syllables earlier than segmenting by phonemes. The results were described by G.T. Gillon (2004) as:

"Children more readily segmented words into syllables at each grade level. At the nursery level (average age 4 years, 11 months) 46% of the children could segment words into syllables. By the end of first grade (average age 6 years, 11 months) 90% of the children had mastered the syllable segmentation task and 70% successfully completed the phoneme segmentation task."

Unit 1 Objectives

In this unit children will—
- Deconstruct compound words into two smaller words
- Build compound words by combining two smaller words
- Identify the syllables in names
- Count syllables in multi-syllabic words
- Segment syllables in words
- Join syllables to form words

Skills Connection

Children become aware of how groups of sounds, or syllables, operate in words in spoken language. This awareness forms the groundwork for young readers to look for familiar patterns and use familiar sound chunks from known words to decode or spell unfamiliar words. Chunking sounds makes the reading and spelling process more effective and efficient.

English Language Learners

Focus on syllable awareness by helping children listen for long words and short words. To distinguish between multisyllabic and single syllable words, children enjoy clapping, snapping, or tapping while saying the syllables in words. To make the activity playful, use percussion instruments, such as a drum, a xylophone, or maracas.

Home-School Connection

Dear Parent,
To help your child recognize syllables in words, have fun together speaking in syllables like a robot. Model for your child how Robot Mom or Robot Dad might talk, such as "Ja-son, turn off the tel-e-vi-sion. It's al-most time for soc-cer prac-tice." As your child gets ready, spend a few minutes speaking together like robots.

On-the-Go Assessment for Word Awareness

As each child gets ready to line up, say a two-syllable word slowly, in two parts. Ask the child to put the two parts together and say the word. You say _cup...cake_; the child says _cupcake_.

Unit 2 Syllable Level Chart of Manipulatives

Activity	A—Compound Word Puzzles	B—Puppet Talk	C—Syllable Pocket Chart	D—Fruit and Bugs	E—Syllable Spinner	F—Mystery Bag
Reading Rods® Picture Rods	●					
BLM 2-1, 2-2, 2-3 Compound Word Puzzle Cards	●					
SunSprouts® Wolf Puppet		●				
Large Pocket Chart			●			
Reading Rods Phonological Awareness Pocket Chart Cards			●			●
Insect and Arachnid Learning Place® Game Cards			●			
Fruity Fun Counters				●		
Bug Counters				●		
Segmenting, Blending and Sorting Mats				●		
Game Spinner					●	
Fruits and Vegetables Learning Place Game Cards					●	
BLM 2-4 4- and 5- Syllable Animal Cards					●	
BLM 2-5 Elkonin Boxes						●

Unit 2 Activity A

Compound Word Puzzles

Notes

Materials

- Reading Rods® Picture Rods
- BLM 2-1, 2-2, 2-3 Compound Word Puzzle Cards

Skill

Segment compound words into syllables

Objective

To recognize that compound words are made up of two smaller words

Purpose

To learn to separate compound words into two smaller words and combine smaller words into compound words, children use picture rods and picture puzzles.

Activity Overview

Children use compound word picture cards to segment compound words into two smaller words. Children join the two picture words back together to form the compound word.

Getting Ready

Introduce the activity using Reading Rods Picture Rods. Possible compound words include:

catfish   cowgirl
doghouse   sunhat
dollhouse   sunfish
handball   sunlamp

Build Background

- *Let's talk about snacks. When we have two halves of a snack bar, each part is a snack. When both parts are put together, it makes one large snack.*

- *Some large words are made of two smaller words put together. Some larger words can be divided into two smaller words.*

- *To show this, let's use picture rods. When we put together the picture of the dog with the picture of the house, we make the word <u>doghouse</u>. Say the compound word <u>doghouse</u>.*

- *When we take the large word apart, there are two smaller words. Say the two smaller words <u>dog</u> and <u>house</u>.*

- *Repeat the activity, if needed.*

        StarLIT™ Literacy Intervention Toolkit

Model the Activity

Use 3 pairs of Compound Word Puzzle Cards to model the activity.

Copy the Compound Word Puzzle Cards onto card stock. Cut out the cards.

Review the names of the pictures with children before you begin.

Continue the Activity Together

Distribute Compound Word Puzzle Cards.

Practice segmenting the words and then joining the two pieces back together with children.

Ask them to say the two smaller words and the compound words aloud.

Watch Me Play

- *Here is how to play the game using Compound Word Puzzle cards. Place the cards on the table.*
- *I look at the pictures to find two pictures that fit together to make a compound word.*
- *Here is a picture of a dog and a picture of a house.*
- *The two pieces of the puzzle card can fit together to make the compound word <u>doghouse</u>. See the dog and the house on separate cards.*
- *I fit the pictures together. I see the picture of the doghouse.*
- *When I take the cards apart, there are two words: <u>dog</u> and <u>house</u>.*

Play the Game with Me

- *Let's do this activity together. Look at the puzzle cards and think about a compound word.*
- *What two cards can join together to make a compound word? Let's say the compound word.*
- *Now, pull the two pieces apart and look at the two pictures. Say the two words with me.*
- *Put the two picture words back together. What compound word does it make? Say the compound word with me.*
- *Let's try that again.*

Unit 2 Activity A

Compound Word Puzzles

Notes

Independent Activity

Distribute 3–4 pairs of Compound Word Puzzle Cards to the children.

On Your Own

- *Look at the cards on the table.*

- *What two cards can make a compound word? Put them together and say the word.*

- *Pull the two pieces of the word apart and look at the two pictures. Say the two words.*

- *Join the pieces back together again. What compound word does it make? Say the compound word.*

- *Can you make another compound word?*

- *Continue playing until you have used up all of the Compound Word Puzzle Cards.*

Assess Understanding

Select Reading Rods® Picture Rods and ask each child to form a compound word. Have the child say the compound word and the two smaller words aloud.

Monitor whether each child can segment and join parts of compound words.

Note any difficulties and at what point the difficulties became evident.

Show What You Know

- *Listen to the compound word. Say the compound word.*

- *[Child's name], can you hear the two smaller words? Say the two words for the group.*

- *Who can think of a compound word with the word* book? [Notebook, cookbook, bookcase, bookstore, bookmark, bookworm]

Compound Word List

butterfly

cupcake

matchbook

football

sunflower

mailbox

toothbrush

doorbell

snowman

pinecone

ladybug

doghouse

cowboy

wheelchair

armchair

lighthouse

starfish

pinwheel

rainbow

drumstick

pancake

clothespin

horseshoe

popcorn

Extend and Adapt

Meet Your Match

Create compound word picture cards by pasting pictures on index cards. Distribute one card to each child. Have children find the child whose card will form a compound word with their cards. (For an odd number of children, the teacher should also take a card.) Invite pairs of children to stand together to show and say their compound words for the group. Have each pair of children segment and join the pieces of their compound word as the whole group says the word.

Pick a Pair

Separate ten compound word picture cards and place the pieces in a bowl. Have children take turns selecting two pieces from the bowl to create a compound word. If the pieces form a compound word, the child lays the compound word on the table and says the word for the group. Then the child can choose two more cards and try again. If the pieces do not form a compound word, the child keeps one of the pieces and returns the other to the bowl.

Compound Concentration

Arrange 6 pairs of Compound Word Puzzle Cards upside down in an array on the table. Each child turns over two pieces to try to form a compound word. If the child forms a compound word, he shows the picture and says the word. If they do not form a word, the child returns the pieces to the array. Continue until all cards are used to form compound words.

I'm Thinking Of...

Take turns playing the game to think of compound words for specific places, such as the classroom, playground, bedroom, bookstore, etc.

Clapping Names and Puppet Talk

Notes

Materials

- SunSprouts® Wolf puppet

Skill

Segment children's names into syllables

Objective

To recognize that words are made up of syllables

Purpose

To demonstrate knowledge that words are made up of syllables, children move a puppet mouth and clap hands for each syllable they hear.

Activity Overview

Children practice hearing syllables in names by saying and clapping for the syllables.

Getting Ready

Have children sit in a circle on the floor.

Introduce the wolf puppet and tell children that Mr. Silly Bill has a strange way of saying names.

Build Background

- *Mr. Silly Bill has a funny way of saying names. Listen to Mr. Silly Bill say the name* <u>Jason</u>.

- *Ja-son. How does he say it? Mr. Silly Bill breaks the name into 2 pieces, like this:* <u>Ja</u>-<u>son</u>.

- *Listen to Mr. Silly Bill say other names.*

- *For this game, we use our ears and our hands to make our puppets talk. Then we use our hands to clap the syllables.*

StarLIT™ Literacy Intervention Toolkit

Model the Activity

The teacher always says the name blended, and the puppet always says it segmented.

Continue the Activity Together

You may wish to have children take turns with the puppet, or children may use their hands to form a talking puppet mouth.

Continue the activity together and provide support as needed.

Watch Me Play

- *Here is how to play the game.*
- *Mr. Silly Bill wants to say my name.*
- *I tell Mr. Silly Bill my name. My name is _____.*
- *Mr. Silly Bill says my name in his special way.*
- *I listen as Mr. Silly Bill says the sound units— called syllables—of my name.*
- *I follow along and repeat my name. Now I say it again in parts, the way that Mr. Silly Bill says it.*
- *I can help Mr. Silly Bill by clapping the parts of names with him. Now I say the parts again, and clap once for each part.*
- *How many times did I clap?*
- *There are _____ syllables in my name.*
- *Now Mr. Silly Bill wants to say another name. Who would like to be next?* (Model again, as needed.)

Play the Game with Me

- *Let's use our talking puppet mouths to say a name together. Who wants to be first?*
- [Child's name], *say your name aloud for us. Let's repeat it all together.*
- *Listen to our puppet say your name again slowly. You clap the syllables in your name to help Mr. Silly Bill hear the syllables.*
- [Child's name], *how many claps did you hear? Let's say the name one more time. Listen carefully and tell us if we are correct.*
- *Let's try it again with someone else's name. Who wants to be next?* (Repeat several times.)

Unit 2 Activity B

Clapping Names and Puppet Talk

Independent Activity

After using first names for the activity, try using last names or middle names, if appropriate.

On Your Own

- *When it is your turn, say your first name aloud for the group.*

- *The group repeats the name slowly.*

- *Say your name with the group and clap your name, or move your hands like a talking puppet.*

- *How many claps do you hear? How many syllables do you hear?*

- *Now it is someone else's turn to say his name while our puppet mouths the name.*

Assess Understanding

Monitor whether each child can hear the syllables in a name. You may ask a child to segment the syllables in the name of a favorite movie or TV character.

Note any difficulties in completing the task and at what point the child shows hesitancy.

Show What You Know

- *Listen as I say a one-syllable name:* <u>Bert</u>. *If you have a one-syllable name, clap your name with me.* (Repeat for 2-, 3-, and 4-syllable names: <u>Barney</u>, <u>Tinkerbelle</u>, and <u>Cinderella</u>.)

- Secretly select the first name of a child in the class. Clap that child's name. Invite all the children whose names have the same number of syllables as the identified child to stand up and say their names. Repeat with other names.

1-syllable names

Kurt   Kate

Sam   Grace

Brett   Juan

George   Shawn

2-syllable names

Oscar   Angel

Raymond   Emma

Annette   Dora

Peter   Tyrell

3-syllable names

Pamela

Edwardo

Jamileh

Christopher

Lydia

Muhammad

Armando

Jennifer

4-syllable names

Alexander

Antonio

Victoria

Elizabeth

Emmanuel

Gabriela

Extend and Adapt

Counting Names

Use Craft Sticks, tongue depressors, or any other counters to represent the number of syllables in names. The child says his name (or a friend's name) and then says it again more slowly as he pushes a counter forward for each syllable in the name. The child can check to see if he has the correct number of counters by saying the name again slowly as he touches a counter for each syllable in his name.

It's a Snap

A variation of the clapping activity, children snap their fingers for each syllable in a name. Children take turns snapping their fingers to the syllables in their middle or last names.

Tap a Name

Children use rhythm sticks or drums to tap out the syllables in their names. To vary the activity, children might enjoy tapping out the names of their family members.

In Shape

Each child says his name and chooses the correct number of geometric shapes to represent the syllables in his name. The child uses the shapes to build a design to represent his name. To check himself, the child repeats his name slowly as he touches each piece of the design. Children enjoy comparing the colorful designs that represent the syllables in their names. Vary this activity by having children build designs using color names, pet names, or street names.

Unit 2 Activity C
Syllable Pocket Chart

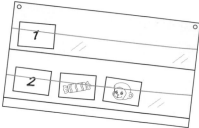

Materials

- Large Pocket Chart
- Number Cards
- Insects and Arachnids Learning Place® Game Cards
- Blank Reading Rods® Phonological Awareness Pocket Chart Cards

Skill

Segment words into syllables

Objective

To recognize the number of syllables in multisyllabic words

Purpose

To show the number of syllables in multisyllabic words, children place blank cards in a pocket chart to represent each syllable they hear.

Activity Overview

Children demonstrate their understanding of how many syllables there are in multisyllabic words, by placing each picture card in the correct row of the pocket chart.

Getting Ready

Cut off the ½ card picture side of the Insects and Arachnids Learning Place Game Cards.

Review the names of the cards with the children.

Use a marker to number blank pocket chart cards.

Build Background

- *Let's have fun with bugs. For this game we use Insects and Arachnid Game Cards and a pocket chart.*
- *Let's say the names of the bugs together before we start.*
- *These picture cards show pictures of words that have between 1 and 4 syllables.*
- *Let's number the rows of the pocket chart 1–4.*

Model the Activity

Write numbers 1–4 on blank Reading Rods® Pocket Chart Cards to number the rows of the large pocket chart.

Place the pile of picture cards upside down on the table.

Refer to the list of syllables in Appendix IV, if needed.

Continue the Activity Together

Allow enough time to do the activity with the children. Provide support as needed. Gradually release responsibility to children.

Watch Me Play

- *Here is how to play the game. I pick a card from the top of the pile.*
- *My word is* <u>butterfly</u>.
- *I say the word slowly and clap the number of syllables:* <u>but</u>–<u>ter</u>-<u>fly</u>.
- *I hold the card at the top step of the pocket chart beside the number 1. I say the word slowly and "walk the picture card down the steps" of the pocket chart:* <u>but</u> *(1),* -<u>ter</u> *(2),* -<u>fly</u> *(3).*
- *How many syllables do I hear? (3) I place the picture of the butterfly card in row 3.*
- *To check to see if this is correct, I say the picture word and touch the rows of the pocket chart.*
- *I clap the syllables again:* <u>but</u>–<u>ter</u>-<u>fly</u>. *I clapped 3 syllables. Therefore, the butterfly picture card is in row 3.*
- *Let's do one together.*

Play the Game with Me

- *Let's play the game together. Who would like to pick the next card?*
- *Look at the picture card and say the word with me.*
- *Let's clap the syllables and say the word again. How many claps did you hear?*
- *Let's hold the card near the top of the chart, beside the number 1.*
- *As we say the word together again, let's "walk the card down the steps," of the chart, one step for each syllable.*
- *At the step where we say the last syllable in the word is where we place the card in the chart*
- *Is the card in the correct row? Let's clap the syllables as we say the word slowly one more time.*

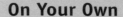

Notes

Independent Activity

When the group is ready, have children take turns. The rest of the group confirms the response by saying and clapping the word together.

On Your Own

- *When it is your turn, pick a card and say the word.*

- *"Walk the card down the steps" of the pocket chart to the correct row.*

- *Listen as the rest of the group says and claps the word together.*

- *Is the number of claps the same as the number of the row on the pocket chart?*

- *The next player continues play by choosing a new card.*

Assess Understanding

Monitor whether each child can easily identify words with a designated number of syllables.

Show What You Know

- [Child's name], *tap out the name of the person sitting next to [behind, in front of] you.*

- [Child's name], *tell me how many syllables you hear in your two favorite colors.*

Insects and Arachnids Game Cards

<u>1-syllable words</u>
ant
bee
flea
fly
moth
wasp

<u>2-syllable words</u>
beetle
termite

<u>3-syllable words</u>
bumblebee
butterfly
dragonfly
grasshopper
ladybug
mosquito
scorpion
lightning bug

<u>4-syllable words</u>
tarantula
rhino beetle
garden spider

Extend and Adapt

Thinking of a Word

Spread the cards on the table, face up. Children take turns by saying, "I'm thinking of a word with [1–5] syllables." The rest of the group looks at the picture cards and guesses a word with that number of syllables. The group confirms the word by repeating the word slowly as they clap out the syllables.

Spin a Word

Use a spinner numbered 1–5. Children take turns spinning for a number. Each child must think of a word with the designated number of syllables. The rest of the group confirms the number of syllables in the word by repeating and clapping the syllables in the word.

Spin and Think

Children may work in pairs or in a small group. One child spins for a number, shares the number with the group, and then thinks of a word with that number of syllables. He keeps the word to himself and gives his partner (or the rest of the group) a hint about the word. The partner uses the hint to think of the word. The whole group confirms the number of syllables by saying and clapping the word.

Syllable Picnic Plate

Provide each child with a paper plate, old magazines, paste, and scissors. Each child writes the number of syllables in his first name in the center of the paper plate. The child cuts out magazine pictures with that number of syllables and pastes them on the plate (*cheese*—1 syllable; *pizza*—2 syllables; *strawberry*—3 syllables; *macaroni*—4 syllables). Children will have fun creating strange combinations of picnic food on their picnic plates.

Unit 2 Activity D

Fruit and Bugs

Materials

- Fruity Fun™ Counters
- Bug Counters
- Mystery Bag
- Segmenting, Blending, and Sorting Mat (side 1)

	1	2	3	4	5

Segmenting, Blending, and Sorting Mat
Side 1

Skill Segment words into syllables units

Objective To recognize that words are made up of syllables and be able to segment them

Purpose To demonstrate understanding of the number of syllables in words, children sort counters by the number of syllables in their names.

Activity Overview Children select a counter form the Mystery Bag, say its name, and clap the number of syllables in the name of the counter. The children place the counter on the mat in the column that represents the number of syllables in the word.

Getting Ready

Gather the Fruity Fun and Bug Counters and review the names with children.

Place the counters in the Mystery Bag.

Use side 1 of the Segmenting, Blending and Sorting Mat (columns labeled with numbers 1–5).

Build Background

- *Are you ready to play with bugs? Let's name the Bug Counters:* grasshopper, bumblebee, beetle, spider, dragonfly, *and* caterpillar.

- *Bugs like fruit because it is sweet. Let's name the Fruit Counters:* banana, apple, orange, grape, strawberry, *and* lemon.

- *The counters go in the Mystery Bag.*

- *We also use a mat with numbered columns. Each number stands for the number of syllables in a word.*

- *Some words have only one syllable. Others may have 2, 3, 4, or 5 syllables. The columns on the mat will let us show how many syllables are in the name of each counter.*

Model the Activity

Tell children that they will use the mat to show how many syllables are in a word.

Watch Me Play

- *Here is how to play the game. Reach into the Mystery Bag and pull out a counter.*

- *I say the name of the counter and place it on the table.*

- *I say the name again and clap out the syllables. Example:* ap-ple—*2 claps.*

- *Did you hear 2 syllables in the word* apple*? I place the counter on the mat in column 2.*

- *Is it correct? I say the name of the counter* [apple] *and clap the syllables* [ap-ple].

- *That is 2 claps. The counter belongs in the second column.*

- *Let's try it again with a different counter.*

Continue the Activity Together

Continue the activity with the children and provide support as needed.

Gradually release responsibility to children.

Play the Game with Me

- *Try this activity with me.* [Child's name]*, reach in the bag and pick out a counter.*

- *Which one did you pick? Let's all say the name of the counter.*

- *Place the counter on the table.*

- *Now say the name again and clap the syllables. How many claps did you hear?*

- *Where does the counter belong on the mat? If the word has 2 syllables, place it on the column labeled with the number 2. Let's place it in the _____ column.*

- *How can we check to see if we are correct? Let's say the name again and clap the syllables. How many times did you clap? Is that the number on top of the column where you placed the object?*

- *Who wants to choose the next counter from the bag?*

Fruit and Bugs

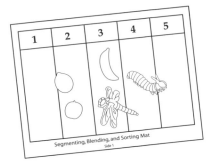

Independent Activity

Continue play until all the fruit and bug counters are out of the bag and on the mat.

Extend the game by placing picture cards in the Mystery Bag.

Assess Understanding

Give two picture cards or small classroom objects to each child. Ask children to place them in the correct columns on their mats.

Monitor whether each child can clap the syllables in a word. Note any difficulties.

On Your Own

- *Take turns choosing a counter from the bag and placing it on the table.*

- *Say the name of the counter and clap the syllables. How many claps did you hear?*

- *Place the counter in the correct column on the mat, according to the number of syllables in the name.*

- *Check your response. Say the name again as you clap the syllables. Is your counter in the correct column?*

Show What You Know

- *Listen to the word* pineapple. *Say the word and clap out the syllables.*

- *[Child's name], how many syllables do you hear in the word?*

- *Who can think of the name of a bug with 2 syllables? 3 syllables? 1 syllable? Say the name and clap out the syllables.*

- *Play the game: I am thinking of something with* [number] *syllables. [Child's name], say and clap out the name of a* [number]-*syllable word.*

Number of syllables:

grasshopper (3)

bumblebee (3)

beetle (2)

spider (2)

dragonfly (3)

caterpillar (4)

banana (3)

apple (2)

orange (2)

grape (1)

strawberry (3)

lemon (2)

Extend and Adapt

Name That Fruit

Taking turns, a child reaches into the bag and feels a fruit counter. He keeps the name of the counter secret. The child claps the number of syllables in the name of the fruit. The group must guess which fruit counter the child picked. If the group cannot guess the name, the child may provide two other hints, such as "It starts with" or "It is yellow." When the group guesses correctly, the fruit is removed from the bag and all clap the syllables.

Bugs Like Fruit

Place the grape, apple, and strawberry counters on the table to represent the 1, 2, and 3 columns. Place all the Bug Counters (except the caterpillar) in the Mystery Bag. Each child takes a turn and picks one bug from the bag, says the name, and claps out the syllables. The child matches the bug counter to the piece of fruit with the same number of syllables. For example, *spider* (2 syllables) goes with *apple*. Play again using different fruit counters (*orange* (1), *lemon* (2), and *banana* (3)).

Unit 2 Activity E

Syllable Spinner

Notes

Materials

- Game Spinner
- Fruits and Vegetables Learning Place® Game Cards
- BLMs 2-4 Four-and-Five Syllable Picture Cards

Skill

Segment words into syllables

Objective

To recognize that words are made of sound units called syllables

Purpose

To learn to distinguish the number of syllables in words, children select a picture card with a given number of syllables.

Activity Overview

Children spin for a number and choose a picture from a group of picture cards that has the same number of syllables as the number shown on the spinner.

Getting Ready

Use the spinner with numbers 1–5. Arrange 6–8 Fruits and Vegetables Learning Place Game Cards right-side up on the table.

Build Background

- *Fruits and vegetables are good for us. They are healthy foods. Fruits and vegetables can also be fun.*
- *Let's say the names of the fruits and vegetablespictures together.*
- *What is your favorite fruit or vegetable? How many syllables do you hear in their names? Let's clap the syllables.*

Model the Activity

Continue to model the activity as needed.

Watch Me Play

- *Watch me play the game.*
- *First, I spin for a number.*
- *Next, I look for a picture card with the same number of syllables.*
- *I place the card on the table and clap the syllables in the name of the picture.*
- *If the number of claps and syllables matches the number on the spinner, I keep the card.*
- *Then it is the next player's turn to spin for a number.*

Continue the Activity Together

Continue the activity with children. Offer support as needed.

If children are ready for more challenge, copy and cut apart 4- and 5-syllable Picture Cards on BLMs 2-4 and 2-5.

Play the Game with Me

- *Place a different set of 6–8 picture cards right-side up on the table.*
- *Let's try this activity together. Who would like to spin first?*
- [Child's name], *spin the number _____.*
- *Let's help* [Child's name] *find a picture word with _____ syllables.*
- [Child's name], *pick up the picture card and place it in front of you.*
- *Let's see if* [child's name] *is right. Let's clap the syllables in the picture name.*
- *How many times did we clap? How many syllables are there in the word?*
- *Does it match the number on the spinner? If it matches,* [child's name] *gets to keep the card.*
- *Who would like to spin for a number next?*

Unit 2 Activity E

Syllable Spinner

Independent Activity

Use a different set of picture cards (Insects and Arachnids Learning Place® Game Cards or Reading Rods® Phonological Awareness Pocket Chart Cards).

Assess Understanding

Monitor whether each child can select a picture name with a designated number of syllables.

Note any difficulties and at which point they begin to occur.

On Your Own

- *Look at the picture cards on the table.*
- *Spin for a number.*
- *Pick up a picture card with the designated number of syllables and place it in front of you.*
- *Clap the syllables in the picture name.*
- *Does the number of claps and syllables match the number on the spinner?*
- *If it matches, keep the card.*
- *Then it is the next player's turn to spin.*

Show What You Know

- [Child's name], *can you think of a vegetable name with ___ syllables? Clap the vegetable name. How many syllables do you hear?*
- [Child's name], *what is my technology word? Join these syllables together to make a word:* <u>com</u>-<u>put</u>-<u>er</u>. *How many syllables do you hear?*

  Use other words, such as

sat-el-lite	vid-e-o
tel-e-vi-sion	ra-di-o
tel-e-phone	mov-ie
disc	key-board
mi-cro-phone	mon-i-tor
print-er	speak-er

Fruits and Vegetables Learning Place Game Cards:

2-syllable words

apple

cabbage

carrots

cherries

spinach

lettuce

onions

3-syllable words

apricots

artichokes

broccoli

lemons

oranges

pineapple

potatoes

radishes

strawberries

4-syllable words

cauliflower

watermelons

Extend and Adapt

Counter Moves

Use Reading Rods® Picture Rods, your choice of counters, and side 2 of the Segmenting, Blending, and Sorting Mat. Place a Picture Rod in the circle at the top of the mat. Place 6–8 counters in the circle. The child says the word and moves one counter for each syllable down the mat. Ask the child to say the picture word and clap the syllables. Does the number of claps and syllables match the number of counters on the mat?

Thinking of a Word

Each child plays with a partner. One child spins for a number and thinks of a word with the designated number of syllables. The child says, "I'm thinking of a word…" and gives his partner a hint about the word. The partner must guess the word and clap the number of syllables. The number of claps must match the number on the spinner.

Spin a Name

A child spins for a number and then asks who in the group has the designated number of syllables in his name. Both children clap the child's name to confirm the number of syllables. The game can be played using names of brothers or sisters or pet names (real or imaginary).

Unit 2 Activity F

Pass the Mystery Bag

Materials

- BLM 2-5 Elkonin Boxes
- Reading Rods® Phonological Awareness Pocket Chart Cards
- Mystery Bag

Skill

Blend syllables or sound units to make words

Objective

To recognize that syllables blend together to make words

Purpose

To distinguish the syllables in words, children listen to the segmented syllables of a word and blend the syllables to say the word.

Activity Overview

Children choose a picture from the Mystery Bag and say the segmented syllables slowly for the group. The rest of the group blends the syllables together and says the word aloud.

Getting Ready

Begin the activity by placing 2-syllable animal picture cards in the Mystery Bag.

2-syllable cards
camel
lion
monkey
rabbit
tiger
turtle
zebra
ostrich
inchworm

Build Background

- *Let's talk about our favorite kinds of animals. What animals have you seen at the zoo, on a farm, in the wild?*
- *Who had a pet? What kinds of animals make good pets?*
- *For this activity, we can use animal picture cards.*
- *Let's look at the picture cards and say the animal names.*

Model the Activity

Model the activity as needed.

When children are able to do 2-syllable words, add 3-syllable animal picture cards to the Mystery Bag.

3-syllable cards

gorilla

octopus

kangaroo

elephant

Continue the Activity Together

Fill the Mystery Bag with 2-, 3-, and 4-syllable animal picture cards.

4-syllable cards

salamander

barracuda

tarantula

rhinoceros

alligator

armadillo

Watch Me Play

- *Here is how to play the game.*
- *Reach in the Mystery Bag and take a card. Hold it so that no one else can see the picture.*
- *I look at the card and think about the syllables in the picture word.*
- *I say the word slowly in syllables. For example, mon-key.*
- *Then I ask the group, "What is the word?"*
- *The group blends the syllables to say the word, monkey.*
- *Is it the correct word?*
- *I show the picture to the group to see if they are correct.*
- *To play again, the next person takes a card from the Mystery Bag.*

Play the Game with Me

- *Let's fill the bag with 2- and 3-syllable words and play the game together.*
- *Choose a picture card and hold it so that no one else can see the picture.*
- *Think about the word and say the name of the picture by saying each syllable.*
- *Who would like to try? Say the name of the picture by saying each syllable. Ask the group, "What is the word?"*
- *Blend the syllables together and say the name of the picture.*
- *Were we correct? Show us the picture.*
- *Who would like to take a turn to choose a picture card?*

Pass the Mystery Bag

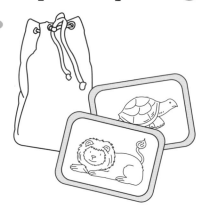

Notes

Independent Activity

Review the names of the animals and add 5-syllable cards to the Mystery Bag.

5-syllable cards
hippopotamus
bottlenose dolphin
found on BLM 2-4

You may wish to continue the activity with a combination of 2–5 syllable cards.

Assess Understanding

Use a copy of BLM 2-5 Elkonin Boxes and the children's choice of counters.

Note any hesitancy or reliance on others in the group.

On Your Own

- *Are you ready to try it on your own?*
- *When it is your turn, take a picture card from the Mystery Bag.*
- *Say the name of the picture for the group by saying each syllable.*
- *Ask the group, "What is the word?"*
- *Then show the picture to the group. Were they correct?*
- *Pass the Mystery Bag to the next player.*

Show What You Know

- *[Child's name], when I show you a picture, say the name of the picture and then say the syllables in the name. For example, I show you a picture of a table. You say the word* <u>table</u>*. Then you say the syllables,* <u>ta</u>-<u>ble</u>*. How many syllables do you hear in the word* <u>table</u>*?*[2]
- *Place a set of counters in the circle at the top of the page. Move the correct number of counters down the page into the boxes as you say the syllables. How many syllables are in the word?*
- *[Child's name], I will say the syllables in a word. You say the word. For example, I say* <u>va</u>-<u>ca</u>-<u>tion</u>*. You say the word,* <u>vacation</u>*.*

Elkonin Boxes

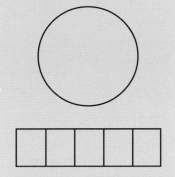

1-syllable cards

cow

cat

dog

duck

fish

fox

goat

goose

horse

mouse

pig

seal

Syllable Slide

Make copies of the Elkonin Boxes in BLM 2-5. Use picture cards with 1–5 syllable names, and 1–5 counters. Children place their counters in the circle. Taking turns, each child chooses a picture card and says the name of the picture. Next the child segments the name and slides the counters, one for each syllable, into the columns on the card. Finally, the child checks his response by saying the syllables in the word as he touches each counter on the card.

Picture Sort

Place all picture cards in the Mystery Bag. Each child selects a card and sorts the card into groups by number of syllables. To extend the activity, children can fold a piece of drawing paper into columns and label the columns 1–5. Using the picture cards, children can draw small pictures in the correct column to show how many syllables are in each picture name. For example, children would draw a tomato in column 3.

Theme Pictures

Create picture cards that correspond with a theme, such as rooms in a house, sports equipment, animals, seasonal items, and so on. Use these cards for syllable activities.

Phonological Awareness at the Onset and Rime Level

Onsets and rimes are parts of spoken language that are smaller than syllables but larger than phonemes. The onset is the initial consonant in a one-syllable word. Rime includes the remaining sounds, including the vowel and any sounds that follow. For example, in *kite*, the /k/ is the onset, and the /īt/ sound is the rime.

Rhyme awareness is the understanding that certain word endings sound alike, and therefore contain the same sounds, such as the short /a/ and /p/ sound in *cap* and *map* or the long /i/ and /t/ combination in *fight* and *kite*. To recognize and generate rhyming words, children must understand the concept of rhyme. Children must know which part of the word is important for rhyming. Instruction and modeling, segmenting, deleting, substituting, and blending sounds to create rhymes are key components of rhyme awareness. Alliteration is the occurrence of two or more words having the same initial sound in a line or phrase, such as *She sells sea shells at the seashore*.

A Word from the Experts

"Knowledge of nursery rhymes positively influences rhyme awareness. In turn, rhyme awareness in prereaders (e.g., 4-year-old children) has some influence on early reading and spelling development, possibly via its contribution to stimulating phoneme awareness."

G.T. Gillon, *Phonological Awareness: From Research to Practice, 2004*

Unit 3 Objectives

In this unit children will—
- Recognize words with the same beginning sound
- Recognize similar sounds at the ends of words that rhyme
- Develop auditory discrimination skills to distinguish between rhyming words and words that do not rhyme
- Supply a missing word that fits a rhyming pattern
- Recognize and supply words that rhyme with a target word
- Recognize rhyming words in text

Skills Connection

The ability to rhyme orally is helpful for children to be successful in using word parts for reading and spelling. Children learn to look inside words to find familiar patterns based on rhyme patterns to help them to decode and spell unfamiliar words.

English Language Learners

Choose books for read-alouds that provide good examples of alliteration and rhyme. Help students focus on the ending sounds. Point out to children which words rhyme. Talk about how rhyming words sound the same at the end. Segment words between the onset and rime so children can hear how the rime sounds in both words. Reread the text and leave out the second rhyming word. Have children supply the missing rhyming word and make up other words to complete the rhyme.

Home-School Connection

Dear Parents,
Please support your child as he/she recognizes rhyming pattern. Enjoy songs, rhymes, and poems with your child. Point out rhyming words. Talk about how to recognize words that rhyme with one another. Improvise to create nonsense rhymes. Sing songs, such as "A-Shopping We Will Go" to the tune of "A-Hunting We Will Go" and have your child supply names of objects that rhyme.

On-the-Go Assessment for Word Awareness

As children get ready to line up, say a rime sound orally, such as /ăt/. Then say a beginning sound, such as /k/. Ask the child to tell the word that is made with those sounds. Change the beginning sound /m/ and ask the next child to say another word.

Unit 3 Onset/Rime Level Chart of Manipulatives

Activity	A—Complete My Sentence	B—Rhyming Pictures	C—Three in a Row	D—Erase a Rhyme! Draw a Rhyme!	E—Rhyming Bingo	F—Eeny Meeny Miney Mouse
Reading Rods® Picture Rods	●					
BLM 3-1 through 3-8 Rhyme Picture Cards		●	●		●	
Large Pocket Chart			●			●
Student Pocket Chart			●			
Write 'N' Wipe Board				●		
BLM 3-9, 3-10 Erase a Rhyme! Draw a Rhyme!				●		
BLM 3-11, 3-12, 3-13 Rhyming Bingo Cards					●	
Quiet Counters					●	
StoryBlossoms® Small Book Eeny Meeny Miney Mouse						●
Blank Cards						●

Unit 3 Activity A

Complete My Sentence

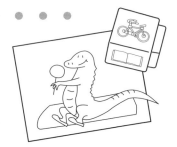

Materials

- Reading Rods® Picture Rods

Skill

Recognize words with the same beginning sound, which are also called alliterative words

Objective

To develop auditory skills to recognize words that begin with the same sound

Purpose

To recognize words with the same beginning sound, children generate sentences using alliterative words.

Activity Overview

Children recognize and generate sentences that use alliteration in order to call attention to the initial sounds in words.

Getting Ready

Engage children in word play by creating short sentences using children's names. For example, *Jack jumps, Carlos cooks,* or *Rakesh runs races.*

Distribute two Reading Rods® picture rods to each child.

Build Background

- *Let's have fun with words that begin with the same sound.*

- *Think about the sound you hear at the beginning of your name.*

- *What other words begin with the same sound as your name?*

- *Let's make up a sentence for each of our names.*

- *Listen to the similar sounds at the beginning of the words.*

- *Each Reading Rod Picture Rod shows pictures that begin with the same sound.*

- *Who can say a sentence that uses the names of all the pictures on the rod?*

StarLIT™ Literacy Intervention Toolkit

Model the Activity

Point out to children that alliterative sentences begin with the same initial sounds.

Watch Me Play

- *Here is how to play the game. Listen to the sentence:* <u>Lucy Lizard likes lollipops.</u>

- *What sound do I hear at the beginning of each word?* (/l/)

- *Now I leave off the last word in the sentence.* <u>Lucy Lizard likes</u> _____.

- *I think of another word with the same beginning sound to complete the sentence.*

- <u>Lucy lizard likes</u> _____. *What word can I use to complete the sentence?* [<u>ladybugs</u>, <u>letters</u>, <u>ladders</u>, <u>leaves</u>, <u>licorice</u>, <u>lilacs</u>, <u>lemons</u>]

- *I need a word that begins with /l/ to complete the sentence. Who can help me?*

- *Then I listen to the next sentence:* <u>Tall Tom took two</u> _____.

- *I think of words that begin with the /t/ to complete the sentence.* [<u>turtles</u>, <u>telephones</u>, <u>tents</u>, <u>tickets</u>, <u>tortillas</u>, <u>tubas</u>]

- *Words that do not begin with /t/ cannot be used. Even though other words would make sense—for example, <u>rides</u>, <u>pencils</u>, and <u>cookies</u>—they do not begin with /t/.*

Continue the Activity Together

Create alliterative sentences and say them aloud for children.

Children enjoy word play with alliteration. Accept silly but appropriate responses.

Play the Game with Me

- *Let's listen to a new sentence:* <u>Sammy saw a sailboat.</u>

- *Repeat the sentence. What sound do we hear at the beginning of each word?*

- *Let's leave off the last word and think of another word that begins with /s/ to complete the sentence.* <u>Sammy saw a</u> _____.

- *Would the word <u>bus</u> fit in the sentence?* <u>Sammy saw a bus.</u> *<u>Bus</u> makes sense, but it does not have the /s/ at the beginning.*

- *Who can think of another word that begins with /s/?* <u>Sammy saw a</u> _____ [<u>sock</u>, <u>seal</u>, <u>sun</u>].

- *Let's listen to another sentence.*

Unit 3 Activity A   Complete My Sentence

Independent Activity

Children enjoy word play. Accept appropriate responses. Use sentences on the following page or enjoy creating your own.

On Your Own

- Listen to the next sentence and think about the sound you hear at the beginning of the words. <u>Big brown bear bought bread.</u>

- Take away the word <u>bread</u>.

- Take turns saying a new word with the same beginning sound that will fit the sentence.

- The rest of the group can give a "Thumbs up" sign if the word fits.

Assess Understanding

Monitor whether each child can recognize and say sentences made of words with the same beginning sound.

Note any difficulties and at what point the difficulties became evident.

Show What You Know

- Make up first names for animals that begin with the same sound as the name of the animal. For example, if <u>dog</u> is the last name, a first name should also begin with /d/. [<u>Darla Dog</u>]

- Say a first name for another animal, such as a horse, goat, camel, kangaroo, or zebra.

- Brainstorm an alliterative sentence for each animal, such as <u>Darla Dog dreams about dinosaurs.</u>

1. Sally Seal sings songs about_____ (soup, supper, sunshine, seagulls).

2. Pink pigs play with _____ (pumpkins, pencils, paper clips).

3. Walter Wombat wanted a _____ (well, watch, wig, wagon).

4. Happy horses hurry home for_____ (hay, hats, honey).

5. Careful Kangaroo carries a _____ (cane, candle, coat).

Extend and Adapt

Finish My Sentence

Each child works with a partner to think of a subject and verb that begin with the same sound, such as *Santo sips* _____. The rest of the group brainstorms how to complete the sentence.

Add a Word

Children stand in a circle. The teacher says a 2-word sentence aloud, such as *Tina tastes*. The child to the teacher's right, repeats the sentence, and adds an alliterative word *(Tina tastes tacos)*. The sentence lengthens as play continues around the circle.

Character Name Alliteration

Many nursery rhymes, storybook and cartoon characters have alliterative names. Have fun creating a list of the names of these characters with the children. Examples include Daisy Duck, Old King Cole, Black Beauty, and so on.

Materials

- Rhyme Picture Cards BLM 3-1, 3-2, 3-3, 3-4, 3-5, 3-6, 3-7, 3-8

Skill
Recognize pairs of words that rhyme

Objective
To match rhyming pairs

Purpose
To develop awareness of the sounds in words, children listen to words that end with the same sound.

Activity Overview
Children distinguish a rhyming pair of picture cards from a group of cards.

Getting Ready

Cut out the Rhyme Picture Cards.

Name each picture card for the group.

Select 4 pairs of Rhyme Picture Cards. Mix up the cards and place them on the table.

Build Background

- *Let's use Rhyme Picture Cards to play a rhyming game.*

- *Before we play the game, let's look at the pictures and say their names.*

- *Listen carefully to the sound you hear at the end of the picture names.*

- *If the cards rhyme, the sounds at the end of both picture names sound the same.*

- *Can you hear a rhyming pair?*

Model the Activity

Choose 4 different pairs of Rhyme Picture Cards.

Continue to model the activity, as needed.

Watch Me Play

- *Here is how to play the game.*
- *There are eight cards on the table. Pick a card and say the picture name.*
- *I say the names of the other pictures on the table.*
- *I listen for a picture word that rhymes with the first picture card.*
- *Then, I pick up the card and put it next the first card.*
- *I repeat the two picture names and listen to the ending sounds.*
- *Do the names of the picture cards rhyme?*
- *I continue the activity by choosing another card and repeating the steps.*
- *At the end of the activity, I have four pairs of rhyming cards.*

Continue the Activity Together

Choose 8 new Rhyme Pictures Cards and place them on the table.

Look at the pictures with children and say the name of each card.

Continue until the group has matched all four rhyming pairs of picture cards.

Play the Game with Me

- *Let's place 8 new cards on the table. Say the name of each card with me.*
- *Who would like to choose a card?*
- *[Child's name], say the picture name for the group.*
- *Point to the remaining pictures as we say the names of the remaining pictures together.*
- *Listen for the sounds at the ends of the words.*
- *Who can find a card that rhymes with the first card?*
- *[Child's name], put the cards next to each other and say the rhyming names.*
- *Let's all say the picture names to see if they rhyme. Do the picture cards rhyme?*
- *Let's play again. Who would like to choose the next card?*

Notes

Independent Activity

Use a new set of 4 pairs of Rhyme Picture Cards.

Observe children as they complete the activity independently.

Assess Understanding

Monitor whether each child can match the Rhyme Picture Cards.

Note any difficulties and at what point the difficulties became evident.

On Your Own

- *Place a new set of Rhyming Picture Cards on the table and say the names of the pictures.*

- *Choose a card and say its name.*

- *Say the names of the remaining cards.*

- *Choose the card that rhymes with the selected card.*

- *Put the cards together and say the names of the two picture cards.*

- *Do they rhyme?*

- *Continue until all 4 rhyming pairs have been matched.*

Show What You Know

- *Look at the cards on the table. Listen as I say a word. Pick up a card that rhymes with my word and say the rhyming pair.*

- *Who can think of a word that rhymes with_____?*

- *I ask a question using the word, and you answer. For example,* <u>Teacher says,</u> <u>Do you know a word that rhymes with *tree*?</u>
<u>You answer,</u> <u>I know a word that rhymes with *tree*.</u>
<u>My rhyming word is *bee*.</u>

Support children as they listen for ending sounds to create rhyming pairs. You may wish to use the following phonograms.

-ack	-ap
-ail	-ash
-ain	-at
-ake	-ate
-ale	-aw
-ame	-ay
-an	-ank
-eat	
-eil	
-est	
-ice	-ing
-ick	-ink
-ide	-ip
-ight	-it
-ill	-in
-ock	-uck
-oke	-ug
-op	-ump
-ore	-unk
-ot	

Extend and Adapt

The Last Word

The teacher says a rhyme with a missing word. Children supply the rhyming word to complete the line. For example,

Pig, pig	Goat, goat	Whale, whale
Dance a _____.	Wear a _____.	Has a _____.

I Know a Word

Children sing a song that has a rhyme in it. The teacher begins by singing *I have a word that rhymes with* <u>cat</u>. The child on the right repeats the song and supplies a new rhyming word *I have a word that rhymes with* <u>hat</u>. The next child repeats the song and supplies a new rhyming word *I have a word that rhymes with* <u>bat</u>. The song continues until it gets back to the teacher who says *And that word is* <u>cat</u>. The teacher sings the song again using a new rhyme *I know word that rhymes with* <u>pet</u>.

I Spy

Have children sit in a circle on the floor. Use rhyming word cards or have children look around the room for rhyming pairs of objects. Create a short sentence with two rhyming words (for example, *I spy a* <u>floor</u> *and a* <u>door,</u> or *I spy a* <u>boy</u> *with a* <u>toy</u>. Invite children to take turns creating their own "I Spy" sentences.

Notes

Materials

- Rhyme Picture Cards BLM 3-1 through 3-8
- Large Pocket Chart
- Student Pocket Charts

Skill

Distinguish between rhyming words and words that do not rhyme

Objective

To use auditory skills to distinguish between words that rhyme and words that do not rhyme

Purpose

To learn to recognize words that rhyme, children focus on the parts of words that sound alike.

Activity Overview

Children identify a set of 3 words that rhyme and place them in a row of a pocket chart.

Getting Ready

Review the names of the Rhyme Picture Cards before you begin the activity.

Separate two sets of three Rhyme Picture Cards.

Use the Large Pocket Chart to model the activity.

Build Background

- *Let's have fun with rhyming picture cards.*
- *Look at the pictures on the Rhyme Picture Cards and say the picture names with me.*
- *When we think about rhyming words, we pay attention to the parts of the words that sound alike.*
- *Words that rhyme have the same sound at the end.*
- *Let's look at the cards on the table and say their names.*
- *Now we can play the game. Do any of these words rhyme? Do any cards end with the same sounds?*

Model the Activity

Place two sets of three Rhyme Picture Cards face up on the table.

Model an example of placing a rhyming word in the row of the pocket chart and placing a nonexample in another row of the pocket chart.

Continue to model the activity as needed.

Continue the Activity Together

Place another group of 6–7 Rhyme Picture Cards face up on the table.

Provide support and gradually release more responsibility to children.

Watch Me Play

- *Here is how to play the game. I select 2 cards that rhyme from the group of picture cards on the table.*

- *I say the names of the rhyming pair. What is the ending sound? I place the two rhyming picture cards in a row in the pocket chart.*

- *I select a third card and explore whether it rhymes with the two cards in the chart.*

- *If the card rhymes with the pair in the pocket chart, I place the new card in the same row.*

- *If the picture card does not rhyme, I return it to the table.*

- *When I find a third rhyming card, I add it to the same row in the pocket chart.*

- *Then I select two new rhyming picture cards from the table.*

- *Let's continue the activity.*

Play the Game with Me

- *Let's look at these new pictures and say their names together. Listen for the rhyming sounds.*

- *[Child's name], choose 2 Rhyme Picture Cards. Say their names and place the cards in a row in the pocket chart.*

- *Who can find another card that rhymes with the two cards in the pocket chart?*

- Nonexample: *If a card does not have the same ending sound, we put the card back and choose another one.*

- Rhyme: *This card has the same ending sound. Let's place it next to the other 2 cards in the pocket chart.*

- *Now we have three rhyming cards. Let's say their names together.*

- *Let's begin again. Who would like to choose two rhyming cards?*

Notes

Independent Activity

Provide each child with a Student Pocket Chart and a group of 7 Rhyme Picture Cards. Cards should include 2 sets of 3 rhyming cards and 1 nonrhyming card.

Assess Understanding

Examples:

ring, king	(sing)
fox, ox	(box)
rose, nose	(toes)
wig, pig	(fig)
up, cup	(pup)
sock, clock	(lock)
cake, make	(take)
bag, flag	(tag)
mop, stop	(hop)
bug, rug	(snug)
hand, band	(sand)
tie, my	(pie)
ice, mice	(nice)
sun, fun	(bun)
jet, met	(pet)

On Your Own

- *Use a Student Pocket Chart and aset of cards.*
- *Place the cards face up on the table.*
- *Choose 2 cards that rhyme and say the names of the pictures.*
- *Place both cards in a row in the pocket chart.*
- *Choose a third card and say the name.*
- *If the picture rhymes with the cards in the pocket chart, place the card in the same row.*
- *If the picture does not rhyme, put it back and try another card.*
- *Continue until you have three cards in the row.*
- *Then pick two more rhyming words from the table. Continue the activity.*
- *When you are finished, say the names of the words in each row aloud for the group.*

Show What You Know

- *Listen to a pair of rhyming words I say. Say another word that rhymes with the two words.*

Rhyme Picture Cards:

<u>track</u>	tack	sack
<u>run</u>	bun	sun
<u>clap</u>	cap	map
<u>jar</u>	star	car
<u>chest</u>	vest	nest
<u>brick</u>	stick	sick
<u>nail</u>	pail	mail
<u>van</u>	fan	pan
<u>bat</u>	rat	cat
<u>dig</u>	wig	pig
<u>net</u>	wet	jet
<u>log</u>	frog	dog
<u>snake</u>	rake	lake
<u>pill</u>	grill	hill
<u>plate</u>	skate	eight
<u>well</u>	shell	bell
<u>twin</u>	violin	pin
<u>swing</u>	sing	ring
<u>dice</u>	ice	rice
<u>boat</u>	coat	goat
<u>mop</u>	stop	pop
<u>run</u>	bun	sun
<u>lock</u>	clock	sock
<u>rug</u>	bug	mug
<u>nose</u>	rose	toes

Extend and Adapt

Thumbs Up!

Say a pair of words aloud for each child. If the two words rhyme, the child gives the "Thumbs up" sign. If the two words do not rhyme, the child gives the "Thumbs down" sign.

<u>Rhyming Pairs</u>		<u>Nonrhyming Pairs</u>	
fox-box	toad-road	bug-bag	pen-pig
bed-Ted	toast-roast	hair-hat	toad-red
sack-snack	fill-bill		

Fish for a Rhyme

Attach paper clips to rhyming picture cards to create fish and place them in a baking pan—a make-believe pond. Tie a string with a magnet on the end to a stick to serve a fishing pole. In turn, each child uses the fishing pole to fish for a picture card. Then the child fishes for another card that rhymes with the first. If the child "catches" a rhyme, he keeps the cards. The child with the most rhyming fish wins the game.

Three-Way Match

Place 12 picture cards face down in a 3 x 4 array on the table. In turn, each child turns over 3 picture cards. If all 3 cards rhyme, the child keeps the cards. If the 3 words do not rhyme, the child turns the cards over and the next child takes a turn.

Erase a Rhyme!
Draw a Rhyme!

Notes

Materials

- Write 'N' Wipe Board

- BLM 3-9: Erase a Rhyme!, and BLM 3-10: Draw a Rhyme!

- Rhyming stories for teacher read-alouds found in Appendix IV.

Skill

Identify words that rhyme

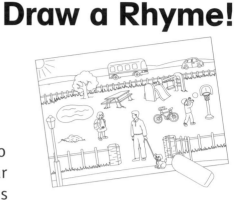

Objective

To develop auditory skills to recognize similar rhyming patterns

Purpose

To discriminate between words that end with the same sounds, children supply rhyming words to complete a rhyming pattern.

Activity Overview

Children listen to an incomplete rhyming pattern and select the name of an object with the same ending sound to complete the rhyme.

Getting Ready

Draw the picture shown on BLM 3-9 on the dry erase board or a chalkboard and have children erase parts of the picture. As an alternative, provide children with a copy of BLM 3-9 and have children color parts of the picture.

Build Background

- *Look at this picture of a park. What do you like to do when you visit a park? How do you have fun?*

- *Let's say the names of the objects that we see in this park.*

- *For this activity, we will make parts of this picture disappear (or color some of the objects in the picture.).*

- *Listen to the story Going to the Park and look for objects in the picture that complete the rhymes.*

Model the Activity

Draw children's attention to the changes in the picture as they erase or color.

Continue modeling the activity as needed.

Continue the Activity Together

As you continue the activity with children, repeat the rhymes, using the names of the objects.

Gradually release responsibility as you continue the activity together.

Watch Me Play

- *Here is how to play the game. Listen to the first set of rhymes:* <u>Come with us</u>: <u>erase (color) the</u> _____.
- *The last word in the rhyme is missing. Something in the picture completes the rhyme.*
- *I listen for the ending sound that makes the rhyme. Look for an object in the picture that rhymes with us.* [<u>bus</u>]
- *I say the rhyme again to see if the name of the object completes the rhyme.*
- *When I find the name of an object that completes the rhyme, I erase (color) it from the picture.*
- *If the name of the object does not complete the rhyme, I continue looking at the picture until the rhyming word is found.*
- *How will the picture change?*

Play the Game with Me

- *Let's do the activity together.*
- *Listen to the story. When I stop reading, think about what object in the picture would fit the rhyming pattern.*
- *Who's ready to try?*
- *Listen and then look for the name of the object with the same ending sounds. Does it complete the rhyme?*
- *If the name does not complete the rhyme, find another object in the picture that has the same ending sounds.*
- *If the word does complete the rhyme, ask a volunteer to erase the object from the picture.*
- *Let's listen to the rest of the rhymes and see how our picture changes.*

Unit 3 Activity D

Erase a Rhyme! Draw a Rhyme!

Independent Activity

Provide each child with a copy of BLM 3-10: Draw a Rhyme!

Offer support and modeling for children by doing the first 3–4 examples together.

Observe children as they complete the activity.

Encourage children to quickly draw the outline of the alien's body parts. They can color and add details later on.

Assess Understanding

Monitor whether each child can recognize ending sounds that rhyme and can supply another word to complete a rhyme.

Note any difficulty and at what point it became evident.

On Your Own

- *Use a new picture and a different set of rhymes for this activity.*
- *Instead of erasing (coloring)objects, draw the parts of an alien from outer space.*
- *Who knows what an alien looks like?*
- *Listen very carefully as I read the rhyme. The rhyme will tell you how the alien looks.*
- *Draw the parts of the alien that fit the rhyme.*
- *What parts of the alien fit the rhyme?*
  <u>An alien landed from outer space</u>
  <u>With a puzzled look on his egg-shaped</u> _____.
- *What body part completes the rhyme?* [face]
- *Listen once again to how the alien looks.*
- <u>Face</u> *completes the rhyme. Did you draw an egg-shaped face?*
- *The alien now has a face, let's listen to the next rhyme and draw another part of the alien.*

Show What You Know

- *Let's sit in a circle on the floor. Listen to the word.*
- *When I toss the beanbag (or a foam ball), catch it and say a word that rhymes with the word.*
- *Then toss the beanbag to someone else. That child catches the beanbag and says another rhyming word.*
- *Let's see how many rhyming words we can say.*

Children may enjoy creating rhyming sentences using pairs of words. For example,

Click, <u>clack</u>,
The train went down the <u>track</u>.

snap/trap

man/van

bake/cake

snack/sack

dip/drip

shop/pop

more/store

bump/lump

Extend and Adapt

Who Has the Rhyme?

Children stand in a circle. Each child has a picture card with different ending sounds. Read a pair of rhyming sentences that end with a missing word. The child who has the picture card that completes the rhyme repeats the rhyming sentences aloud and adds his word. If it rhymes, the child sits down. Continue until all children are sitting.

Draw It

Read short rhymes to the children. Leave off the last word of the rhyme. Have children draw a picture of an object that would complete the rhyme. For example, *The shivering goat/Forgot his <u>coat</u>*, or *Dad used a wrench/To fix the <u>bench</u>*.

Rhyme Collection

Give each child a target picture word to start a collection. The child can draw the target picture word on a small paper bag or cut out a magazine picture of the word and paste it on the bag. Have each child cut five pictures from old magazines that rhyme with the target word and place them in the bag. Later, have each child share the pictures with the group.

Rhyming Bingo!

Notes
Materials

- BLM 3-3, 3-4, 3-5, Rhyming Bingo Cards
- Quiet Counters
- Rhyme Picture Cards BLM 3-1 through 3-8

Skill

Recognize words that rhyme with a target word

Objective

To focus on ending sounds of words, children select names of pictures that rhyme with a target word

Purpose

To gain awareness of rhyming sounds in words children listen for words that end in the same sounds.

Activity Overview

Children listen to target words and cover pictures on their bingo cards that rhyme with the target word.

Getting Ready

Provide each child with a Rhyming Bingo Card and Quiet Counters.

Review the images on the set of picture cards to avoid any confusion about picture names.

Teacher Note: Use these target word cards:

track	dig
clap	pill
chest	shell
nail	swing
bat	boat
net	pop
snake	jar
plate	van
twin	lock
dice	rug
log	nose
run	brick

Build Background

- *Let's have fun playing Rhyming Bingo.*
- *Who knows how to play Bingo?*
- *Each of us has a bingo card and some counters.*
- *There is a smiley face in the middle of your card.*
- *Let's say the names of the pictures on our bingo cards. Listen to the sounds at the ends of the names.*
- *Raise your hand of you hear words that rhyme.*

StarLIT™ Literacy Intervention Toolkit

Model the Activity

Target word cards show a shaded triangle in the lower corner.

Establish the name of the selected picture card as the target word.

Model the activity as needed.

Continue the Activity Together

Reshuffle the picture cards and place them in a pile on the table.

Remind children that the card that is chosen is the target word.

Redistribute the Bingo cards.

Coach the children until they are ready to play independently.

Watch Me Play

- *Here is how to play the game. I take one picture card from the pile. I look at the picture and say the name. This is the target word.*

- *I repeat the target word and listen to the ending sound.*

- *Now I look for a picture on my Bingo card that rhymes with the target word. I use a counter to cover up the word that rhymes with the target word.*

- *Then I take another picture card from the pile and repeat the steps until a whole row of pictures is covered on the Bingo card.*

- *I say "Bingo!" to win the game.*

- *Then I say the picture names that are covered on my card. Does each one rhyme with a target word?*

Play the Game with Me

- *Let's play together. We each have a Bingo card.*

- *Let's take turns choosing a picture card from the pile and saying the name of the target word.*

- *Let's all say the target word together.*

- *Let's look at our Bingo cards to find a picture word that rhymes with the target word.*

- *If the word rhymes with the target word, cover the picture with a counter.*

- *The next player takes a card and says the target word.*

- *Let's look at the open pictures on our cards. Cover the picture that rhymes with the target word.*

- *Continue until someone in the group has covered a complete row of pictures and says "Bingo!"*

Rhyming Bingo!

Rhyming Bingo

Independent Activity

Vary Rhyming Bingo! by covering the corner pictures, the outside perimeter pictures, the top and bottom rows of pictures, or all of the pictures on the Bingo cards.

On Your Own

- *Exchange Bingo cards.*
- *Reshuffle and stack the pile of target picture cards.*
- *Choose a picture card and say the target word for the group.*
- *Find a picture on your card that rhymes with the target word.*
- *Cover each rhyming picture with a counter until a complete row of picture words is covered.*
- *Say "Bingo!" to win the game.*

Assess Understanding

Monitor whether each child can provide a word that rhymes with a target word.

Note any difficulties and at what point the difficulties become evident.

Show What You Know

- *Let's all sit together in a circle. Look at the picture card and listen to the word.*
- *Can you think of another word that rhymes with the target word?*
- *When I toss a sponge ball (or a beanbag) to someone in the group, that child says a rhyming word. Then he tosses the ball to another child, who says another word that rhymes with the target word.*
- *We continue to play until we cannot think of any more rhyming words.*
- *The child with the ball begins with a new word, and the game starts all over again.*

StarLIT™ Literacy Intervention Toolkit

Reading Rods®
Pocket Chart Cards
Animal Pictures

cat	dog
duck	fox
frog	goat
horse	mouse
pig	camel
lion	monkey
rabbit	tiger
turtle	zebra
gorilla	seal
ant	ox
inchworm	ostrich
elephant	octopus

Rhyme Card
Animal Pictures

bat	rat	cat
snake	goat	bug

Insects and
Arachnids
Game Cards

beetle	flea
mosquito	bee
dragonfly	ant
bumblebee	fly
tarantula	ladybug
butterfly	termite
scorpion	moth
grasshopper	wasp
rhino beetle	
monarch butterfly	
garden spider	
lightning bug	

Extend and Adapt

Rhyme Partners
Use a small set of rhyming pairs of picture cards. Give one card to each child. Children circulate to find the other person in the group with the picture card that rhymes with his card. The two children say their pair of rhyming words aloud for the group. Shuffle the cards and repeat.

Pocket Chart Rhymes (See left column)
Use animal picture cards. Invite children to choose a card and think of a short rhyme with the name of the animal. For example *The* snake *swam in the* lake, or *The* pig *wore a purple* wig. Extend the activity by inviting children to add two rhymes, such as *When the* snake *started to* bake*, he jumped in the* lake.

It's Raining, It's Pouring; The Old Man Is Snoring
Improvise on the words of the familiar song. Replace *He went to bed and bumped his head* with other rhyming words. For example, *He bumped his* hand *on a rubber* band, or *He bumped his* toe *on a pile of* snow. Children will enjoy making up silly verses and ending the song with *And he couldn't get up in the morning.*

Unit 3 Activity F

Eeny Meeny Miney Mouse

Materials

- Story Blossoms™ small book *Eeny Meeny Miney Mouse*
- Large Pocket Chart
- Blank Cards

Getting Ready

Show children the title of the book, *Eeny Meeny Miney Mouse* by G. Pascoe and S. Williams.

Skill

Recognize rhyming words in a story

Objective

To develop auditory discrimination skills to recognize words that rhyme

Purpose

In order to learn to distinguish rhyming words in text, children arrange blank cards in a pocket chart and use color to show which words rhyme.

Activity Overview

Children listen to text and place cards in a pocket chart to represent each word. They use color to discriminate the rhyming words from other words.

Build Background

- *Here is a fun book to read aloud. Let's sit together and listen to the story* Eeny Meeny Miney Mouse *by Gwen Pascoe and Simone Williams.*

- *What do you think this book will be about?*

- *What does the title remind you of?*

- *Did you think of a way of choosing someone or something called* Eeny meeny miney moe?

- *Help me say* Eeny meeny miney moe *and listen for the words that rhyme:*

    Eeny meeny miney moe,
    Catch a tiger by the toe.
    If he hollers, let him go.
    Eeny meeny miney moe.

- *Did you hear the rhyming words? What part of the words sounded the same—the beginning or the ending?*

- Moe, toe, *and* go *have the same ending sound.*

- *Listen for the rhyming words as I read this story aloud.*

Model the Activity

Read page 4 aloud to the children.

This activity may require a great deal of modeling.

Watch Me Play

- *Listen to my favorite part of the story. Do you hear rhyming words?* [Eeny, meeny; moo, shoe]

- *I place blank cards in the pocket chart to model the words in the story.*

- *I use red cards for words that rhyme and blue cards for words that do not rhyme.*

- *Here is the first line:* Eeny, meeny, miney, moo. *How many cards will I need? There are four words, so I will need four cards.*

- *Do any of these words rhyme?* Eeny, meeny, miney, moo. *Yes,* eeny *and* meeny *are rhyming words. I need two red cards.*

- *Watch as I place cards in the chart. Two red cards for* Eeny, meeny. *Two blue cards for* miney, moo. *Is that correct?*

- *I say the words as I touch the cards* Eeny, meeny, miney *and* moo.

- *Listen to the rest of the words:* Have you been hiding in my shoe? *How many cards do I need?* [7]

- *Another word rhymes with* shoe. *Which word is it? Go back and check the words.* Eeny, meeny, miney, moo—have you been hiding in my shoe?

- Shoe *rhymes with* moo. *I need red cards for these rhyming words.*

- *I need six blue cards and one red card.*

Continue the Activity Together

Continue the pocket chart activity using the text from page 10.

Repeat the activity using children's favorite parts of the book.

Play the Game with Me

- *Let's read the text aloud and continue the activity. Help me find the rhyming words.*

- *How many cards do we need for the pocket chart? How many red cards? How many blue cards?*

- *Who would like to point to each card as we repeat the text together?*

- *Let's review the rhyming words together.*

Unit 3 Activity F

Eeny Meeny Miney Mouse

Independent Activity

Show the picture and read the text on page 6 aloud.

The audiotape of *Eeny Meeny Miney Mouse* is available from ETA/Cuisenaire®. Visit our website at www.etacuisenaire.com

Assess Understanding

Monitor whether each child can recognize rhyming words at the end of sentences.

Remember that rhyming can be a difficult activity for some children. Try to help the child hear the part of the word that rhymes by accenting the ending as you say the word.

If a student cannot master rhyming, do not hold back from working on initial sounds.

On Your Own

- *Look at the picture and listen for the rhyming words.*

- *Name the words that rhyme.* [Eeny, meeny; mole, hole] *How many red cards do you need?* [4]

- *How many words do not rhyme? How many blue cards do you need?*

- *Place the cards in the pocket chart.*

- *Point to the cards as the group says the words together.*

Show What You Know

- *Let's take an imaginary safari. We can take two items.*

- *Listen to the name of one item. Can you think of another item that rhymes with it?*

- *I say, "I'm going on a safari, and I am taking a sack and a _____." You take turns adding another item that rhymes with sack.* [snack]

- *Later we can use other rhyming words or we can bring two rhyming words.* [snack, tack]

- *Take turns making up imaginary trips and thinking about the items you can bring along.*

Rhyming words in *Eeny Meeny Miney Mouse:*
Rhyming words *eeny* and *meeny* appear in each section.

pp. 1-2	mouse/house
p. 4	moo/shoe
p. 6	mole/hole
p. 9	mums/crumbs
p. 10	munch/lunch
p. 12	moan/phone
p. 14	mat/cat
pp. 15-16	mouse/house

I'm going to the mountains, and I am taking a_____ and a _____.

I'm going to the desert, and I am taking a _____ and a _____.

I'm going to the seashore, and I am taking a _____ and a _____ .

Extend and Adapt

I Found a Word

Sing a song that has a riddle in it. Children listen to the song and suggest a rhyming word to complete the riddle.

> *I found a word that rhymes with <u>cake</u>,*
> *I found a word that rhymes with <u>cake</u>,*
> *I found a word that rhymes with <u>cake</u>,*
> *My rhyming word is _____.*
> > [<u>lake</u>, <u>rake</u>, <u>snake</u>, <u>bake</u>, <u>Jake</u>]

Puppet Fun

Read the story aloud to the children. Allow children to take turns with the pupet. Ask the child to make the puppet perform a specific gesture when he hears the rhyming word at the end of each sentence. The puppet can open its mouth wide, get shy, pop up, or dance happily when it hears a rhyming word.

Phonological Awareness at the Phoneme Isolation Level

Phonemes are the smallest units of sound in a word. The English language has about 41 phonemes. Most words have more than one phoneme. A student with phonemic awareness hears the three distinct sounds in the word *bat*: /b/ /ă/ /t/.

Phoneme awareness plays an important role in the development of the alphabetic principle—that a word is simply a means of applying a letter code to the sounds of the spoken word. The ability to hear, identify, and manipulate individual sounds is important to learning to read and spell.

A major component that determines a child's readiness to learn to read is an understanding of how sounds work together. There are many different sounds in the English language. When two or more sounds are put together, a word is created. It is important for children to understand that words are blended sounds.

A Word from the Experts

66 You should provide your students with instruction that is appropriate for their level of literacy development. If you teach younger children or less able, older readers, your instruction should begin with easier activities, such as having children identify and categorize the first phonemes in words. When the children can do these activities, move them on to more difficult ones. 99

B.B. Armbuster, F. Lehr, & J. Osborn, *Put Reading First: The Research Building Blocks for Teaching Children to Read,* 2001.

Unit 4 Objectives

- Identify the beginning, ending, and middle sounds in words
- Categorize the beginning, ending, and middle sounds in words
- Distinguish between the beginning, ending, or middle sounds in words

Skills Connection

By looking inside words for individual sounds, children can later attend to them in print. To be able to isolate sounds encourages invented or temporary spelling and forms the foundation for early writing.

English Language Learners

Read aloud and shared reading experiences provide opportunities to focus on particular aspects of word play. Select words from a story that have three or four sounds. Say the words, sound by sound. Pick a word from a story or poem. Ask children to put on their "construction hats" to help build a word. For example, say the segmented sounds /c/ /ă/ /t/, and ask the children to construct the sounds to say the word *cat*.

Home-School Connection

Dear Parents,
Support your child as he/she learns to identify beginning, middle, and ending sounds in words. This game can be played at home or in the car. Ask your child to name three objects that begin or end with a particular sound. For example, "Name three objects that you see that begin with /s/". [*sink, salt, soup*] Challenge your child to name three objects that have the same middle sound, such as *cat, bag,* and *rack*.

On-the-Go Assessment for Word Awareness

As children get ready for dismissal, ask each child to tell you the sound at the beginning, middle, or end of a word. For example, "Tell me the sound you hear at the end of apple." [/l/]

Unit 4 Phoneme Isolation Chart of Manipulatives

Activity	A—Sound Bus	B—Picture Card Sound Match	C—Mystery Sound Bag	D—Feed the Animals	E—Sound Chart	F—Sound Concentration
Reading Rods® Phonological Awareness Pocket Chart Cards	●	●			●	●
BLM 4-1, 4-2 Sound Bus	●					
BLM 4-2 Two Sounds Chart		●				
Mystery Bag	●		●			
Choice of Picture Cards			●		●	●
BLM 4-3 Animal Head Cutouts				●		
BLM 4-4, 4-5, 4-6, 4-7 Food Picture Cards				●		
Large Pocket Chart					●	

Unit 4 Activity A

Sound Bus

Notes

Materials

- BLM 4-1, 4-2 Sound Bus
- Mystery Bag
- Reading Rods® Phonological Awareness Pocket Chart Cards

Skill

Phonemic Isolation and Categorization

Objective

To identify and categorize initial sounds in words

Purpose

To determine if two sounds are the same or different, children isolate and categorize words by initial sound.

Activity Overview

Children say a word, segment the initial sound, compare the sound to a target sound, and determine if the two sounds are the same or different.

Getting Ready

Discuss children's past experiences riding a bus. Ask a volunteer to describe what it is like to ride on a public bus. Explain that people wait at the bus stop to board the correct bus. They must have a ticket, a token, or pay a fare to ride the bus.

Build Background

- *Who can tell us what it is like to ride on a bus?*
- *People who want to ride a bus wait at the bus stop.*
- *When the right bus stops, they board the bus. If another bus stops, they wait at the bus stop until the right bus comes along.*
- *When people board the bus, they pay a fare.*
- Show the picture of the bus on BLM 4-1, 4-2 and the picture cards. *We can use this picture of a bus and four picture cards to play a game called Sound Bus.*

Model the Activity

The target sound is /b/. Select pictures cards for *ball*, *book*, *banana* and *moon* and set them aside.

When modeling this activity, choose picture cards that show objects that begin with two sounds that are not at all alike. (See Appendix II Maximal Pairs.)

First model what to do when the picture starts with the target sound. Then model what to do when the picture does not start with the target sound.

Continue the Activity Together

Check that each child understands the instructions and knows how to isolate and compare initial sounds. Select a new set of cards and model again.

Watch Me Play

When the sounds match: Pick up the picture card and say *ball*.

- *Here is how to play the game. This is a picture of a ball.* Ball *starts with /b/. Repeat the word and sound.*

- *This is the /b/ bus, so I place the picture of the ball in the driver's seat.*

- Pick up a second picture of an item that starts with the target sound—book. Book *begins with /b/. I say the picture word and say the beginning sound /b/.*

- Ball. Book. *Do they begin with the same sound?* Ball /b/; book /b/.

- *They both start with /b/ so* book *can ride the /b/ bus. I put the picture of the book on the /b/ bus.*

Pick up another picture card that begins with /b/. Give children more time to think about the answer. Repeat the same cues while modeling aloud to help children understand what to do.

When the sounds do not match: Select a picture of a word (*moon*) that does not begin with the target sound.

- *What is this picture? I say the word* moon *and say the beginning sound /m/.*

- *I heard /b/ at the beginning of* ball *and /m/ at the beginning of* moon. *Are /b/ and /m/ the same?*

- *They are not the same. Does* moon *ride the /b/ bus? No.*

- *I put the picture of the moon over here to wait at the Bus Stop.*

Play the Game with Me

- *Let's use a different set of picture cards.*

- Choose the card for *table* and place it in the driver's seat. *This is a picture of a table, so this is the /t/ bus.*

- *Let's choose another picture card. Let's say the name, and say the beginning sound aloud.*

- *Does it begin with the /t/ sound?*

- *Does it match? If it does, the card can ride the bus. If not, let's make it wait at the bus stop.*

Unit 4 Activity A

Sound Bus

Notes

Independent Activity

Choose new cards and allow children to play the game independently. Observe how each child uses the strategy to determine if the initial sound of the picture word matches the target sound.

Assess Understanding

Monitor whether each child correctly segments the initial sounds and knows if the sounds are the same.

Keep notes about the sounds used and whether each child was able to complete the task.

Note any difficulties and plan to use that sound again another day.

On Your Own

- *Now you are ready to play the game on your own.*
- *Remember to choose a card, say the name, and say the beginning sound aloud.*
- *Then compare it to the bus driver's sound.*
- *If the sound matches, the card can ride the sound bus. If the sound does not match, the card must wait at the bus stop.*

Show What You Know

- *[Student name], do you agree or disagree that this picture belongs on the /t/ bus?*
- *Say the sound of the bus and the sound of the word on the picture card.*
- *Can you think of other objects around the room that might ride on the /t/ bus?*
- *Whose first name begins with the same sound as the driver's sound? Who can ride the bus?*

Selected picture cards for matching final consonant sounds:

/l/

ball	girl
doll	camel
needle	turtle
bicycle	apple
seal	pencil
well	

/k/

duck	book
sock	milk

/t/

cat	feet
goat	hat
jet	nest
quilt	rabbit
ant	elephant
kite	rowboat

/s/

grapes	horse
house	mouse
octopus	dice
necklace	

/n/

queen	lion
pumpkin	wagon
valentine	sun
violin	yarn
xylophone	van
television	moon

/p/

cup	lamp
up	jeep
envelope	

/g/

dog   frog   pig   wig

/r/

jar	tiger	zipper
quarter	under	

Extend and Adapt

More Than One Bus
Place two buses on the table and use picture cards that begin with two different sounds. Ask children to take a card from the Mystery Bag and place it on one of the buses. Ask children to repeat the target word in the driver's seat and the word for each card that is already on the bus. Then ask children to say the word for each new card before placing the new card on the bus.

Pairs of Sounds with Minimal Contrast
Choose two sounds that are more alike, such a /m/ and /n/ or /s/ and /z/. See Appendix II Minimal Pairs.

Closed Sort to Open Sort
Add more than two sounds to the pile of picture cards, such as /m/, /n/, and /b/.

A Bus for Each Child
Place about 20–25 cards on the table and place a bus in front of each child. Ask children to select only the cards from the table that belong on his or her bus.

Final Consonant Sounds (Refer to Notes in the left column.)
Ask children to perform the same activity, matching the final consonant sounds in words, such as *cat* and *jet*.

Medial Vowel Sounds
Extend the activity by sorting picture cards by medial vowel sound, such as *pan* and *cat*.

Unit 4 Activity B

Picture Card Sound Match

Notes

Materials

- BLM 4-2 Two Sounds Chart
- Reading Rods® Phonological Awareness Pocket Chart Cards

Skill
Phoneme Isolation and Categorization

Objective
To recognize and distinguish initial sounds

Purpose
To isolate and categorize words by initial sound, children sort picture cards into two categories.

Activity Overview
Children sort picture cards into two columns by initial sound.

Getting Ready

Choose a set of 6 Reading Rods Phonological Awareness Pocket Chart Cards with two widely different initial sounds. See Appendix II Maximal Pairs.

Show children the cards and say the names of the pictures together.

Build Background

- *Let's use our imaginations to have some fun. Let's imagine that everything around us begins with the same sound as our names.*

- *What colors would you see? What kinds of food would you eat? What kind of pet would you have? Where would you live?*

- *Can you imagine how many things begin with the same sound as your name? Sometimes it's fun to make up stories about ourselves and include words that begin with the same initial sound.*

- *For example, My name is Ben. My best friend is Brad. My favorite color is blue. I live on Birch Bend, and my house is made of bricks. I like bananas, but I don't like broccoli.*

- *For today's activity, we listen to the beginning sounds of picture card words. Then we can sort the cards according to their beginning sounds.*

Model the Activity

Begin with words that have two distinctly different initial sounds (maximal pairs).

Because each card can be categorized in one of the columns, this is a called a closed sort.

Watch Me Play

- *Here is how to play the game. First, I shuffle the picture cards and place them face down on the table.*

- *I look at the Two Sounds Chart. Pictures that begin with the same sound go in the same column.*

- *I take a card and say the name of the picture—* milk—*aloud. I listen for the beginning sound.*

- *This is a picture of milk. What is the first sound I hear in the word* milk? *The beginning sound is /m/.*

- *I place* milk *in the first column. This is the /m/ column. Pictures that begin with /m/ go in this column under the picture of milk.*

- *I take a second card and say the name of the picture—* table. *What sound do I hear at the beginning? [/t/] Do I hear the same beginning sound as I heard in* milk, */m/? Does this card belong in the same column as the word* milk?

- Milk *begins with /m/, and* table *begins with /t/. The words do not have the same beginning sound, so* table *goes in the second column. This is the /t/ column.*

- *When all of the cards are on the chart, I check by saying the names of the picture cards in each column.*

Continue the Activity Together

Provide additional support by asking a child to say the sounds of the pictures at the top of each column and compare that sound to the initial sound of the picture card the child chose.

Play the Game with Me

- *Let's look at a new set of picture cards together and say the names of the pictures.*

- *Let's mix up the cards and place them on the table. Let's choose a card and say the picture name.*

- *We sort the picture cards by beginning sound.*

- *Say the picture names in each column with me. Do we hear the same beginning sound in each picture name in the column?*

Notes

Independent Activity

Provide each child with a set of 6–8 Reading Rods® Phonological Awareness Pocket Chart Cards and a copy of BLM 4-2 Two Sounds Chart.

Children may work alone or with a partner. Observe children as they work independently.

If children place a card in error, ask them to say the names of the picture cards in each column. Allow children a chance to try again.

Assess Understanding

Place a set of 10 cards with 3 or 4 different initial sounds face up on the table.

Monitor whether each child can segment the initial sounds of words and recognize words with the same initial sounds.

Note any difficulties in your intervention logs and plan to teach the concept or specific sounds again.

On Your Own

- *Use a new set of picture cards and a chart.*

- *Say the names of the picture cards to yourself or to your partner.*

- *Then shuffle the cards and place them face down on the table.*

- *Choose a picture card, say the picture name, and listen for the beginning sound.*

- *Where does the card belong on the chart?*

- *After you place each card on the chart, say the names of the pictures in each column.*

- *Do all of the words begin with the same sound? Do you need to make any changes?*

Show What You Know

- *Look at all of the cards on the table.*

- *Which picture cards belong in the same column as the word I say?* (Milk—*children look for picture names that begin with /m/.*)

- *Name some objects around the room that belong in the /m/ column.*

- *Can you think of someone's name that would go in the /m/ column?*

Vary the activity by using Rhyme Picture Cards, Learning Place® Game Cards, or Compound Word Puzzle Cards.

Extend and Adapt

Three Column Sort

Use a set of 9 or more cards with three distinct initial sounds and a 3-column chart. Have children sort picture cards into three columns.

Picture Card Dominoes

Children take turns taking a card, saying the picture name, and arranging cards with matching initial sounds end-to-end like a domino game.

Open Sort

Use a set of picture cards with multiple initial sounds and a 3-column chart. Have children sort the cards for two distinctive initial sounds and place words that don't begin with the two sounds into a third "Doesn't Fit" column. Extend the open sort further by using a 4-column chart to sort words with three initial sounds and a fourth "Doesn't Fit" column.

Unit 4 Activity C　　Mystery Sound Bag

Notes

Materials

- Mystery Bag
- Small objects from the classroom
- Your choice of Picture Cards

Skill　Phonemic Isolation and Categorization

Objective　To recognize and distinguish initial sounds

Purpose　To isolate initial sounds, children select and sort objects and picture cards by initial sound.

Activity Overview　Children select objects from the Mystery Bag, isolate the initial sound of the name of the object, and categorize them by initial sound.

Getting Ready

Choose objects that begin with two different sounds. Refer to Appendix II Minimal and Maximal Pairs.

If you cannot find enough small objects, you may wish to use Picture Cards.

Build Background

- *Let's pretend that we are on vacation at the beach. Let's imagine that we are going on a scavenger hunt to find objects that begin with the same sound.*
- *What objects could we find that begin with /s/?*
- *We might find sand, shells, seaweed, sunscreen saltwater, sunglasses, and so on.*
- *All of these objects begin with the /s/.*
- *For this activity, we use 8–10 small objects (or picture cards) and the Mystery Sound Bag.*
- *Let's practice listening for the beginning sound of each object before placing them in the Mystery Sound Bag.*

Model the Activity

Model the activity for the children.

Continue the activity until the objects are sorted into two groups by initial sounds.

Watch Me Play

- *Here is how to play the game. I reach into the Mystery Sound Bag and pull out an object.*

- *I show the object and say its name. Then I say the beginning sound.*

- *I place the object on the table. That is where objects with that same beginning sound go.*

- *I reach back into the Mystery Sound Bag, pull out another object, and show it.*

- *I say the beginning sound. If it is the same sound as the first object, I place it on the table with the first object.*

- *If it begins with a different beginning sound, I place it in another spot on the table.*

- *I continue to take objects from the bag until all have been sorted according to their beginning sounds.*

- *Then I say the names of all the objects in each pile and check that each object is sorted correctly.*

Continue the Activity Together

Place another group of 8–10 objects that begin with maximal pairs of initial sounds in the bag.

Play the Game with Me

- *Let's play the Mystery Sound Bag game together.*

- *Who would like to select an object from the bag, show it to the group, and say its name?*

- *Place it on the table. This is the place for objects that begin with that sound.*

- *Select another object, show it, and say its name.*

- *Does it begin with the same sound as the first object? If it does, place it in the same place. If not, start a new pile.*

- *Pass the bag to the next player. When all the objects have been sorted, say the names of all the objects in the pile. Are they sorted correctly?*

Unit 4 Activity C

Mystery Sound Bag

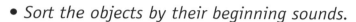

Independent Activity

Refill the bag with objects. Have children play the game independently.

On Your Own

- *The Mystery Sound Bag is refilled.*
- *Pass the bag around the group so that each person can take a turn.*
- *Sort the objects by their beginning sounds.*
- *Check by saying the names of the objects in the piles and listening for the beginning sounds.*
- *Are all the beginning sounds the same? Do you need to make any changes?*

Assess Understanding

Monitor whether each child can isolate an initial sound and find four objects around the room with the same initial sound.

Note any difficulties in your intervention log so that this skill can be reviewed.

Show What You Know

- *Each of us has a special sound. Think of your sound now but don't say it aloud.*
- *When it is your turn, say your sound and name four objects that begin with your special sound.*
- *Name objects from one of the following places that begin with the same sound:*

  school
  campground
  backyard
  playground
  garage
  farm
  jungle

After children are successful in sorting objects or pictures by the initial sound, ask them to sort by final sound.

Then ask children to sort by medial, sound.

Extend and Adapt

Many Sounds

Place objects with many different initial sounds in the bag. Have each child choose an object from the Mystery Sound Bag and name two people, places, or things that begin with the same sound.

Ending Sounds

Place two or more groups of objects with the same ending sound in the Mystery Sound Bag. Pass the bag around the group and have children choose objects from the bag and cooperate to sort them by ending sound.

Medial Sounds

Place two or more groups of objects with the same middle sound in the Mystery Sound Bag. Pass the bag around the group and have children choose objects from the bag and cooperate to sort them by medial sound.

Fill the Mystery Bag

Give each child a small paper bag and an initial sound. (Children should not reveal their initial sounds.) Ask each child to fill the bag with five small objects with that initial sound. Ask children to trade bags with another child. Children open their Mystery Sound Bags and guess the initial sound of the names of the objects. Repeat the game using final or medial sounds.

Unit 4 Activity D

Feed the Animals

Materials

- BLM 4-3 Animal Head Cutouts
- Small paper bags
- BLM 4-4, 4-5, 4-6, 4-7 Food Picture Cards

Skill Phonemic Isolation and Categorization

Objective To recognize and distinguish initial sounds

Purpose To identify initial sounds that are the same and those that are different, children sort picture cards.

Activity Overview Children recognize the initial sounds of animal names and match them with the initial sounds of the names of food.

Getting Ready

Cut out the Animal Head Cutouts on BLM 4-3. Attach the animal heads at the back of the top of the small paper bags (behind the opening), as if the animal is looking into the bag when it is open.

Each animal has an alliterative name, using a high utility consonant sound.

Cut apart the Food Picture Cards on BLM 4-4, 4-5, 4-6, and 4-7.

Build Background

- *Let's talk about our favorite foods. What are some of your favorites?*

- *Who knows what a bear's favorite food is? What would a mouse's favorite food be?*

- *Let's play a game called Feed the Animals.*

- *These animals will only eat foods that have the same beginning sound as their names.*

- *Let's begin by saying the names of the foods on the picture cards.*

- *The names of the animals are Pedro the Pony, Sasha the Seal, Toby the Toucan, Benny the Bear, Carla the Cat, and Mandy the Monkey.*

- *Say their names with me and listen to the beginning sounds.*

Model the Activity

Show children the bag for Pedro the Pony. Talk with children about the sound they hear at the beginning of Pedro's name—/p/.

Tell children that Pedro only likes foods that begin with the initial sound in his name.

Model the activity for the children using the Food Picture Cards on BLM 4-4, 4-5, 4-6, 4-7.

Continue to model the game as needed.

Continue the Activity Together

Choose another set of Food Picture Cards and a different animal bag. Review the names of the foods and place the cards face down on the table.

Introduce the animal and ask children to say the animal's name. Talk about the beginning sound.

Watch Me Play

- *Here is how to play the game. Place the Food Picture Cards face down on the table.*

- *This animal is Pedro the Pony. The sound at the beginning of Pedro's name is /p/.*

- *Pedro will only eat foods that begin with the same sound as his name.*

- *To play the game, I pick up a card and look at the picture. The food name is* <u>pineapple</u>.

- *What sound do I hear at the beginning of* <u>pineapple</u>? *I hear /p/.*

- *Is it the same sound I hear at the beginning of Pedro and Pony?*

- *Does Pedro the Pony like pineapple? Yes, he does. The pineapple picture card goes in Pedro the Pony's bag.*

- *Now I am ready to turn over another food card. This one's name is* <u>banana</u>. *It starts with /b/.*

- *Does* <u>banana</u> *begin with the same sound as* <u>Pedro</u> *and* <u>Pony</u>? *No, it does not. Pedro the Pony does not like bananas, so I put the food card back on the table.*

Play the Game with Me

- *Let's play the game together. Our new hungry animal is Toby the Toucan. What beginning sound do you hear in his name? What food does Toby the Toucan like?*

- *Let's say the names of the food and place the Food Picture Cards face down on the table.*

- *Pick up a card. Does the name of the food begin with the same beginning sound that we hear in Toby the Toucan?*

- *If the beginning sound is the same, place the Food Picture Card in Toby's bag. If it does not begin with the same sound, return the card to the table.*

- *Who would like to pick the next card?*

Feed the Animals

Independent Activity

Review the names of the animals and give each pair of children an animal bag and a set of 6–10 Food Picture Cards.

If needed, review the names of the food. Place the Food Picture Cards face down in front of the children.

Partners take turns until all the cards have been selected. Then partners say the names of each card in the bag to check themselves.

Assess Understanding

Monitor whether each child can isolate initial sounds by asking each member of the group to name two or three foods that begin with the same sound as his name.

On Your Own

- *Choose a partner for this activity. Use an animal bag and a set of Food Picture Cards.*

- *Review the names of the foods on the cards with your partner. Then place the cards face down in front of you.*

- *Take turns selecting a card, saying the name of the food, and the beginning sound.*

- *Does the food have the same beginning sound as your animal's name? If it does, your animal likes that food. Place the Food Picture Card in the bag.*

- *If the beginning sound is not the same, return the card.*

- *When you have seen all the cards, take turns with your partner and say the names of all the foods that your animal likes. Do they all have the same beginning sound?*

Show What You Know

- *Roscoe the Rat likes foods that begin with the same sound as his name. For example, Roscoe likes <u>radishes</u> and <u>rice</u>.*

- *Can you name other foods that begin with /r/ that Roscoe Rat likes to eat?*

Extend and Adapt

Multiple Animals

Use the same bags and Food Picture Cards, although this time place two or more animal bags out at the same time. Children can pick up a card, and decide whether or not it belongs in one of the bags displayed.

Favorite Colors

Use colored markers to draw large purple, red, green, and blue circles on a large piece of drawing paper. Give children a set of 12–15 picture cards of objects that begin with *p, r, g,* and *b*. Have children stack the cards face down on the table. Each player selects a card and says the name of the object and its initial sound. The player places the card in the circle of the color with the same initial sound.

I Found a Treasure Chest

Pretend that you found an old treasure chest in the attic. This treasure chest is unusual because it contains only objects that begin with the same sound. Tell children the target initial sound is /d/. Start the game by saying, *I found a treasure chest. The treasure chest is filled with diamonds.* In turn, children add objects to the treasure chest and add to the statement. For example, *I found a treasure chest filled with diamonds and dandelions.* The game continues until someone cannot think of another /d/ object. Then choose a new target initial sound and play again.

Unit 4 Activity E

Sound Chart

Notes

Materials

- Large Pocket Chart
- Reading Rods® Phonological Awareness Pocket Chart Cards
- Choice of Picture Cards
- Student Pocket Charts

Skill

Phoneme Isolation and Categorization

Objective

To recognize and distinguish initial sounds

Purpose

To identify the individual sounds in words, children sort Picture Cards by initial sound.

Activity Overview

Children match the initial sound on Picture Cards with the initial sound of the target card.

Getting Ready

Gather a set of Reading Rods Phonological Awareness Pocket Chart Cards.

Build Background

- *Let's have fun with Picture Cards and the Large Pocket Chart.*
- *We can put cards with the same beginning sound in a row on the pocket chart.*
- *Help me look at the Picture Cards and say their names.*
- *This Picture Card [monkey] is the target sound, so I'll place it here in the pocket chart. What is the beginning sound of this picture? [/m/]*
- *Now we can look for other cards that begin with the target sound, and place them in the same row. [milk, moon, mouse]*

Model the Activity

Review the names of the objects on the Picture Cards.

Place a Picture Card in the left side of the pocket chart. [monkey] The initial sound of the object on the Picture Card becomes the target sound. [/m/]

Stack the remaining Picture Cards in a pile, face down on the table.

Continue to model the activity as needed.

Continue the Activity Together

Ask children to help you say the beginning sounds of each picture name.

Continue play until all the cards are used.

Check by saying the names of all the cards in the chart.

Select a new target sound card and play again.

Watch Me Play

- *Here is how to play the game. Look at the pictures on the left of the pocket chart. These picture names begin with the target sound.*

- *I stack the rest of the cards and place them face down on the table. I take a card from the stack and say the name of the picture.*

- *I listen for the beginning sound and say the sound. Does this picture name begin with the same sound as the target sound?*

- *If the beginning sound is the same, I place the card in the chart to the right of the target sound card.*

- *If the picture does not begin with the same sound, I place the card in the discard pile.*

- *I continue to take a card from the stack and say the name. I say the beginning sound and decide if the sound is the same as the target sound.*

- *When there are no more cards in the stack, I check by saying all the picture names in the chart next to the target sound card. Do all the names begin with the same sound?*

- *I check the discard pile to see if any other cards that begin with the target sound were missed.*

Play the Game with Me

- *Let's play together. Choose one card to be the target sound. Say the target sound with me.*

- *Let's mix up the cards and stack them face down on the table. Who will pick the first card?*

- *Say the name of the picture for us. What is the beginning sound? Is that sound the same as the target sound?*

- *If it is the same beginning sound, we place the card in the chart. If it is not the same beginning sound, we place the card in the discard pile.*

- *When all cards are used, we can check by saying the names of all the cards in the chart.*

Notes

Independent Activity

You may wish to use the Large Pocket Chart for the group or provide each child with an individual Student Pocket Chart and a set of Picture Cards.

Have children select a new Picture Card to become the target sound.

When all the cards are used, children say the target sound and the names of the other cards in their charts.

Assess Understanding

Monitor whether each child can sort words by initial sounds.

You may ask children to think of names of other objects that begin with the same target sound.

On Your Own

- *Use your pocket chart and the Picture Cards to do the activity on your own.*

- *Choose one card for your target sound and place it in the chart.*

- *Stack up the remaining cards and place them face down in front of you.*

- *Pick up a card, say the name, and listen for the beginning sound.*

- *If the picture begins with the same sound as the target sound, place the card in the chart.*

- *If the picture begins with a different sound, place the card in the discard pile.*

- *When you have used all the cards, check by saying the target sound and then saying the names of all the Picture Cards in the chart.*

- *Check the discard pile for any words with the target sound that may have been missed.*

Show What You Know

- *Place two cards with the same beginning sound in the pocket chart.*

- *Spread out the remaining cards face up on the table.*

- *Take turns finding other cards that begin with the same sound as the cards in the pocket chart.*

- *Can you say two other words that are not on the Picture Cards that begin with the same sound?*

Picture Cards sorted by final sound:

/l/—ball, bicycle, camel, doll, girl, apple, needle, pencil, seal, turtle, well

/t/—cat, feet, goat, hat, jet, ant, elephant, kite, nest, quilt, rabbit, rowboat

/s/—dice, grapes, horse, house, mouse, octopus

/k/—book, duck, milk, question mark, sock

/p/—cup, jeep, envelope, lamp, up

/n/—lion, moon, pumpkin, queen, sun, valentine, van, violin, wagon, exit sign, xylophone, yarn

/r/—jar, quarter, zipper, under

Extend and Adapt

Not Like the Others
Set up rows of the pocket chart in advance and keep them hidden. Place three cards in each row, two with the same sound as the target sound, and one that does not begin with the same sound. Uncover a row, and ask children to find the picture that does not belong.

Match the Sounds
Place two or three target words in each child's individual pocket chart. Have each child determine where to place the Picture Cards so that words with the same initial sound are placed together in a row.

Final and Medial Sound Variations
Repeat the original or extension activities, sorting words by final or medial sounds.

Sound Concentration

Notes

Materials

- Reading Rods® Phonological Awareness Pocket Chart Cards

- Your choice of Picture Cards

Please Note:

Sound Concentration takes a significant amount of time to play. This activity is not intended for everyday use. It is an appropriate Friday game or can be adapted for a holiday or curriculum theme game.

Skill

Phoneme Isolation and Categorization

Objective

To recognize and isolate sounds in words

Purpose

To learn to separate the individual sounds in words, children isolate the initial sounds.

Activity Overview

Children recognize and match picture names with the same initial sounds to play Sound Concentration.

Getting Ready

Select 6–8 pairs of Picture Cards with the same initial sounds.

Show the Picture Cards and say their names.

Then ask the children to repeat the names and say the initial sounds.

Build Background

- *Who knows how to play matching games? Memory or Concentration are fun matching games.*

- *Does anyone play matching games at home?*

- *We can have fun playing Sound Concentration. To make a match we turn over two cards that have the same beginning sound.*

- *Let's say the names of the Picture Cards for this game. Listen for the beginning sounds.*

StarLIT™ Literacy Intervention Toolkit

Model the Activity

Mix up 6 pairs of cards and place them in an array face down on the table.

The object of the game is to turn over two cards with the same initial sound.

Advise children to concentrate on the placement of cards revealed by other players. It might help them to create a matching pair later on.

Continue to model the activity as needed.

Continue the Activity Together

Review the names of 6 new pairs of Picture Cards with the children.

Provide support as you play the game with children. Gradually release more responsibility to them.

Watch Me Play

- *Here is how to play Sound Concentration. First, I mix up the cards and place them in an array, face down on the table.*
- *I turn over two cards and say the picture names. Listen carefully as I say the beginning sounds.*
- *If the two pictures begin with the same sound, it is a match. I keep both cards in front of me*
- *If the two pictures begin with different sounds, I return them to their places.*
- *It is important to pay attention to where the cards are on the table.*
- *Later on, I might need a card that begins with that sound to make a match.*
- *I continue to play until all the cards have been matched.*

Play the Game with Me

- *Let's take turns playing Sound Concentration.*
- *Who would like to be first to turn over two cards?*
- *Let's say the names of both cards. Do the names begin with the same sound?*
- *If both picture names have the same beginning sound, we keep the cards.*
- *If the picture names begin with different sounds, we return the cards to the table.*
- *Let's try to remember where these cards are on the table because they may help us make a match later on.*
- *Who would like to take the next turn?*
- *Let's play until all the Picture Cards have been matched.*
- *How many pairs of cards can we find?*

Sound Concentration

Notes

Independent Activity

Review the names of a new set of Picture Cards.

Observe children as they do the activity independently.

On Your Own

- *Begin with a new set of cards. Look at the cards and say the picture names. Think about the beginning sounds.*

- *When it is your turn, pick up two cards. If the picture names begin with the same sound, keep the pair of cards.*

- *If the picture names do not begin with the same sound, place the cards back in their original places face down on the table.*

- *Continue to play until all the Picture Cards are matched. The player with the most cards wins the game.*

Assess Understanding

Monitor whether each child can distinguish initial sounds.

Show What You Know

- *Sit together in a circle on the floor.*

- *When it is your turn, select a card from the stack of cards and say the initial sound of the picture name.*

- *Then say five other words you know that begin with the same initial sound.*

- *The rest of the group will give a "High Five" to show that they agree with your choice of words.*

Extend and Adapt

Add-To Concentration

Play the game as described in the activity. After making a matching pair, the player says the picture names aloud. Then, in turn, each player says another word that begins with the same initial sound. You may wish to go around once or several times. You might limit the choices of words to categories, such as food, toys, sports, and so on.

Triple Concentration

Use 12, 15, or 18 Picture Cards that contain sets of three cards with the same initial sound. After reviewing the names of the pictures with the children, place the cards face down on the table. Each player turns over three cards to match three cards with the same initial sound. If the cards do not match, all three cards must be returned to the table. Players should concentrate on the placement of each card as it is revealed. At the end of the game, the player with the most triple match cards wins.

Variation: To increase student concentration, place Picture Cards face down on the table in different patterns. You may wish to place them in a circle, triangle, smiley face, or other pattern.

Find It

Say a sentence that contains words with the same initial sound. Ask each child to supply 3 words to complete the sentence.

<u>Gary</u> *cleaned out the* <u>garage</u> *and found* _____.
(Children supply words that begin with /g/.)

<u>Dorrie</u> *looked behind her* <u>dresser</u> *and found* _____.
(Children supply words that begin with /d/.)

<u>Ben</u> *went down to the* <u>basement</u> *and found* _____.
(Children supply words that begin with /b/.)

Unit 5

Phonological Awareness at the Phoneme Segmentation and Blending Level

Phoneme segmentation and blending develops children's understanding of the positions of sounds in words. At this stage of phonological awareness, children bridge the gap between the knowledge of sounds and the position of those sounds. Some children may perceive a word as one big sound or hear it as a group of randomly selected sounds without order or sequence. As they practice segmenting and blending sounds, children begin to understand that each sound within a word has a specific position within the word.

Children generally have an easier time blending sounds to form words than they have isolating sounds. Forming a word that has meaning seems a more logical task to a child. It is best to begin with the blended word, segment the sounds, and then blend the sounds back together again.

A Word from the Experts

66 The theoretical and practical importance of phonological awareness for the beginning reader relies not only on logic but also on the results of several decades of empirical research. Early studies showed a strong association between a child's ability to read and the ability to segment words into phonemes (Liberman et al., 1974). Dozens of subsequent studies have confirmed that there is a close relationship between phonemic awareness and reading ability, not just in the early grades (e.g., Ehri and Wilce, 1980, 1985: Perfetti et al., 1987) but throughout the school years (Calfee et al., 1973; Shankweiler et al., 1995). 99

Catherine E. Snow. M. Susan Burns, & Peg Griffen, *Preventing Reading Difficulties in Young Children*, 1998

Unit 5 Objectives

In this unit children will—
• Segment words into individual phonemes
• Blend phonemes into words
• Segment words into the correct number of phonemes
• Sort picture words by the number of phonemes
• Segment phonemes in a word and accentuate the initial, medial, or final sounds
• Isolate the initial, medial, or final sounds in a word

Skills Connection

Segmenting and blending phonemes has a strong correlation to learning to read. As children learn to read later on, they use letters and sounds as a source of information or as a cueing system as they learn to read and spell. Children need to be able to segment and blend sounds to be successful in using letter-sound knowledge effectively for reading and writing.

StarLIT™ Literacy Intervention Toolkit

Total physical response is a very effective teaching technique. Use movement to help children segment sounds in words. Ask children to stand up and say the sounds of a word: /k/ /ī/ /t/. Have children repeat the sounds together and touch their heads for the beginning sound /k/, their waists for the middle sound /ī/, and their knees for the ending sound /t/. Then all stand up straight and blend the sounds to say the word *kite*.

Home-School Connection

Dear Parent,

Support your child as he/she learns to segment the sounds in words. As your child goes about his/her everyday activities, play a game to focus on the individual sounds in words. Your child may enjoy tapping, snapping, clapping, or using a small hand-held "clicker" from the toy store. For example, at bath time, you and your child might tap out the sounds (/t/ /ŭ/ /b/), (/w/ /ă/ /sh/), (/s/ /ō/ /p/), (/b/ /ŭ/ /b/ /l/ /z/), and so on.

On-the-Go Assessment for Word Awareness

Slowly, say the individual sounds in a word. Ask the child to blend the sounds together and say the word. For example, you say /c/ /ŭ/ /p/. The child says *cup*. Supply a word and ask the child to hop once for each sound, and then blend the sounds back together to say the word.

Unit 5 Phoneme Segmentation and Blending Chart of Manipulatives

Activity	A—Pupet Talk	B—Move It and Say It	C—Chart a Sound	D—Counting Mat	E—Building Words	F—Guess That Object	G—Accent It!	H—Sound Bingo
SunSprouts™ Wolf Puppet	●			●				
Your choice of Picture Cards	●							
Segmenting, Blending, and Sorting Mats		●	●					
Your choice of Counters		●						
BLM 5-1 Fruit Bowl, 5-2 Bears' Den, 5-3 Frog Pond		●						
Large Pocket Chart			●					
Student Pocket Charts			●					
Reading Rods® Phonological Awareness Pocket Chart Cards			●			●		
BLM 5-4 Train Cars, 5-5 Train Car Cards							●	
Reading Rods Picture Rods				●				●
Mystery Bag				●		●		
Link 'N' Learn® Links					●			
Sorting Bowls						●		
Quiet Counters								●
BLM 5-6, 5-7, 5-8 Sound Bingo Cards								●

Unit 5 Activity A

Puppet Talk

Notes

Materials

- SunSprouts™ Wolf Puppet
- Appendix III Syllables and Phonemes

Skill
Phoneme Segmentation and Blending

Objective
To segment phonemes within words and to blend phonemes together to create words

Purpose
To practice isolating and blending phonemes, children segment sounds in words and blend sounds back together to form words.

Activity Overview
Children use a hand puppet to segment the sounds in words to isolate the phonemes. Then they blend the phonemes back together to form the words again.

Getting Ready

Introduce the puppet Wally Wolf to the children.

Refer to the list of Picture Cards with 2, 3, 4 or 5 phonemes in Appendix III.

Build Background

- *Would you to meet a new friend? His name is Wally Wolf. Wally, say hello to everyone.*
- *Poor Wally Wolf is having trouble learning how to say words correctly.*
- *You know a lot about sounds. Maybe you could teach him how to say his words the right way.*
- *Would you like to help Wally?*

Model the Activity

Continue to model the activity as needed.

Watch Me Play

- *Wally Wolf has many animal friends. One of his best friends is a cat, but Wally has trouble saying the word* cat. *I can help him.*

- *What sound do I hear at the beginning of the word* cat? /k/ Move the puppet's mouth and say /k/.

- *What sound do I hear in the middle of the word* cat? /ă/ Move the puppet's mouth and say /ă/.

- *What sound do I hear at the end of the word* cat? /t/ Move the puppet's mouth and say /t/.

- *Wally, the sounds in the word* cat *are* /k/ /ă/ /t/. Move the puppet's mouth three times saying /k/-/ă/-/t/.

- *This is how to put those sounds back together to say the word correctly,* cat.

- *See that, Wally, you can say it!* /k/ /ă/ /t/, cat!

- *Wally has another friend, a dog. Wally, do you need help learning how to say* dog?

Continue the Activity Together

Invite children to help Wally Wolf say words correctly.

Children may like to take turns with the puppet or form a puppet mouth with their hands.

Pass the puppet to another child and repeat the activity for the words *hen* and *bug*.

Continue the activity as needed.

Play the Game with Me

- *Let's help Wally Wolf say his words correctly. Who would like to take a turn holding Wally?*

- *Another one of Wally's friends is a pig. Let's help Wally say the word* pig *correctly.*

- *Who can say the beginning sound of the word* pig? *Say the beginning sound with Wally.* [/p/]

- *Who can say the middle sound of the word* pig? *Let's all say the middle sound with Wally.* [/ĭ/]

- *Who can say the ending sound for us? Let's all say the ending sound.* [/g/] *You too, Wally.* [/g/]

- *Let's say all the sounds* /p/ /ĭ/ /g/. *Now let's put those sounds together to help Wally:* pig.

- *Wally, can you say the word correctly with us?*

- *Who would like to help Wally Wolf next?*

Puppet Talk

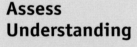

Independent Activity

Continue the activity using other words from the list.

On Your Own

- *Wally Wolf would like to learn to say other words correctly.*

- *Listen to the next word. Take turns with the puppet or use your hands as a puppet mouth.*

- *Say the word and move your puppet mouth for each sound in the word.*

- *Then put the sounds back together and say the word correctly for Wally.*

Assess Understanding

Monitor whether each child can segment and blend sounds in words correctly.

Ask the child to show you how he/she can help Wally Wolf say words correctly.

Note any difficulty and at what point it became evident.

Show What You Know

- *Take turns teaching Wally Wolf how to say words.*

- *Hold Wally Wolf and listen to the word.*

- *Say the sounds and move Wally's mouth for each sound in the word.*

- *Blend the sounds back together and make Wally say the complete word again.*

- *Everyone give a Thumbs Up if Wally says the sounds and the word correctly.*

Reading Rod® Pocket Chart Card Animals: (Wally Wolf's Friends)

cat   /k/ /ă/ /t/
dog   /d/ /ŏ/ /g/
pig   /p/ /ĭ/ /g/
duck   /d/ /ŭ/ /k/
fish   /f/ /ĭ/ /sh/
cow   /k/ /ow/
fox   /f/ /ŏ/ /k/ /s/
frog   /f/ /r/ /ŏ/ /g/
goat   /g/ /ō/ /t/
horse   /h/ /or/ /s/
mouse   /m/ /ou/ /s/
pig   /p/ /ĭ/ /g/
camel /k/ /ă/ /m/ /l/
lion   /l/ /ī/ /ən/
monkey
/m/ /ŏ/ /n/ /k/ /ē/
rabbit
/r/ /ă/ /b/ /ĭ/ /t/
tiger   /t/ /ī/ /g/ /er/
turtle   /t/ /ur/ /t/ /əl/
zebra
/z/ /ē/ /b/ /r/ /ə/
gorilla
/gə/ /r/ /ĭ/ /l/ /ə/
seal   /s/ /ē/ /l/
ant   /ă/ /n/ /t/
ox   /ŏ/ /k/ /s/
inchworm
/ĭ/ /n/ /ch/ /w/ /or/ /m/
ostrich
/ŏ/ /s/ /t/ /r/ /ĭ/ /ch/
elephant
/əl/ /ĕ/ /f/ /ă/ /n/ /t/
octopus
/ŏ/ /k/ /t/ /ō/ /p/ /ŭ/ /s/

Extend and Adapt

Stand for a Sound

Supply a word (or show a picture card) to the group. Repeat the word as you tap a child on the shoulder for each sound in the word. Ask the children who were tapped to stand in the order of the sounds in the word. Ask children to say their sounds in order, and then all say the word together for the rest of the group. Later on, choose a child in the group to tap the shoulders of the other children who will stand and represent the sounds in the word.

What's in a Name?

Tell children that Wally Wolf needs help learning to say children's names. Have children take turns with the puppet as other children use their hands. Use short names, such as Pam, Tom, Jim, Bill, Dan, or Kim.

Side 2

Notes

Materials

- Segmenting, Blending, and Sorting Mats

- Fruity Fun™, Bear, and Frog Counters

- BLM 5-1 Fruit Bowl, 5-2 Bears' Den, 5-3 Frog Pond

Skill

Phoneme Segmentation and Blending

Objective

To segment words into individual phonemes and blend phonemes back into words

Purpose

To segment words into phonemes and then blend the phonemes back into words, children move a counter for each phoneme in a word.

Activity Overview

Children listen to a word and segment the phonemes by moving a counter for each phoneme in the word. Then they blend the phonemes back together in the correct order to say the word.

Getting Ready

Children place counters in the Home Base circle at the top of side 2 of the Segmenting, Blending, and Sorting Mat.

Explain to children that they will line up their counters in a left-to-right direction on the arrow at the bottom of the mat. Point out that when we learn to read, we read in the direction of the arrow.

Build Background

- *Sometimes when we play, we take things apart, and then we put them back together again.*

- *We might take a puzzle apart and then put it together again.*

- *For some people, taking things apart and rebuilding them is part of their jobs. For example, a mechanic may take apart a machine to repair it and then put it back together.*

- *For this activity, we practice taking words apart and putting them back together.*

- *Let's look at side 2 of the mat. To begin, the activity counters go in the circle at the top of the mat. The circle is called "Home Base."*

- *At the bottom of the mat is an arrow. We line up each counter on the arrow, beginning on the left side.*

- *When we separate the sounds in a word, the first counter goes on the left, the middle one in the middle, and the last sound is here (point to the right), closest to the end of the arrow.*

- *The sounds of words go in order in the direction of the arrow.*

Model the Activity

Place counters in the Home Base circle on the sorting mat.

Use the following words: *mat, pan, lid, sun, kit,* and *top*.

Demonstrate how to slide your finger under the arrow from left to right as you blend the sounds in the word back together.

Choose another word and model for the children as needed.

Continue the Activity Together

Provide each child with a Segmenting, Blending, and Sorting Mat and 5 or 6 Counters. Use side 2 of the sorting mat.

Watch Me Play

- *Here is how to play the game. All of the counters are in the Home Base circle.*

- *Listen to the word* <u>cup</u>. *I move one counter from Home Base to the arrow for each sound in the word* <u>cup</u>.

- *Watch me. The beginning sound in the word* <u>cup</u> *is /k/. I move one counter down to the left side of the line and say /k/.*

- *The next sound in the word cup is /ŭ/. I move another counter down to the line and say /ŭ/.*

- *The last sound in the word cup is /p/. I move a third counter down to the line and say /p/.*

- *Look at the three counters for the beginning, middle and end sounds on the line for /k/ /ŭ/ /p/.*

- *I slide my finger from left to right under the arrow while blending the sounds together and saying the word* <u>cup</u>. *I repeat the word* <u>cup</u>.

- *Then, I return the counters to Home Base and listen for a new word.*

Play the Game with Me

- *Let's review this activity together. Place the counters in the Home Base circle.*

- *The word is* <u>sun</u>. *Listen to the sounds.*

- *Let's say the beginning sound. Show me the spot where the counter for the first sound, /s/, will go. Move a counter to that spot.*

- *Let's say the next sound. Where will we place the counter for the next sound, /ŭ/?*

- *What is the ending sound? [/n/] Where will we place the last counter?*

- *Did we place all the counters on the arrow from left to right?*

- *Now, let's slide our fingers under the arrow as we blend the sounds back together. This step is very important. Say the word with me.*

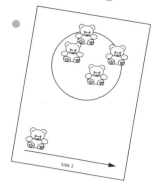

Notes

Independent Activity

Provide each child with a mat and a set of counters. Say a word for the children.

Children may work alone or with a partner for this activity.

Vary the activity by using BLM 5-1, 5-2, 5-3 and corresponding counters in place of the Segmenting, Blending, and Sorting Mat.

Assess Understanding

Say a word for each child. Ask the child to tap the sounds on the table or take a giant step for each sound. Then ask the child to put the sounds back together again to say the word.

On Your Own

- *Place your counters in the Home Base circle.*
- *Listen to the word and say the word.*
- *Slowly, say the sounds in the word.*
- *Take your time to slide a counter from Home Base to the arrow for each sound in the word.*
- *Remember to place the counter in the correct spot on the arrow.*
- *Then slide your finger under the arrow and blend the sounds together to form the word again.*
- *Repeat the word.*

Show What You Know

- *Listen to the word and say the word.*
- *Think about the sounds you hear in the word.*
- *Take one giant step forward as you say each sound you hear in the word.*
- *Then blend the sounds back together and say the word again.*

Instead of Picture Cards, use a collection of objects from the classroom. Ask each child to select an object and say its name. Use body movements to segment the phonemes and then blend the sounds to form the name of the object again.

Extend and Adapt

Stand Up Phonemes
Say a word to the group and select a child to repeat the word. Ask the child to select a child from the group to represent each sound in the word. Children stand side-by-side in a line. Then the child taps the shoulder of each child in the line as he blends the sounds to form the word again.

Adding Phonemes
Refer to the list of words with more than three phonemes in Appendix III to increase the difficulty of the activity.

A Special Home
Make copies of BLM 5-1, 5-2, or 5-3 and use specific counters for this activity. Children will have fun using the Fruit Bowl with the Fruity Fun™ Counters, the Bears' Den with the Bear Counters, and the Frog Pond with the Frog Counters.

Chart a Sound

Notes

Materials

- Large Pocket Chart
- Student Pocket Charts
- Reading Rods® Phonological Awareness Pocket Chart Cards
- Appendix III Syllables and Phonemes

Getting Ready

Refer to the list of phonemes in the names of Picture Cards in Appendix III.

Write numbers 1 through 5 on blank Reading Rods Phonological Awareness Pocket Chart Cards and place them along the top row of the Large Pocket Chart.

Review the picture names on the cards with the children before starting the activity.

Skill

Phoneme Segmentation

Objective

To segment words into the correct number of phonemes

Purpose

To isolate phonemes within words, children sort Picture Cards according to the number of phonemes in the picture word.

Activity Overview

Children use their fingers to count the number of phonemes in a word and place the picture card in the appropriate column of the chart, according to the number of phonemes.

Build Background

- *Let's have fun using the Large Pocket Chart to show how many sounds we hear in words.*

- *We can place cards with numbers 1–5 at the top of the Pocket Chart. The numbers stand for the number of sounds we hear in the names of the pictures.*

- *Some picture names have just one sound. Some may have 2, 3, 4, or 5 sounds.*

- *If a word has two sounds, it goes under the number 2 in the chart. If the word has three sounds, it goes under the number 3, and so on.*

- *Let's say the names of the pictures before we begin.*

- *Then we can stack up the cards and place them face down on the table.*

Model the Activity

Choose 6 picture cards to begin modeling the activity.

If children have difficulty raising their fingers individually, they may use the fingers on the opposite hand to touch their fingers as they count.

Continue to model the activity until all Picture Cards are placed in the chart.

Continue the Activity Together

Select another set of Picture Cards and review their names with children. Place the pile of cards face down on the table.

Invite children to do several practice times with you.

If more support is needed, select another set of cards and continue the activity together.

Watch Me Play

- *Here is how to play the game. I choose a Picture Card and say its name. This is a picture of a van.*

- *Using my fingers, I count the sounds that I hear in the word* van, /v/ /ă/ /n/. *I hear three sounds. Let me check:* /v/ /ă/ /n/.

- *See that I have three fingers raised. So, I place the picture of the van in the chart under the number 3.*

- *Then I pick another card. This time I pick a picture of a cup.*

- *Counting on my fingers, I say the sounds in the word* cup, /k/ /ŭ/ /p/. *I hear three sounds.*

- *Let's check that again:* /k/ /ŭ/ /p/. *I count my fingers. How many are raised?*

- *Where do I place the picture of the cup in the chart? Yes, I place it under the number 3.*

- *I continue playing until all the cards are in place on the Pocket Chart.*

Play the Game with Me

- *Let's play the game together using another set of Picture Cards. First, let's say the names of the pictures together.*

- *Who would like to choose the first card and say the name of the picture for us?*

- *Let's all say the name of the picture together.*

- *Now let's count the sounds on our fingers.*

- *Let's do that once again to check. How many sounds did you hear? How many fingers?*

- *Next, we place the card in the chart under the correct number.*

- *Who is ready to choose another Picture Card?*

- *Let's find out where the rest of the cards belong on the Pocket Chart.*

Notes

Independent Activity

Provide a Student Pocket Chart and a set of 6–8 picture cards for each child.

Observe each child's ability to do the activity with ease.

Assess Understanding

Monitor whether each child can correctly count the number of phonemes in words.

You may ask each child to count the number of phonemes in a color word [red, pink, tan, black, lime] and tell you where the word belongs in the chart.

Note any difficulty and at what point it became evident.

On Your Own

- Use your Student Pocket Chart and a set of Picture Cards to do the activity.
- Stack up your cards and place them face down on the table.
- Choose a card and say the name of the picture. Count the number of sounds you hear on your fingers.
- Check yourself by counting again. Then place the card in the correct column of the chart, according to the number of sounds.
- Continue until all of your cards are in your chart.

Show What You Know

- There are number cards in several areas of the room. Let's try to find them. Who can see a number card?
- After identifying all numbers in the room say, I will place one Picture Card face down in front of you.
- At the signal, turn over your card, say the picture name, and count the sounds on your fingers.
- Move to the area of the room with the number of sounds in your picture name.
- I will ask you to show me how to count the number of sounds in your picture name.
- Leave your card in that area of the room.
- Come back to the table for another card and repeat the activity.

Use Fruits and Vegetables Learning Place® Game Cards, Insect and Arachnid Learning Place Game Cards, Rhyme Picture Cards, or your choice of picture cards to extend these activities.

Extend and Adapt

Guess a Word

After all cards have been placed in Student Pocket Charts, children can play a game to get rid of their cards. Each child tilts his chart so the others cannot see it. Taking turns, a child gives three clues about a single picture and asks the rest of the group to guess the word. For example, the child may say, *I'm thinking of a word that has three sounds and begins with a /b/. It is something that you carry*. The child who guesses the word [*bag*] removes the picture from the first child's Pocket Chart and places the card in front of him on the table. The object of this game is to give good clues so that all of a child's cards are gone.

Variations on Guess a Word

Vary the number of clues that children can give to the group. Or have children choose a partner to play the game. It is important that one of the clues is the number of sounds in a word, since the purpose of this activity is to practice segmenting sounds. If another clue is about the sound at the beginning of the word, this activity also provides a review of initial sounds.

Unit 5 Activity D

Counting Mat

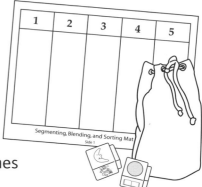

Notes

Materials

- Segmenting, Blending, and Sorting Mats
- Reading Rods® Picture Rods
- Mystery Bag
- Number cards
- Self-stick notes
- Small removable stickers

Skill Phoneme Segmentation

Objective To sort picture names by the number of phonemes

Purpose To segment phonemes in words, children sort Picture Rods according to the number of phonemes.

Activity Overview Children segment picture names into individual phonemes, count the phonemes, and place each Picture Rod on a chart according to the number of phonemes.

Getting Ready

Use stickers to cover the images on the Reading Rods Picture Rods that you may not want to use for this activity.

Name each picture on the rods that remains uncovered.

Place the Picture Rods in the Mystery Bag.

Use side 1 of the Segmenting, Blending, and Sorting Mat (5 columns).

Build Background

- *Let's have fun playing a game using our Mystery Bag and some Reading Rods Picture Rods.*

- *Each Picture Rod has four pictures. Some of the pictures on the rods are covered up with stickers.*

- *Let's look at the uncovered pictures and say their names.*

- *Let's place the Picture Rods in the Mystery Bag.*

- *Look at side 1 of the Segmenting, Blending and Sorting Mat. The columns are numbered 1–5.*

- *The numbers at the top of the mat stand for the number of sounds in a word.*

- *For this game, we place each Picture Rod in one of the columns on the mat.*

StarLIT™ Literacy Intervention Toolkit

Model the Activity

Cover the following Reading Rods® Pictures Rod images:

banana	bicycle
gorilla	jump
rope	kangaroo
light bulb	monkey
necklace	paper clip
pencil	pumpkin
quarter	question mark
television	vacuum
valentine	violin
exit sign	xylophone
yo-yo	elephant
envelope	inchworm
Indian chief	octopus
ostrich	umbrella

Continue the Activity Together

Continue the activity together to provide support as needed.

Gradually release responsibility to children.

Watch Me Play

- *Here is how to play the game. I take a Picture Rod from the Mystery Bag and choose a picture that is <u>not</u> covered by a sticker.*

- *I chose the picture of the zoo. I say the word <u>zoo</u>, and then segment the sounds in the word: /z/ /oo/. How many sounds do I hear?*

- *I use my fingers to count the sounds or tap out the sounds.*

- *I repeat the sounds /z/ /oo/. There are two sounds, so I place the Picture Rod in column 2.*

- *Then I choose another Picture Rod from the bag. This rod has a picture of a cat. I say the word <u>cat</u> aloud.*

- *I segment the sounds in the word—/k/ /ă/ /t/ and count the sounds—/k/ /ă/ /t/. <u>Cat</u> has three sounds.*

- *I place the Picture Rod on the mat under the number 3.*

Play the Game with Me

- *Let's do this activity together. There are two Picture Rods on the mat.*

- *Who would like to choose the next Picture Rod?*

- *[Child's name], select which picture on the rod you want to use and show it to us. Say the picture name.*

- *Who can help [child's name] segment the sounds in the picture word?*

- *Let's all say the sounds as we count the number of sounds on our fingers.*

- *How many sounds did we hear? Let's try it again to make sure we are right.*

- *[Child's name], place the Picture Rod under the correct number on the mat. Now who would like to try it next?*

Unit 5 Activity D

Counting Mat

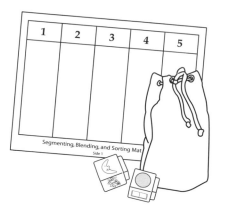

Independent Activity

Provide mats and counters to each child or have children choose a partner and share counters and a mat.

Observe children as they work independently.

Assess Understanding

Monitor whether each child can segment the sounds of words and count the number of sounds.

Say a word for each child. Ask the child to *stretch out* the word (segment the phonemes) and count the number of sounds on his fingers.

Note any difficulty and at what point it became evident.

On Your Own

- *Choose a Picture Rod from the Mystery Bag and select one of the pictures on the rod.*

- *Show the picture and say the word aloud.*

- *Segment the sounds in the picture word as you count the number of sounds on your fingers.*

- *Place the Picture Rod in the correct column on the mat.*

- *Continue the activity until the Mystery Bag is empty.*

- *Once all the Picture Rods are placed on the mat, say the sounds in each word and count the sounds again.*

- *If you are working with a partner, your partner can help you check your responses.*

Show What You Know

- *When I point to a Picture Rod on your mat, say the picture word and segment the sounds of the word.*

- *Stretch out the word and say the sounds aloud as you count them on your fingers.*

StarLIT™ Literacy Intervention Toolkit

Reading Rods®
Picture Rods

3 phonemes:

ball	/b/ /ă/ /l/
moon	/m/ /oo/ /n/
dog	/d/ /ŏ/ /g/
doll	/d/ /ŏ/ /l/
duck	/d/ /ŭ/ /k/
feet	/f/ /ē/ /t/
goat	/g/ /ō/ /t/
hat	/h/ /ă/ /t/
leaf	/l/ /ē/ /f/
yarn	/y/ /ar/ /n/

4 phonemes:

fox	/f/ /ŏ/ /k/ /s/
queen	/k/ /w/ /ē/ /n/
hand	/h/ /ă/ /n/ /d/
nest	/n/ /ĕ/ /s/ /t/
lamp	/l/ /ă/ /m/ /p/
milk	/m/ /ĭ/ /l/ /k/
table	/t/ /ā/ /b/ /l/
needle	/n/ /ē/ /d/ /l/
camel	/c/ /ă/ /m/ /l/
frog	/f/ /r/ /ŏ/ /g/

5 phonemes:

zebra
/z/ /ē/ /b/ /r/ /ă/
monkey
/m/ /ŏ/ /n/ /k/ /ē/
rabbit
/r/ /ă/ b/ /ĭ/ /t/

Extend and Adapt

Add Up the Sounds
At the end of the activity, work with children to add up the total number of sounds of the picture words on the Segmenting, Blending, and Sorting Mats.

Variations
Draw picture cards or small objects from the Mystery Bag instead of Picture Rods. Use any type of counter to place in the columns on the mat to indicate the number of phonemes.

Unit 5 Activity E

Building Words

Materials

- Link 'N' Learn® Links

- Appendix III Syllables and Phonemes

Skill

Segment and Blend Phonemes

Objective

To segment and count the number of phonemes in words and blend the sounds to form the word again

Purpose

To isolate phonemes in words, children build chains of links to represent each phoneme.

Activity Overview

Children segment the sounds in a word, and then assemble a string of Link 'N' Learn Links to represent the number of sounds. Then children form the word again by blending the sounds back together.

Getting Ready

Use the list of phonemes in Picture Card names provided in Appendix III.

Show children how to connect the links by matching the opening in each link and pressing them together, also called "going through the gate."

Build Background

- *Let's have some fun with our Link 'N' Learn Links.*

- *Do you remember how to put them together and take them apart?*

- *Watch me. Hold the links so that the open spaces touch. Then press the links together. Remember to "go through the gate" to connect the links.*

- *Let's practice joining the links.*

Notes

Model the Activity

Be sure that children use left-to-right directionality as they say the sounds and slide their fingers under the chain to say the word.

Provide support and continue to model the activity children as needed.

Continue the Activity Together

Continue the activity, using other words from the list. As the children are ready, use words with more sounds.

Provide support and gradually release more responsibility to children.

Watch Me Play

- *Here is how to play the game. The first word is* hat.
- *I say the word slowly and count the sounds I hear on my fingers: /h/ /ă/ /t/.*
- *Count the number of fingers. I count three.*
- *I connect three Link 'N' Learn® Links to make a chain of three.*
- *I place the chain on the table.*
- *To see if I am correct, I start with the link on the left and say the sounds while I touch each link: /h/ /ă/ /t/.*
- *I start on the left and slide my finger under the chain of links, blending the sounds to say the word:* hat.
- *Now I am ready to listen to a new word.*

Play the Game with Me

- *Let's do the activity together. Listen to the word. The word is* bat.
- *Let's say the word slowly and count the number of sounds in the word* bat *on our fingers.*
- *How many fingers and how many sounds are there? [3] How many links do we need to make a chain for the sounds in the word* bat*? [3]*
- *Who would like to join the links? Let's place the chain on the table and point to each link as we say the sounds in the word* bat: /b/ /ă/ /t/. *Do we have the right number of links?*
- *We slide our fingers under the chain of links and blend the sounds together to say the word.*
- *Let's leave this chain on the table and make another chain for the next word.*
- *Then we can compare the length of the two chains of Link 'N' Learn Links to see which one is longer.*

Unit 5 Activity E

Building Words

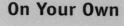

Notes

Independent Activity

Provide each child with a set of Link 'N' Learn® Links. Say a different word for each child.

On Your Own

- *Listen to the word and say the word slowly.*
- *Count the number of sounds you hear on your fingers and make a chain of links for the number of sounds you hear.*
- *When your chain is on the table, say the sounds slowly as you touch each link.*
- *Is the number of links correct?*
- *Slide your finger under the chain and blend the sounds back together to say the word again.*
- *Then listen for the next word.*

Assess Understanding

Monitor whether each child can segment phonemes, create a physical representation, and blend the sounds back into a word.

Show What You Know

- *Listen to the sounds in the word. Blend the sounds to say the word. For example,*

    /s/ /ĭ/ /t/, <u>sit</u>
    /r/ /ŭ/ /n/, <u>run</u>
    /h/ /ŏ/ /p/, <u>hop</u>
    /s/ /k/ /ĭ/ /p/, <u>skip</u>
    /r/ /ĕ/ /s/ /t/, <u>rest</u>

- *Stretch out the sounds of a word by pretending to hold a rubber band in front of your lips as you say each word. For example,*

    <u>frog</u>, /f/ /r/ /ŏ/ /g/
    <u>cow</u>, /k/ /ow/
    <u>pond</u>, /p/ /ŏ/ /n/ /d/
    <u>duck</u>, /d/ /ŭ/ /k/
    <u>fish</u>, /f/ /ĭ/ /sh/

Vary the activity by asking children to isolate phonemes in the names of other Picture Cards. Refer to the list of phonemes in each picture name found in Appendix III.

Extend and Adapt

Line Up the Sounds

Say a word for the children. Have children work together to decide how many sounds they hear in the word. Then have the correct number of children stand side-by-side to represent the number of sounds they hear in the word. The teacher (or another child) taps a child while saying individual sounds and then blends the sounds together again.

Variation I

You may have each child think of objects in the gym (net, ball, rope, mat, bat, etc.) or other area. Ask the children to segment the phonemes, create a chain of links, and then blend the sounds together again to form the word.

Compare the Words

Children can save their chains of links for several words. Later they can compare the length of the chains of phonemes. Children will enjoy seeing the differences between words.

Variation II

To vary the activity children may use craft sticks placed end-to-end in a line in place of Link 'N' Learn® Links. Vary the activity further by using sets of fruit, bug, bear, or Quiet Counters.

Unit 5 Activity F

Guess That Object

Materials

- Reading Rods® Pocket Chart Cards
- Mystery Bag
- Sorting Bowls
- Rubber bands
- Appendix III Syllables and Phonemes

Skill

Phoneme Segmentation and Blending

Objective

To segment words into phonemes and then blend phonemes into words

Purpose

To sequence units of sounds into comprehensible units, children blend individual sounds together to form words.

Activity Overview

Children listen to segmented phonemes and blend them into words.

Getting Ready

Use the list of phonemes in Picture Card names provided in Appendix III.

Choose a Picture Card from the list and hide it in the Mystery Bag.

Build Background

- Demonstrate using different sizes of rubber bands. *Rubber bands are useful to us because they stretch out to fit around things. When we remove a rubber band, it shrinks back to its original smaller size.*

- *We can have fun pretending to stretch out the sounds of a word in the same way that we can stretch a rubber band.*

- *When we blend the sounds back together again to say a word, it is the same as the rubber band shrinking back to its original size.*

- *Let's pretend to hold rubber bands in front of our mouths. Carefully stretch out your imaginary rubber band and then let it shrink back again.*

- *If a word has many sounds, the rubber band will stretch very far. If there are only a few sounds, the rubber band will stretch just a little.*

- *When the sounds are blended together, the rubber band shrinks back to its original size.*

Model the Activity

Say the segmented sounds of the picture word /l/ /ă/ /m/ /p/ hidden in the Mystery Bag.

Show children how to blend the sounds to form the word again. Say the word *lamp*.

Confirm the word by taking the Picture Card of the lamp from the Mystery Bag and showing it to the children.

Continue to model the activity, as needed.

Continue the Activity Together

Hide a Picture Card in the Mystery Bag.

Invite children to play the game with you.

Continue the activity by choosing another word from the list and hiding the Picture Card in the Mystery Bag.

Give each child a turn to blend sounds into words.

Gradually release responsibility to the children.

Watch Me Play

- *Here is how to play the game. I listen to the separate sounds of a word: /l/ /ă/ /m/ /p/*

- *I stretch out my imaginary rubber band for the sounds I hear: /l/ /ă/ /m/ /p/*

- *Now I shrink my rubber band as I blend the sounds back together to say the word: /l/ /ă/ /m/ /p/,* <u>lamp</u>. *The word is* <u>lamp</u>.

- *To check, I reach into the Mystery Bag and take out the Picture Card.*

- *It is a picture of a lamp. I was correct, so I keep the card in my Sorting Bowl.*

- *A new Picture Card is hidden in the Mystery Bag.*

- *I listen to the sounds and pretend to stretch my rubber band again to continue the activity.*

Play the Game with Me

- *There is a new Picture Card hidden in the Mystery Bag. Are you ready with your rubber bands?*

- *Let's do the activity together. Listen as I say the sounds of the word. Let's stretch out our rubber bands as we say the sounds.*

- *Now, blend the sounds with me as we shrink our rubber bands back down to say the word. What word do you hear? Who would like to say the word?*

- *Do you agree or disagree? Let's give a Thumbs Up or a Thumbs Down.*

- *Let's see if we were correct. Who would like to reach into the Mystery Bag for the picture?*

- *Show the Picture Card to the group and say the word. Were we correct?*

- *Let's try it again with another word.*

Guess That Object

Notes

Independent Activity

Choose another word from the list and hide the Picture Card in the Mystery Bag.

Distribute a Sorting Bowl to each child.

You may wish to ask the child who blended the word correctly to hide the next picture and say the segmented sounds for the rest of the group.

Assess Understanding

Monitor whether each child can blend phonemes into words.

Hide a small object in the Mystery Bag and say the segmented sounds of its name for the child.

Ask the child to blend the sounds into a word. Then ask the child to take the object from the bag to confirm it.

On Your Own

- *There is a new Picture Card in the Mystery Bag.*
- *Listen to the sounds I say and think about the word they make when they are blended together.*
- *Raise your hand if you know the word.*
- *[Child's name], say the word. The group will give a Thumbs Up or Thumbs Down to show if they agree or disagree.*
- *[Child's name], take the picture card from the Mystery Bag and show it to the group to confirm that your word is correct.*
- *[Child's name], is correct, so he keeps the Picture Card in his Sorting Bowl.*
- *I'll hide another Picture Card, and let's continue the activity with the next player.*

Show What You Know

- *Let's pretend that we have been on a shopping trip. We have items in our shopping bag.*
- *When it is your turn, take an object from the bag and say the name of the object aloud.*
- *Segment the sounds in the name of the object.*
- *Then, blend the sounds back together again to say the word.*
- *If you are correct, you may keep the object with you for a while.*
- *If you are incorrect, put the object back in the bag and try again at your next turn.*

Children enjoy these activities on the playground or outdoors where there is more freedom of movement.

Extend and Adapt

Blending and Bending

Begin with two- or three-phoneme words, such as *no* or *yes*. Have children stand in an area that allows free movement. Model touching your head for the first sound, your waist for the second sound, and your knees for the third sound. As you stand up straight raise both arms above your head and say the blended word. For example, /y/ (head), /ĕ/ (waist), /s/ (knees), and as you stand up say the blended word *yes*. When using words with more phonemes, have children touch their shoulders or toes for the other sounds.

Hop a Word

Draw a rectangle on a large piece of paper or make a rectangle on the carpet or floor with masking tape. Divide the rectangle into 3–5 boxes, depending on the number of phonemes in the words used. Have children take turns and slowly hop one box for each sound in the word. Then ask the child to hop out of the rectangle and say the blended word.

Unit 5 Activity G

Accent It!

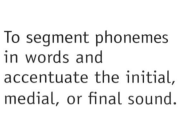

Materials

- Reading Rods® Phonological Awareness Pocket Chart Cards
- Game Spinner
- BLM 5-4 Engine, Boxcar, Caboose
- BLM 5-5 Train Car Cards

Skill

Phoneme Segmentation and Placement

Objective

To segment phonemes in words and accentuate the initial, medial, or final sound.

Purpose

To isolate the individual sounds in words and identify the initial, medial, and final sounds, children use hand gestures to accent sound placement.

Activity Overview

Children make a hand gesture for the sound at a particular place (initial, medial, or final sound) in a word.

Getting Ready

Cut out the Engine, Boxcar, and Caboose from BLM 5-4.

Choose a set of gestures for children to use to accentuate sounds in words. Practice the gestures with the children.

You may wish to begin by accentuating the initial sound and then do the activity for the final sound and then the medial sound.

Build Background

- *We can have fun using hand gestures for this activity.*
- *Let's practice some hand gestures: thumbs up, high five, wave, finger snap, hand clap, etc.*
- *For this activity, sometimes we accent the beginning sound. Other times we accent the ending or the middle sounds.*
- *We need to listen carefully to the sounds in words and use the gestures at just the right time.*

Model the Activity

Show the children that for the word *mop*, you clap for /m/ /ŏ/ /p/— 3 claps.

To accent the sound at a particular place in the word, use a different gesture or motion.

Model the activity to accent the initial, final, and middle sounds of words.

Continue the Activity Together

Invite children to do the activity with you.

Be sure to practice isolating ending and middle sounds.

Repeat the activity together, as needed.

Watch Me Play

- *Here is how to play the game. The word is* mop.
- *I stretch out the sounds of the word and say the sounds: /m/ /ŏ/ /p/.*
- *Then, I clap for the sounds of the word. I clap for the /m/, clap again for /ŏ/, and clap one more time for /p/.*
- *To accent the beginning sound, I use a different gesture: I snap my fingers for that sound. Watch me snap my fingers instead of clap for the beginning sound of the word* sun: *Snap for /s/, clap for /ŭ/, and clap for /n/.*
- *The next word is* net. *I separate the sounds /n/ /ĕ/ /t/. To accent the middle sound, I clap for /n/, snap for /ĕ/, and clap for /t/.*

Play the Game with Me

- *Let's do the activity together. We can begin by clapping the sounds of the word I say.*
- *The word is* cart. *Let's say the sounds of the word together. Now let's clap the sounds for the word* cart. *(/k/ /ar/ /t/)*
- *Let's accent the middle sound of the word this time. Who can tell us which sound is in the middle of the word* cart? *[/ar/]*
- *[Child's name], what gesture would you like to use for the middle sound?*
- *Let's say the sounds and do the gestures together: clap /k/, snap /ar/, clap /t/.*
- *Let's use a different gesture to show the final sound. Who has an idea?*
- *Show us the way to accent the final sound in* cart: *clap /k/, clap /ar/, snap /t/.*

Unit 5 Activity G

Accent It!

Independent Activity

Count around the group to give each child a number.

Assess Understanding

Cut apart the Engine, Boxcar, and Caboose from BLM 5-4 and place them on the table. Place Picture Cards in a pile face down.

Engine–beginning sound (Engineer pulls the horn.)

Caboose–ending sound (Trainman waves.)

Boxcar–middle sound (Move arms in a locomotive motion.)

On Your Own

- *Let's count off to give each of us a number.*
- *Now I'll spin. [Child's name] has that number, so he/she chooses a hand gesture and tells us what part of the word to accent.*
- *Listen to the word. Everyone clap the sounds of the word together.*
- *Now use the gesture that [child's name] chose to accent the part of the word.*
- *Let's repeat the word, using the same hand gesture.*
- *[Child's name], spin the spinner to see who goes next.*
- Repeat the activity, changing the accented part of the word and the hand gestures for each word.

Show What You Know

- *Use these pictures to stand for the sounds of a word. The Engine stands for the beginning sound. The Caboose stands for the ending sound. The Boxcar stands for the middle sound.*
- *Begin with the picture of the Engine and accent the beginning sound.*
- *First, take a Picture Card and clap the sounds of the word. What special gesture can we use to accent the beginning sound?*
- *The train's engineer rides in the engine. Let's use the gesture of the engineer pulling the horn to accent the beginning sound. Pull the horn to accent the beginning sound and clap the other sounds.*
- *Choose another Picture Card and repeat the activity using the Caboose or the Boxcar. What gestures can you use to accent these ending or middle sounds?*

Rhyme Picture Cards
Initial sounds
differ:

car/jar

bug/hug

mail/nail

well/bell

tack/sack

Ending sounds
differ:

wet/well

pin/pill

cap/cat

bug/bun

rug/run

Middle sounds
differ:

sack/sick

map/mop

cat/coat

dig/dog

pin/pan

sack/sick

Extend and Adapt

Stand Up for Sounds

Begin the activity with children seated on chairs. Tell children that they should stand for a particular sound placement. For example, ask a child to say the sounds of the word and stand for the ending sound.

Accent the Vowel Sound

Choose a hand gesture to accent the vowel sounds in words. Supply a word to the group. Ask a volunteer to segment the word and suggest a hand gesture for the group to use to accent the vowel. Children say the segmented sounds of the word together and perform the gesture when they hear the vowel sound. For example, for the word *bike*, a child would say /b/ /ī/ /k/ and might suggest snapping fingers for the vowel sound. Children would all say /b/, snap their fingers as they say /ī/, and then say /k/.

Which Sound Changes

Cut out Train Car Cards from BLM 5-5. Give each child an Engine, Boxcar, and Caboose card. As children listen to a pair of words, have them show whether the beginning, ending, or middle sound is different by placing the correct Train Car Card on the table.
(car/jar—initial sounds differ—Engine)
(wet/well—ending sounds differ—Caboose)
(sack/sick—middle sounds differ—Boxcar)

Unit 5 Activity H

Sound Bingo

Notes

Materials

- BLM 5-6, 5-7, 5-8 Sound Bingo Cards
- Quiet Counters
- Reading Rods® Picture Rods

Skill

Phoneme Segmentation and Blending

Objective

To isolate the sounds in a word (beginning sound, ending sound, or middle sound)

Purpose

To distinguish the number of sounds and the position of sounds in words, children use word clues to play Sound Bingo.

Activity Overview

Children isolate the sounds of words and cover a picture on a Sound Bingo Card with the same beginning, ending, or middle sound.

Getting Ready

This activity may require more modeling than is usually required.

Begin this activity with the list of Sound Bingo clues found in Appendix IV.

Build Background

- *Let's have fun playing Sound Bingo.*
- *Let's look at the pictures on the Sound Bingo Cards and say their names.*
- *We can listen to the clues and find a picture on the card that matches the clues.*
- *Listen to the clues carefully. There are two parts to each clue.*
- *When we find a picture that matches the clue, we cover the picture with a counter.*
- *When a whole row is covered with counters, say Sound Bingo!*

Model the Activity

Use a Sound Bingo Card and Quiet Counters to model this activity.

Name the pictures on the Sound Bingo Card. Cover the Smiley Face picture with a counter.

Help children attend to both parts of the clue.

Continue to model the game until you have a row of pictures covered with counters. Say Sound Bingo!

Continue the Activity Together

Use a different Sound Bingo Card and a set of Quiet Counters.

Children may need more coaching with this activity. Provide support as needed and work with children on clues to find beginning, ending, and middle sounds.

Help children think through both parts of the clues.

Gradually release responsibility to the children.

Watch Me Play

- *Here is how to play the game. I cover the smiley face in the middle of the card.*
- *Listen to the first clue:* <u>Cover a picture with a three-sound name that begins with /g/.</u>
- *First, I look for any pictures that start with /g/. I see a goat.* <u>Goat</u> *starts with /g/.*
- *The second part of the clue said that the word has three sounds.*
- *Does the word* <u>goat</u> *have three sounds? I say the sounds /g/ /ō/ /t/ as I count on my fingers.*
- *Yes,* <u>goat</u> *begins with /g/, and it has three sounds. I place a counter on the picture of the goat.*
- *I continue to play until a whole row of pictures is covered on the card. Then I say Sound Bingo!*
- *I check the pictures with the clues to make sure.*

Play the Game with Me

- *Let's play the game together. Cover up the smiley face in the middle of the card.*
- *Listen carefully to the clue.* <u>Cover a picture with a three-sound name that ends with /l/.</u>
- *Let's listen to that clue again and think about it.* <u>Cover a picture with a three-sound name that ends with /l/.</u>
- *There are two parts to the clue. Can anyone find a picture that ends with /l/?* <u>Camel</u> *and* <u>well</u> *both end in /l/. But we need to think about the other part of the clue.*
- <u>Cover a picture with a three-sound name that ends with /l/.</u> *Does one of those picture names have three sounds? Help me count the sounds on my fingers:* <u>camel</u>*, /c/ /ă/ /m/ /l/;* <u>well</u>*, /w/ /ĕ/ /l/) The word* <u>well</u> *has three sounds.*
- *Which picture do we cover with a counter? Who would like to cover the picture of the well?*
- *Let's listen to the next clue and help each other find the picture.*
- *What do we say when a row is covered? Sound Bingo!*

Notes

Independent Activity

Distribute Sound Bingo Cards and Quiet Counters to each child.

Assess Understanding

Use Pocket Chart Cards to assess understanding of initial sounds.

Give each child two Picture Cards (hat, hand). Give the child two clues and ask the child to choose the right card. For example, Find the picture with a three-sound name that begins with /h/. (hat)

Use Reading Rods® Picture Rods to assess understanding of final and medial

On Your Own

- *Each of us will play the game with our own Sound Bingo Card and Quiet Counters. Cover up the smiley face on your card.*

- *Listen to the clues and look for the picture. You can use your fingers to count the sounds.*

- *I will say the clue again. Be sure to listen to both parts of the clues.*

- *Remember to say Sound Bingo! when you have covered a complete row of pictures.*

Show What You Know

- *Listen to the clues and choose a Picture Card word that fits both clues: Find a picture with a four-sound name that begins with /h/.* [hand, /h/ /ă/ /n/ /d/.]

- *Listen to the clues and choose a Picture Rod that fits both clues: Find a Picture Rod with a four-sound name that ends with /t/.* [nest, /n/ /ĕ/ /s/ /t/]

Extend and Adapt

Reading Rod Sort

Place Reading Rods Picture Rods in the middle of the table. Give each child an ending sound. Have the child connect 3–4 rods with pictures that end with that sound. For example, Connect picture rods that end with /t/. [*goat, cat, jet, rabbit*] Ask the child to say the names of the pictures for the group.

Variation I

Have children work with a partner. Give each pair a clue. For example, Connect Picture Rods with three-sound names that end with /l/. [*well, ball, seal*] Ask partners to say the names of the pictures for the group.

Variation II

Give each child a pink Picture Rod. Have each one say the initial vowel sound. Then have each child connect 2–3 light blue rods with that medial vowel sound. [*cat, van, hand*] Ask each child to say the names of the pictures for the group. Have others in the group verify the collection with a thumbs up or down sign.

Unit 6

Phonological Awareness at the Phoneme Manipulation Level: Phoneme Addition, Deletion, and Substitution

Phoneme manipulation is the addition, deletion, or substitution of sounds in words to create new words. The final stage of phonemic awareness, phoneme manipulation provides children with opportunities to reconfigure sounds in words. Initially children should manipulate sounds at the beginning of words and then move on to working with the ending and middle sounds. It is beneficial for children to learn to manipulate sounds in creative ways to appreciate the playfulness of language.

A Word from the Experts

"Phoneme deletion ability proved to be a strong predicator of both reading and spelling performance."

G. T. Gillon, Phonological Awareness: From Research to Practice, 2004.

Unit 6 Objectives

In this unit children will—
- Segment sounds in words and add sounds to create new words
- Manipulate words by deleting phonemes to form new words
- Change the placement of phonemes to create new words
- Demonstrate an understanding of the placement of the phoneme that is changed to form a new word
- Recognize the placement of the sound that changes in a word when one sound is substituted for another
- Recognize phoneme substitution at the beginning of rhyming words in text

Skills Connection

It is important for children to attend to and manipulate sounds within words. Opportunities to arrange, rearrange, and substitute the sounds in words allow children to enjoy the playfulness of language. The ability to manipulate sounds in words is fundamental to the reading and writing process.

StarLIT™ Literacy Intervention Toolkit

English Language Learners

Children may enjoy playing a sound addition game. Have children stand in a row to represent the sounds in words. Ask a child to add a sound to the word. For example, have three children stand for the sounds /r/ /ă/ /k/. Say, *Add /t/ to the beginning of* [/r/ /ă/ /k/] rack. [*track*] Ask a fourth child to stand at the beginning of the row. Have children say the new word *shop*. Vary the game to practice sound deletion and sound substitution.

Home-School Connection

Dear Parent,
Please support your child as he/she learns to manipulate the sounds in words. Play word games such as *I'm Thinking of a Word* with your child. Select a word and create a riddle, such as "I'm thinking of a word that rhymes with *hen* and starts with /p/" or "I'm thinking of a word that rhymes with *log* and begins with /d/."

On-the-Go Assessment for Word Awareness

To make the most of free moments, show an animal picture or make an animal sound and ask the child to name the animal. Then ask the child to say the name of the animal without the initial sound, without the ending sound, or with a substituted sound. For example, Name this animal. (goat) Say goat without the /g/. [*oat*] Say goat without the /t/. [*go*] Replace the /g/ with /b/. [*boat*]

Unit 6 Phoneme Manipulation Chart of Manipulatives

Activity	A—Changing Sounds: Move It and Say It	B—Those Silly Bugs! Take Away a Sound	C—Stand Up and Change	D—Change That Word Mat	E—Substitute a Sound	F—Fred Told Me
Segmenting, Blending, and Sorting Mats	●			●		
Bear Counters	●				●	
SunSprouts® Wolf Puppet	●					
BLM 6-1 Insect Net		●				
Bug Counters		●				
Fruity Fun™ Counters			●			
BLM 5-1 Fruit Bowl			●			
Quiet Counters				●		
BLM 5-2 Bears' Den					●	
Story Blossoms® small book *Fred Told Me*						●

Unit 6 Activity A

Changing Sounds
Move It and Say It

Materials

- Segmenting, Blending, and Sorting Mats (side 2)
- Bear Counters
- SunSprouts® Wolf Puppet
- Appendix IV Teacher's Notes

Skill   Phoneme Addition

Side 2

Objective   To segment the sounds in words and add sounds to create new words

Purpose   To manipulate the sounds at the beginning, ending, or middle of words and to see the similarities and differences between words, children create new words and enjoy the playfulness of language.

Activity Overview   Children demonstrate how to segment the sounds in words and create new words by changing the beginning, ending, or middle sounds.

Getting Ready

Use the list of Picture Card words and their phonemes in Appendix III.

Use the SunSprouts® Wolf Puppet to segment the sounds in words and add sounds to create new words.

Build Background

- *Here is our friend, Wally Wolf.*
- *Wally Wolf enjoys playing with the sounds in words. He likes to make new words.*
- *Let's have fun helping Wally Wolf make new words by adding sounds to the beginning, the end, or the middle of words.*
- *We can use Segmenting, Blending, and Sorting Mats and Bear Counters to show the sounds in words.*
- *Who is ready to help Wally Wolf?*

Model the Activity

Keep in mind that this is a speaking and listening activity. Children are working with phonemes (sounds), not alphabet letters or correct spellings.

Continue to model the activity as needed.

Continue the Activity Together

Provide support to children and continue the activity together, as needed.

Watch Me Play

- *Watch me help Wally Wolf make new words. Wally's first word is* <u>ice</u>. *I say the sounds in the word* <u>ice</u>. *[/ī/ /s/]*

- *How many sounds do I hear? How many times should Wally Wolf move his mouth? [2]*

- *I place two counters in the Home Base circle to stand for /ī/ and /s/. I help Wally Wolf say the word again and move one counter down to the arrow for each sound.*

- *Now Wally Wolf wants to add /r/ to the beginning of* <u>ice</u>. *What part of the word changes? [beginning sound]*

- *I add another counter to Home Base for the /r/. Then I move it to the line to make /r/ /ī/ /s/. I touch one counter for each sound and help Wally Wolf say* <u>rice</u>.

- *Then I put the counters back on Home Base. I am ready to help Wally Wolf play with a new word.*

Play the Game with Me

- *Let's all help Wally Wolf play with words. Listen to the new word* <u>top</u> *and think about the sounds you hear.*

- *Let's say the sounds and help Wally say them. Choose counters and put them in a row on Home Base to show the sounds /t/ /ŏ/ /p/.*

- *Who can show Wally Wolf how to move a counter to the arrow for each of the sounds?*

- *Now Wally Wolf wants to add /s/ to the beginning of the word* <u>top</u>. *Who can point to the counter where the word changes?*

- *The word changes at the beginning. Let's place another counter at the beginning and help Wally say the sounds of the new word: /s/ /t/ /o/ /p/.*

- *What is the new word? Let's touch the counters and help Wally Wolf say the sounds in the new word.*

- *Now Wally wants to add /s/ to the end of the word. [/s/ /t/ /o/ /p/ /s/]*

- *Who can help Wally with this new word?*

Changing Sounds
Move It and Say It

Notes

Independent Activity

Provide children with Segmenting, Blending, and Sorting Mats and a small set of Bear Counters.

You may wish to have children take turns with Wally Wolf.

Observe whether each child can correctly add phonemes to the beginning and/or ending of a word.

Plan to revisit the activity, if needed.

Assess Understanding

Give each child a word and a sound and have the child add a sound to create a new word.

Sample Clues:
Add /m/ to the beginning of ice to make a word. [mice]

Add /t/ to the end of me to make a word. [meet]

Add /g/ to the beginning of oat to make a word. [goat]

On Your Own

- *Listen to the sounds and say the word.*
- *Take turns helping Wally Wolf move his mouth to say the sounds. Think about how many sounds you hear.*
- *Place your Bear Counters in a row on Home Base to show the sounds in the word.*
- *Move each counter down as you say each sound. Say the word.*
- *When Wally Wolf asks you to change the word, add a counter to the row.*
- *Help Wally Wolf say the new word. Touch your counters and say each sound in the new word.*
- *Listen for another word and help Wally Wolf say the sounds.*

Show What You Know

- *Let's play the Add a Sound game.*
- *When it is your turn, listen to a word and think about the sounds you hear.*
- *Say the word. Then listen for the sound to add to the word.*
- *The clue will tell you to add the sound at the beginning, at the end, or the middle of the word.*
- *Use the clue to add a sound to make a new word.*
- *Here is the first clue. The word is lip. Add /s/ to the beginning of lip to make a new word.* [slip]
- *Here is the next clue. The word is den. Add /t/ to the end of den to make a new word.* [dent]

Phoneme Addition and Deletion

Adding Initial Sounds
all + /k/ = call
lip + /s/ = slip

Adding Final Sounds
men + /d/ = mend
will + /t/ = wilt

Deleting Initial Sounds
small - /s/ = mall
crow - /k/ = row

Deleting Final Sounds
belt - /t/ = bell
drive - /v/ = dry

Phoneme Substitution

Initial Phonemes
Change the /s/ in sand to /h/ = hand
Change the /t/ in top to /m/ = mop

Final Phonemes
Change the /s/ in sip to /z/ = zip
Change the /b/ in bat to /r/ = rat

Medial Phonemes
Change the /a/ in star to /i/ = stir
Change the /u/ in tuck to /a/ = tack

Extend and Adapt

Kids in a Row

Have children sit on chairs (or stand) in a row. Say a word and have children repeat it. Ask children to segment the sounds in the word. Choose children to represent each sound in the word. Ask each child to say his sound. Then say a sound to add to the word. Ask the children where the sound should change? Ask the child in the position where the sound changes to raise his hand. Then have the child select another child to stand before or after him in the row. When that child is in place, all children say the sounds and then blend them together to say the new word. Continue adding, subtracting, or substituting initial, final, and medial sounds to make new words.

Come Out and Play

To vary the activity, use BLM 5-1, Fruit Bowl, 5-2 Bears' Den, or 5-3 Frog Pond in place of the Segmenting, Blending, and Sorting Mats for Activity 6A.

Those Silly Bugs!
Take Away a Sound

Notes

Materials

- BLM 6-1 Insect Net
- Bug Counters
- Appendix IV Teacher's Notes

Skill   Phoneme Deletion

Objective   To manipulate words by deleting phonemes to form new words

Purpose   To create new words and recognize the similarities and differences between words, children manipulate the sounds at the beginning, at the ending, or in the middle of words.

Activity Overview   Children use Bug Counters to delete sounds at the beginning or end of words to form new words.

Getting Ready

Use the list of words for phoneme deletion in Appendix IV.

Build Background

- *Let's have some fun playing with bugs.*
- *Who has ever caught some bugs outdoors in the summertime? What did you catch? How did you catch the bugs?*
- *Did you use a net to catch them? Did you keep the bugs, or did you let them go?*
- *Let's pretend that each of us has caught some bugs in our insect nets.*
- *When I say a word, we can take some bugs out of the net and place them on a stick.*
- *Watch what happens to our word when one of the bugs flies or crawls away!*

Notes

Model the Activity

Use a copy of BLM 6-1 Insect Net and Bug Counters to model the activity for the children.

Place the Bug Counters in the Insect Net on the BLM.

Model at least one example of deleting a final sound and one example of deleting an initial sound.

Continue the Activity Together

Provide each child with a copy of the BLM 6-1 Insect Net and Bug Counters.

Provide support as you continue the activity with the children.

Experience the deletion of both initial and final sounds as you play the game together.

Watch Me Play

- *Here is how to play the game.*
- *Look! I have caught six bugs in my net.*
- *Listen to the first word. The word is* crow.
- *I say the word. I listen for the sounds and say them.*
- *I move one insect onto the stick at the bottom of the page for each sound in the word* crow. */k/ /r/ /ō/*
- *I need to remember to place the first bug on the left side of the stick.*
- *How many sounds are there in the word* crow*? [3] How many bugs are on the stick?*
- *Oh-oh, one of my bugs has flown [crawled] away! The beginning sound, /k/, is gone.*
- *What is my new word? I say the sounds for the bugs that are left on the stick /r/ /ō/.*
- Crow *without the /k/ is the word* row.
- *I touch each bug that is left on the stick and blend the sounds that I hear. The new word is* row.

Play the Game with Me

- *Let's place the bugs back in the net and listen for a new word.*
- *The word is* belt. *Say the word with me and listen to the sounds: /b/ /ĕ/ /l/ /t/. Say the sounds with me.*
- *How many bugs do we need to place on the stick for the word* belt*? [4]*
- *Who would like to line up the bugs for us?*
- *Point to each bug and say the sounds.*
- *Oh-oh! The bug on the end got away! The ending sound is gone.*
- *Who can point to the bugs that are left on the stick and say the sounds? [/b/ /ĕ/ /l/]*
- *Let's say the new word together:* bell.
- *Let's return the bugs to the net and listen for another word.*

Unit 6 Activity B

Those Silly Bugs!
Take Away a Sound

Notes

Independent Activity

Children may work with a partner or in the small group.

Observe children as they do the activity independently.

Assess Understanding

Monitor whether each child can correctly delete the beginning or ending sound of a word to create a new word.

Children enjoy language word play, and it can be fun to delete initial or final sounds to create appropriate nonsense words.

On Your Own

- *Are you ready to play with more bugs? Place your bugs in the net and listen for a new word.*

- *When it is your turn, say the word aloud. Listen to the sounds in the word and say them.*

- *How many bugs will you need to place on the stick? Move the bugs.*

- *Point to each bug and say the sounds.*

- *Now listen for which one of the bugs got away. Which sound is gone? Take away the correct bug.*

- *Say the sounds and the new word aloud.*

- *Let's give* [child's name] *a Thumbs Up! if* [child's name] *says the word correctly.*

Show What You Know

- *Each of us has a crayon (or marker).*

- *Say the name of your color. Say the sounds. Then take away the sound I say.*

- *Say the new color name.*

- *For example,*

  red *without* /r/ *becomes* ed

  yellow *without* /ō/ *becomes* yell

  pink *without* /k/ *becomes* pin

  black *without* /b/ *becomes* lack

  brown *without* /n/ *becomes* brow

  white *without* /t/ *becomes* why

  peach *without* /ch/ *becomes* pea

  tan *without* /t/ *becomes* an

  gray *without* /g/ *becomes* ray

Sample Clues

Delete initial sounds

bring without /b/ [*ring*]

chin without /ch/ [*in*]

send without /s/ [*end*]

shout without /sh/ [*out*]

small without /s/ [*mall*]

trap without /t/ [*rap*]

Delete final sounds

date without /t/ [*day*]

might without /t/ [*my*]

place without /s/ [*play*]

steam without /s/ [*team*]

treat without /tr/ [*eat*]

wilt without /t/ [*will*]

Silly Names

Children enjoy creating nonsense names by deleting the beginning or ending sounds of names. For example, *Mr. Clark* without the /cl/ becomes *Mr. Ark*, and *Emma* without the /ă/ becomes *Em*. It is fun to use some animal names for this activity as well.

Picture Card Fun

Place selected picture cards in the Mystery Bag. Ask each child to take a card and take away a beginning or ending sound to make a new word. For example, delete the beginning sound from the words *ball* [*all*], *cat* [*at*], *cow* [*ow*], and *dice* [*ice*]. Delete the ending sound from the words *zipper* [*zip*], *wagon* [*wag*], *rose* [*row*], and *seal* [*sea*].

I Spy

Show children a magazine picture and tell them that a certain beginning (or ending) sound is not allowed in the picture. Have children look for objects in the picture that begin or end with that sound and say their nonsense names. Say, for example, */b/ is not allowed in this picture. I spy an us for bus, or I spy a ranch for branch*.

Sound Hunt

Give each child a beginning (or ending) sound. Ask the child to find three objects in the room that begin (or end) with that sound. Give each child a turn to take away the beginning (or ending) sound and say the new name of the object. For example, bat and ball become at and all.

Stand Up and Change

Materials

- Fruity Fun™ Counters
- BLM 5-1 Fruit Bowl
- Appendix IV Teacher's Notes

Skill   Phoneme Manipulation

Objective   To change the placement of phonemes to create new words

Purpose   To recognize the similarities and differences between words and to create new words, children substitute sounds at the beginning, at the ending, or in the middle of words.

Activity Overview   Children represent each sound in a word and practice segmenting and blending the sounds to form a word. Children move as the placement of the sound is changed to form a new word.

Getting Ready

Children sit on chairs in a row to represent the left-to-right progression of sounds in words.

Build Background

- *Let's have fun with a new game called Stand Up and Change. Let's pretend that we are the sounds in a word.*

- *We can use a row of chairs. The first chair on the left stands for the beginning sound. The other chairs stand for the rest of the sounds in the word.*

- *First we can listen to a word and think about the sounds we hear.*

- *Then we can count the sounds and decide how many chairs we need in the row.*

- *Are you ready to play Stand Up and Change?*

Model the Activity

Choose a word from the list and say it aloud.

Practice segmenting the sounds and blending them back together.

Be sure to ask each child to say his individual sound as you blend and segment the sounds (left-to-right).

Continue to model the activity, changing the initial or ending sounds.

Continue the Activity Together

Invite children to do the activity with you.

Provide support and continue the activity with the children.

Watch Me Play

- *Here is how to play the game. The first word is* pin. *I say the word and think about how many sounds I hear.* [3]

- *I count three sounds, so three children need to sit in three chairs.*

- *Say the sounds in the word with me as I tap each child sitting in a chair:* /p/ /ĭ/ /n/, pin.

- *I practice segmenting and blending the sounds in* pin.

- *Now I listen for a new word. The new word is* pit. *How many sounds do I hear?*

- *I hear three sounds. I tap each person as I say the sounds:* /p/ /ĭ/ /t/.

- Pin/pit, *one sound is different. The sound that changed has to stand up. Instead of /n/ at the end of the word, I hear /t/. The person in the last chair stands up.*

- [Child's name], *choose another child in the group to take your place.*

- *Help me practice segmenting and blending the sounds in the word* pit: /p/ /ĭ/ /t/, pit.

Play the Game with Me

- *Listen to the word and say it with me. How many sounds do we hear? How many chairs do we need?*

- (Choose children to sit in a row in the order of the sounds.) *The first child on the left represents the beginning sound, the middle one represents the middle sound, and the last one represents the ending sound.*

- *Who would like to tap each child while we say the sounds in the word? Let's blend the sounds and say the word.*

- *Listen to a new word. How many sounds?*

- *What sound is different? Who has to stand up?*

- *Choose another child to sit in your chair. Let's practice segmenting the sounds.*

- *Who would like to tap each child and blend the sounds?*

Stand Up and Change

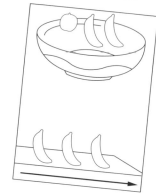

Notes

Independent Activity

Use Fruity Fun™ Counters and BLM 5-1 Fruit Bowl.

Give each child five counters of the same fruit and one counter of a different fruit.

After checking for food allergies, you may use cereal, crackers, raisins, or candy pieces as counters. Children may eat the piece substituted by another.

Assess Understanding

Say a pair of words for each child, such as *goat* and *coat*, *pen* and *pan*, or *hid* and *hit*. Ask the child to tell you the placement of the sound that has changed.

Sample word changes:

pan/nap	rat/tar
meat/team	top/pot
spot/stop	tea/eat
small/malls	star/rats
snail/nails	end/den

On Your Own

- *Place the Fruity Fun counters in the Fruit Bowl.*

- *Listen to the word and say the word. How many sounds do you hear? Place the correct number of counters in a row on the tabletop at the bottom of the page.*

- *Remember to place the counter for the beginning sound on the left.*

- *Point to each counter and segment the sounds.*

- *Then move your finger under the row of counters and blend the sounds together to say the word.*

- *Listen to a new word and show which sound has changed. Replace the correct counter with another kind of Fruity Fun Counter.*

- *Blend the sounds and say the new word.*

Show What You Know

- *Listen to a word and say it. Think about how many sounds you hear.*

- *Place counters in a row to show each sound in the word.*

- *Say the sounds as you point to each counter.*

- *Then listen for a new word. Which sound has changed?*

- *Show which counter changed to form the new word.*

- *Say the sounds and then move your finger under the row of counters to blend the sounds. Say the new word.*

Words with the same sounds in a different order:

cot/tock

tam/mat

lap/pal

bag/gab

tin/knit

tap/pat

bad/dad

pill/lip

cat/tack

let/tell

cap/pack

lit/till

tick/kit

led/dell

kiss/sick

cab/back

light/tile

sight/ties

might/time

rat/tar

net/ten

map/Pam

pan/nap

car/rack

Extend and Adapt

Sit and Change
Do the activity in the opposite way. Children representing the sounds stand up and the child whose sound changes sits down.

What Sound Is Different?
As children are seated in chairs to represent the sounds in a word, another child in the group offers a different word. The child says the word aloud and asks, *What sound is different?* The seated child whose sound has changed stands up to allow the child who gave the word to take that place.

Change and Rearrange
Choose simple words in which the sounds remain the same, but the order of the sounds changes, such as *pan/nap* and *rat/tar*. Say the first word aloud. Have children sit in chairs and say the sounds. Then say the second word aloud. Children change places as the position of the sound in the word changes. You may wish to use the pairs of words listed in the left column.

Unit 6 Activity D

Change That Word Mat

Materials

- Segmenting, Blending, and Sorting Mats (side 1)

- A red, yellow, and green Quiet Counter for each child

- Appendix IV Teacher's Notes

Skill

Phoneme Manipulation

Objective

To demonstrate an understanding of the placement of a phoneme that is changed to form a new word

1	2	3	4	5

Segmenting, Blending, and Sorting Mat
Side 1

Purpose

In demonstrating the similarities and differences in words, children represent phonemes with counters and move counters as the placement of sounds in words is changed.

Activity Overview

Children place red, yellow and green counters to represent the beginning, middle, and ending sounds in words. Children move counters to show which sound changes to form a new word.

Getting Ready

Use side 1 of the Segmenting, Blending and Sorting Mat and a red, yellow, and green Quiet Counter.

Build Background

- *Who can tell us the names of the three colors that we see on a traffic light?*

- *The first color is red, the middle color is yellow, and the last color is green. Red, yellow, and green signal drivers to stop, slow down, or go.*

- *For this activity we use three counters—red, yellow, and green. The colors stand for the beginning sound, the middle sound, and the ending sound in words.*

- *Place the red counter in the first column on the mat for the beginning sound. The yellow one goes in the second column for the middle sound, and the green one goes in the third column for the ending sound.*

Notes

Model the Activity

Use the Segmenting, Blending, and Sorting Mat and three Quiet Counters.

Explain that, just like the colors on a traffic light, the red counter represents the beginning sound, the yellow counter represents the middle sound, and the green counter represents the ending sound of the words.

Move the counter for the sound that changed to the bottom of the mat.

Continue the Activity Together

Give each child a sorting mat and three counters.

pa<u>t</u>/ pa<u>l</u>	ta<u>p</u>/ta<u>n</u>
<u>b</u>at/<u>c</u>at	pa<u>n</u>/ma<u>n</u>
f<u>u</u>n/f<u>i</u>n	c<u>u</u>t/c<u>a</u>t

Provide support as you continue the activity together with the children.

Watch Me Play

- *The first word is <u>bat</u>. I hear three sounds.*
- *I line up three counters and touch each one as I say the sounds: /b/ /ă/ /t/*
- *The beginning sound is /b/ with the red counter, /ă/ is the middle sound with the yellow counter, and /t/ is the ending sound with the green one. I touch each counter and say the sounds again.*
- *Now I listen for a new word. The new word is <u>rat</u>. I line up counters and touch each one as I say the sounds: /r/ /ă/ /t/*
- *What sound has changed? It is the beginning sound, so I move the red counter down to the bottom of the mat.*
- *I remove all the counters from the mat and get ready to play the game again.*
- Model the activity for a second time using a pair of words in which the ending sound changes (<u>man</u>/<u>mat</u>). Model for a third time using a pair of words in which the middle sound changes (<u>hat</u>/<u>hit</u>).

Play the Game with Me

- *Let's do the activity together. Use your mat and three counters. Which color represents the beginning sound? The middle sound? The ending sound?*
- *Let's place our counters on the mat for the word <u>pat</u>. Touch each counter as you say the sounds: /p/ /ă/ /t/.*
- *Listen for the new word. The word is <u>pal</u>. Which sound has changed?*
- *Say /p/ /ă/ /t/ and /p/ /ă/ /l/ with me and point to the counters. We move the green counter to the bottom of the mat to show which sound has changed.*
- *Let's say the sounds and then blend the sounds to say the new word: (/p/ /ă/ /l/, <u>pal</u>).*

Change That Word Mat

Notes

Independent Activity

Monitor that the children place their red, yellow, and green counters in the correct columns on the mat.

Remind children to move a counter for the sound that changes to the bottom of the mat.

Assess Understanding

Ask each child to listen carefully as you say two words. The child places the correct color counter on the table to show which sound changed.

Beginning sound changes
(red counter moves)
pup/cup   tin/pin
van/ran

Ending sound changes
(green counter moves)
cup/cut   tan/tap
men/met

Middle sound changes
(yellow counter moves)
sit/sat   did/dad
ball/bell

On Your Own

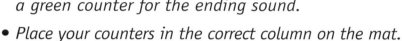

- *Listen to the word and think about the sounds you hear.*

- *Use a red counter for the beginning sound, a yellow counter for the middle sound, and a green counter for the ending sound.*

- *Place your counters in the correct column on the mat.*

- *Then listen to the new word. Think about which sound changed.*

- *Show which sound changed by moving the counter for the sound that changed to the bottom of the mat.*

- *Remember to listen very carefully. Sometimes the beginning sound changes. Sometimes the middle sound changes. Other times the ending sound changes.*

Show What You Know

- *Use a red counter for the beginning sound, a yellow counter for the middle sound, and a green counter for the ending sound.*

- *Listen carefully as I say two words.*

- *Think about which sound changed.*

- *Show which sound changed by placing the correct color counter on the table in front of you.*

Sample Word Changes

Beginning sound:

lot: change /l/ to /p/ (pot)

mad: change /m/ to /b/ (bad)

led: change /l/ to /b/ (bed)

fog: change /f/ to /d/ (dog)

rag: change /r/ to /b/ (bag)

ring: change /r/ to /k/ (king)

Ending sound:

leg: change /g/ to /d/ (led)

men: change /n/ to /t/ (met)

pet: change /t/ to/n/ (pen)

sell: change /l/ to /t/ (set)

sip: change /p/ to /t/ (sit)

top: change /p/ to /t/ (tot)

Middle sound:

cot: change /o/ to /a/ (cat)

far: change /a/ to /u/ (fur)

hot: change /o/ to /i/ (hit)

pack: change /a/ to /i/ (pick)

stir: change /i/ to /a/ (star)

tack: change /a/ to /i/ (tick)

Extend and Adapt

I'm Thinking Of...

Play this game by saying a word and segmenting the sounds. Give clues about a change in one of the sounds and another clue. For example, begin with the word *tall*. Give clues to the children, such as, *I'm thinking of a new word where the red counter changes. It is the name of a place where you go to shop.* The children must think of a word with a different beginning sound that means a place to shop. [*mall*] Later on, children may wish to make up the clues.

Frogs on a Log

Use red, yellow, and green Frog Counters and BLM 5-3 Frog Pond. Ask children to begin by placing their frogs in the pond. Say a word and ask children to place their frogs on the log in the order of the sounds they hear in the word. Ask the children to say the segmented sounds and then blend the sounds together to say the word. Then say another word as the children listen to the sounds. Children show which sound changed by making the correct frog jump off the log.

Unit 6 Activity E

Substitute a Sound

Notes

Materials

- Bear Counters
- BLM 5-2 Bears' Den
- Appendix IV Teacher's Notes

Skill

Phoneme Substitution

Objective

To recognize the placement of the sound that changes in a word when one sound is substituted for another

Purpose

To recognize the similarities and differences between words, children substitute the sounds at the beginning, ending, or middle of words to create new words.

Activity Overview

Children show the placement of sound in words and substitute sounds at the beginning, end, or middle of the word to form new words.

Getting Ready

Use a copy of BLM 5-2 Bears' Den and Bear Counters (3 of the same color and 1 of another color) to model the activity.

Build Background

- *Let's talk about bears. What do you know about bears? What do bears do during the winter?*

- *Bears hibernate in the winter. That means that bears sleep in their dens until spring comes.*

- *For this activity, we can use Bear Counters. Place your counters in the Bears' Den on your paper.*

- *Let's pretend that the bears are asleep in their den. It is almost spring.*

- *For this game we wake up the bears to help us show the sounds in words.*

- *We can line up the bears on the path to show the sounds we hear.*

Model the Activity

Order of increasing difficulty: substitute beginning, ending, middle sounds

First model beginning sound substitution dot: Change /d/ to /c/ (cot)

Model ending sound substitution pen: Change /n/ to /t/ (pet)

Model middle sound substitution hit: Change /i/ to /ă/ (hat)

Continue the Activity Together

Provide a copy of BLM 5-2 Bears' Den and a set of Bear Counters for each child (5 bears of the same color and 1 bear of a different color).

Provide support as you continue the activity together.

Watch Me Play

- *Here is how to play the game. I listen to the word <u>dot</u>. I say the word and think about the sounds I hear. Then I say the sounds: /d/ /ŏ/ /t/*

- *How many sounds do I hear? [3] I wake up three bears of the same color and place them on the path.*

- *I remember to place the first bear on the left side of the path.*

- *Then I point to each bear and say the sounds: /d/ /ŏ/ /t/.*

- *Now I substitute a sound. I change the /d/ to /c/. Which sound has changed? [beginning sound] I take away the first bear.*

- *Now I must wake up a different bear and place it on the path.*

- *I point to each bear on the path and say the new sounds: /c/ /ŏ/ /t/. What is the new word? [<u>cot</u>]*

- *I move all the bears back to their den and listen for a new word to play again.*

- *I need to remember that sometimes the bear at the beginning of the path changes. Other times the last bear or the middle bear changes.*

Play the Game with Me

- *Are your bears asleep in their dens? Let's play the game together.*

- *Listen to the word <u>hit</u>. Say the word. How many sounds do you hear? [3] Let's wake up three bears of the same color and line them up on the path.*

- *Let's begin on the left and point to each bear as we say the sounds in the word: /h/ /ĭ/ /t/. Let's blend the sounds and say the word: <u>hit</u>.*

- *Now we change the /h/ to /b/. Which sound has changed? Take away the bear that has changed.*

- *Let's wake up a different bear and place it on the path.*

- *We point to the bears and say the sounds: /b/ /ĭ/ /t/. Let's say the new word: <u>bit</u>.*

Substitute a Sound

Notes

Independent Activity

Always have the children repeat the word, and then tell children, _Say [the new word] again and change the [sound] to [another sound]. What is the new word?_

Make sure that children say the new word first before they tell which sound changed.

Assess Understanding

Monitor whether each child can substitute the beginning, ending, or middle sound in a word to form a new word.

Note any difficulties and at what point they became evident.

On Your Own

- _Place your Bear Counters in the Bears' Den._

- _Listen to the word and say the word. How many sounds do you hear?_

- _Wake up the correct number of bears and place them on the path. Remember to begin on the left._

- _Say one sound at a time as you point to each bear. Blend the sounds and say the word._

- _Listen to how the word changes. Think about which sound changes._

- _Send the correct bear back to the den and wake up a different bear to replace it._

- _Point to each bear again and say the sounds. Say the new word._

Show What You Know

- _Listen to the word. Say the word._

- _Listen for something to change as I say the new word._

- _Replace the correct sound in the word to form a new word._

- _Say the new sounds. Say the new word aloud._

- _For example,_

    I say, <u>The word is</u> dog.

       <u>Take away the</u> first sound <u>in dog and replace it with</u> /f/.

    You answer, <u>fog</u>.

Manipulate Phonemes

Examples:
Start with *cat*.
Change /t/ to /b/
[*cab*]
Change /ă/ to /ŭ/
[*cub*]
Change /k/ to /t/
[*tub*]

Start with *back*.
Change /b/ to /p/
[*pack*]
Change /k/ to /t/
[*pat*]
Change /ă/ to /ĭ/
[*pit*]
Add /s/ to pit [*pits*]
Delete /p/ [*its*]

Start with *glad*.
Delete /g/ [*lad*]
Change /d/ to /m/
[*lamb*]
Add /p/ [*lamp*]
Add /k/ [*clamp*]
Delete /p/ [*clam*]

Start with *jog*.
Change /j/ to /l/
[*log*]
Change /g/ to /t/
[*lot*]
Change /o/ to /i/
[*lit*]
Add /sp/ [*split*]

Extend and Adapt

Wake Up the Bears

Children pretend to be bears sleeping in a den. When you say a word, ask how many bears will need to wake up. Have the correct number of "bears" line up to represent the sounds in the word. Children stand in a line and say their sounds. Then they blend the sounds to say the word. Ask children to listen to the new word. Change a sound in the word. Ask children to show which sound changed. The "bear" in the place where the sound changed (beginning, middle, or end) returns to the den, and another bear wakes up to take his place. Then all the "bears" say the sounds and say the new word together.

Get On Board

Use a copy of BLM 5-4 Engine, Boxcar, Caboose and 3-letter words for the activity. The train engine represents the beginning sound, the boxcar represents the middle sound, and the caboose represents the ending sound. Children may enjoy placing their bear counters on the cars of the train. As sounds in the words change, children can move the bears from one car of the train to the other or move one bear off the train and replace it with another.

Unit 6 Activity F *Fred Told Me*

Notes

Materials

- Story Blossoms® small book *Fred Told Me*

Skill	Phoneme Substitution
Objective	To recognize the changing sounds at the beginning of rhyming words in text
Purpose	To recognize rhyming pairs of words in text and appreciate the playfulness of language, children listen to a story and find rhyming pairs of words.
Activity Overview	Children recognize pairs of rhyming words in text and isolate the beginning sound as the word changes.

Getting Ready

Build background to set the stage for reading *Fred Told Me* aloud to the children.

Read the text aloud to the children.

Build Background

- *Do you know someone who makes up stories or tall tales? Sometimes, people make up stories just to get attention.*

- *The title of this book is* Fred Told Me. *The story is about a little brother, named Fred, who tells stories to get his big sister's attention.*

- *Should Fred's big sister believe him? What do you predict will happen if the big sister ignores Fred?*

- *Let's listen to the story and look at the pictures together.*

- *Listen for the rhyming words as you listen to what Fred told.*

Model the Activity

Reread each page and show the pictures to the children. (The rhyming words are supported by the pictures on the opposite page.)

Reread pages 1–4.

Continue the Activity Together

Reread pages 6–11.

Review the rhyming pairs by going back to the beginning of the story and showing the pictures.

Have the children say the rhyming words.

Continue the activity together as needed.

Watch Me Play

- *As I read about the first thing [page 1] that Fred told, I listen for the rhyming words.*

- *Rhyming words have the same ending sound. What rhyming words do I hear?*

- *I listen to the sounds in the word <u>frog</u>. Then I listen to the sounds in the word <u>dog</u>.*

- *What sounds are the same? [ending sounds] What sounds are different? [beginning sounds]*

- *The beginning sounds /fr/ and /d/ are different in <u>frog</u> and <u>dog</u>. Both words have the /ŏg/ sound at the end.*

- *I listen for the rhyming words while I read about the next thing that Fred told. [bear/chair]*

- *What sounds are the same? What sounds are different?*

- *Listen to the beginning sounds with me. Do /b/ and /ch/ sound different in the rhyming words <u>bear</u> and <u>chair</u>?*

Play the Game with Me

- *Let's find more rhyming words as I read the story. Listen carefully.*

- *Who can say the words that rhyme for us?*

- *What sound is the same? What sounds are different?*

- *Let's go back to the beginning of the story and look at the pictures. Help me remember the rhymes.*

- *Let's keep reading to find more rhymes.*

- *Who can tell us what sound stays the same and what sounds are different in rhyming words?*

- *Can you think of other words you know that rhyme with <u>fox</u>/<u>socks</u> and <u>whale</u>/<u>mail</u>?*

Fred Told Me

Notes

Independent Activity

Reread pages 12–16.

Encourage children to make up rhymes and use the same format to improvise on the story.

The audiotape of *Fred Told Me* is available from ETA/Cuisenaire®. Visit our website at etacuisenaire.com

Assess Understanding

Ask children to say only the rhyming words as you quickly page through the pictures. Ask children to volunteer another word that rhymes with the pair of rhyming words on the page.

Monitor whether each child can replace beginning sounds to create nonsense rhymes.

This stage of phonemic awareness can be the most playful of all.

On Your Own

- *Listen for the rhyming words as I read the rest of the story. Raise your hand if you hear the words that rhyme.*
- *What part of both words is the same?*
- *What part of both words is different?*
- *What other rhyming stories could Fred tell?*
- *Can you make up more rhymes for Fred?*

> Fred told me
> he saw a _____
> in the _____
> at the _____.

Show What You Know

- *Listen to the word I say.*
- *Choose the two words that rhyme.*
- *Tell me which sounds in the words are different. Which sound is the same?*
- *Say another word that rhymes with the two words you chose.*

Rhyming word pairs in <u>Fred Told Me</u> rhyme with:

frog/dog	log/bog/clog/fog/hog/jog
bear/chair	pear/mare/hair/care/dare/fare/lair/rare/stair
goat/coat	boat/float/moat/note/tote/vote/wrote
snake/cake	bake/fake/Jake/lake/quake/rake/steak/take
fox/box	lox/rocks/knocks/locks/clocks/docks/socks
whale/mail	bale/dale/fail/gale/hail/jail/nail/pail/quail/rail/tail
shark/park	ark/bark/dark/hark/lark/mark
Fred/bed	head/lead/Ned/red/said/Ted/wed/sled

Word play with animal names can be fun. Create nonsense names and enjoy the sounds of oral language. Remember, correct spelling is not be a concern in speaking and listening activities.

Crazy Critters
Examples:

Fog Dog, Mog Dog
Doat Goat, Vote Goat
Veep Sheep,
Beep Sheep
Pen Hen, Len Hen
Rug Bug, Sug Bug
Tea Bee, Zee Bee
Juice Moose,
Loose Moose
Rake Snake,
Hake Snake
Rowl Owl, Growl Owl
Here Deer, Veer Deer
Course Horse,
Borse Horse
Hale Whale,
Rale Whale

Extend and Adapt

Raise Your Hand
Reread the first three lines of a page. Ask children to raise their hands when they hear a word that rhymes with another word on the page. Then ask for a volunteer to say the rhyming pair of words.

Nursery Rhyme Time
Improvise on familiar nursery rhymes by substituting other nonsense rhyming words.
For example, for the nursery rhyme *To Market*,
I say, *To market, to market, to buy a fat pig,*
You say, *Home again, home again, jiggety-jig.*
or
I say, *To market, to market, to buy a gray cat,*
You say, *Home again, home again, jiggety-_____. (jat)*
or
I say, *To market, to market, to buy a brown hen,*
You say, *Home again, home again, jiggety-_____. (jen)*

Use other animals in the nursery rhyme such as dog, goat, sheep, bug, bee, moose, snake, owl, deer, horse, whale.

Crazy Critters
Distribute an animal Picture Card to each child. Tell children that they can create rhyming first names for their animals by changing the beginning sounds in their names. For example, show a picture of a pig and have children change the beginning sound to create a rhyming name, such as Fig Pig, Wig Pig, Zig Pig, or Jig Pig. Children may enjoy drawing their crazy critters.

Planning Intervention Instruction

The StarLIT Literacy Intervention Toolkit for Phonological Awareness is designed to provide everything an intervention teacher needs to teach phonological awareness skills. The toolkit includes activities organized by skill, as well as the manipulatives and tools needed to teach the activities. Although the toolkit is complete in itself, teachers still need to allocate time to complete several stages of planning before launching intervention instruction. First, children must be assessed to determine who needs intervention instruction. After this initial screening, teachers must place at-risk children in small groups. Determining which children to place together and where to begin each group's instruction is a single linked step. Finally, lessons must be planned for each group. This section includes a discussion of assessment and grouping.

Preparing lesson plans for intervention groups is an important part of implementing a well-designed three-tier instructional approach to responding to children with reading skills deficits. Lesson planning is important, yet teachers often have little time to plan for the core lesson, let alone several small intervention group lessons. In order to make lesson planning as efficient as possible, a two-week lesson plan chart and several sample plans are included in this section.

Assessing and Placing Children in Small Groups

One of the most reliable and efficient methods for determining which children are lacking key literacy skills is to use an early literacy screening instrument. Many schools use the Dynamic Indicators of Early Literacy Skills (DIBELS), an assessment instrument that is available free on the Internet at *http://dibels. uoregon.edu*. This assessment enables teachers to screen all K–3 children three times a year to determine if they meet benchmarks for critical literacy skills. There are many other valid and reliable assessment instruments, including the Texas Primary Reading Inventory (TPRI) and the Virginia Phonological Awareness Literacy Screening (PALS). For a list of instruments that meet the criteria for Reading First, see *http://reading.uoregon.edu/assessment/analysis.php*.

After the initial screening is completed, the teacher places children whose skills are below benchmark in small groups for intervention instruction.

While heterogeneous groups are beneficial for much of the core reading instruction time, children involved in intervention instruction need to be grouped homogeneously, based on the specific skill deficits indicated.

If you use the DIBELS assessment, there are several ways to compose groups, depending on whether your school subscribes to the University of Oregon's data management system or uses the PDA version available through Wireless Generation. If your school scores assessments using the paper and pencil method and then enters data into the University of Oregon's DIBELS data management system, one approach is to group children based on the instructional recommendations provided by the system. Obtain a classroom report and look at the far right column called "Instructional Recommendation." The DIBELS data management system evaluates each child's scores on all the indicators assessed at that point and calculates a weighted average to determine which of the three categories to recommend for each child. The Wireless Generation system displays the classroom report by grouping children under these instructional categories. Although the format of this report is slightly different, the data is based on the same calculation for determining which instructional level is recommended for each child.

The three categories in the DIBELS system are identified as *benchmark, strategic,* and *intensive*. Children in the intensive category have the lowest scores, while the strategic group is recommended for some intervention. Presumably, the strategic group will require less intervention than the intensive group. Some teachers group their children by placing the intensive children in one group and the strategic children in another. If there are more children in each category than can be placed in a single group, then teachers need to determine criteria for forming several groups within each category.

If the DIBELS or another early literacy screening instrument that provides recommendations for levels of intervention is not used, then teachers need to determine which children are struggling and place them in small groups based on specific skill deficits. One approach is to use an activity at each level in this kit to assess the skill level of the children. This approach will be described later on. Whichever approach is used to identify children in need of intervention, the process of determining groups is intricately linked with defining an instructional focus for each group. It is critical to articulate exactly what skills will be taught so children can be appropriately grouped. The goal of intervention is to provide targeted instruction: to teach a child only what needs to be learned and not to expect the child to participate in instruction for any skill already mastered.

Determining Where to Start

If you have DIBELS scores, there is information available that helps to determine where to begin a child's intervention instruction. For a kindergarten child who is very low in the DIBELS indicator called Initial Sound Fluency (ISF), the data indicates that the child is struggling in identifying and manipulating a single phoneme in the word. This indicator assesses a child's ability to point to, or name, the picture when asked to select from four pictures and determine which one begins with a target sound. If a child is below benchmark in this skill during the first half of kindergarten, instruction is needed in phonological awareness at the initial sound level of phonemic awareness. If a child is very low in ISF, instruction needs to begin somewhere below this skill on the phonological awareness continuum.

According to the phonological awareness continuum provided on page 20 of this guide, children generally start at the early levels of phonological awareness using larger units of sounds. These include awareness of words, syllables, and onset-rimes. Many children understand units of phonological awareness before they are ready to work on the initial phoneme in a word. Therefore when a child scores very low on the DIBELS ISF measure, often teachers begin their instruction at an easier level and work up to phonemic awareness at the initial sound level.

The next measure of phonemic awareness in the DIBELS system is Phoneme Segmentation Fluency (PSF), which measures the child's ability to segment the sounds in words. Whereas the ISF measure focuses on awareness of only the initial sound in a word, PSF measures the child's ability to segment the initial, middle, and ending sound in a word provided orally by the examiner. Children who are below benchmark in PSF have failed to demonstrate an ability to fluently segment all the sounds in the word. Therefore their instruction should begin with activities to teach phoneme segmentation, or possibly at a lower level along the phonological awareness continuum. If the child is struggling a great deal with segmenting all the sounds in a word, the teacher may need to begin instruction by working on developing awareness of the initial sound first, then move to the ending sound, and finally to the medial vowel sound.

Most children who will receive intervention instruction using this toolkit will be in kindergarten or early first grade. However sometimes older children continue to show a deficit in phonological awareness and may benefit from these activities. The PSF measure is given throughout first grade in DIBELS but is not given as part of the benchmark testing for second grade and beyond. If a child struggles on the Oral Reading Fluency (ORF) measure, it may be necessary to assess the child's ability to decode words. Deficits in rapid and automatic decoding can be caused by a lack of alphabetic principle skills or phonemic awareness skills. Sometimes older children who struggle in reading need the type of intervention provided in this toolkit.

If the DIBELS assessment is not available, then an alternate way to assess a child is by using activities in this toolkit. Teachers can use an activity from each of the first five levels of phonological awareness to observe how well the child performs on the task. Recommended StarLIT activities include:

- Word Level – Bunny Hop – Activity 1A
- Syllable Level - Clapping Names and Puppet Talk - Activity 2B
- Onset-Rime Level – Rhyming Pictures – Activity 3B
- Phoneme Isolation – Picture Card Sound Match – Activity 4B
- Phoneme Segmentation and Blending – Move It and Say It – Activity 5B

When completely uncertain of what phonological awareness skills a child has, begin at the Word Level and move up. With the Bunny Hop Activity (1A), ask the child to hold a bunny placed on a craft stick and hop for each word in a sentence. An alternative is a variation of the Word Card Activity. Lay about five index cards on a table and say a sentence. Ask the child to repeat the sentence while sliding one card for each word. If the child can move cards for each word in a simple 3- or 4-word sentence, then provide more cards and increase the length to sentences with 5 or 6 words.

To assess the Syllable Level using the Clapping Names Activity (2B), ask the child to clap the number of syllables in a child's name. Start with simple names that have only a single syllable and increase to names with three and four syllables. For example, ask the child to clap the following names: Ted (1), Juan (1), Jason (2), Tyrone (2), Elizabeth (3), and Fernando (3).

For the Onset-Rime Level, use the Rhyming Picture Cards Activity (3B). Start by placing four cards on the table that contain pictures of two pairs of rhyming words. If the child can match the rhyming words, then try using eight cards that represent four pairs of rhyming words.

To assess a child's Phoneme Isolation ability, use the Picture Card Sound Match Activity (4B). Begin by placing two picture cards as column headers to represent two different initial sounds. Give the child one card at a time and ask the child to place it in the appropriate column by matching initial sounds.

If a child can complete the Picture Card Sound Match, then try the Move It and Say It Activity (5B) to assess Phoneme Segmentation and Blending skills. Provide the child with counters and ask the child to move one counter at a time on a mat while saying each sound in a word. The mat has a "home base" to store the counters, and a line with an arrow to represent the sounds from left to right, consistent with the direction of reading English text. If the word is *cat*, then the child will move one counter while saying /c/, a second counter while saying /a/, and a third counter while saying /t/. The final step is that the child slides his finger under the arrow while blending the sounds again to say the word.

A teacher will most likely not need to assess a child at the Phoneme Manipulation Level because most struggling readers are lacking lower level skills. However, if a child is successful at the activities above and the teacher wishes to see if the child has more advanced phonemic skills, then an easy way is to give the child an oral phoneme deletion task. To do this say a word, and then ask the child to say it again without one sound to make a different word. For example, say *ice*. Now say it again without the /c/ sound; ask, *What's the new word?* [I] Deleting a sound from a blend can be more difficult. [*stop* to *sop*]

Once the teacher has decided where on the phonological awareness continuum a child's skills begin to break down, the point to begin instruction has been determined. Place several children together who need to start at the same skill level. Plan to teach children at the entry point on the phonological awareness continuum and continue teaching higher and higher skills on the continuum as children demonstrate mastery at each level.

Determining Appropriate Group Size

Phonological awareness is best taught in small groups rather than with the whole class or individually. Experience shows that the ideal size of an intervention group for phonological awareness instruction is three children. Although it is possible to teach groups of four or five children for many other skills, when teaching phonological awareness it is critical to hear each child's voiced response and be able to provide immediate feedback. This error correction technique becomes more difficult even as group size increases from three to four children.

Determining Appropriate Pacing

The most important skill for reading and spelling is Phoneme Segmentation. Therefore teachers need to move through instruction on skills at the lower portion of the phonological awareness continuum as quickly as possible. It is important not to get bogged down waiting for a child to master the Word Level; it is best to think of the Word Level as a useful warm-up to listening for sounds in speech units. It is not as important—in fact, some researchers advise not to bother—to explicitly teach the segmentation of words in a sentence as a separate skill.

Rhyming can be a very difficult skill for some children. Some struggling readers never hear rhyming words well, and yet they can be taught to segment all the phonemes in a word. Therefore, if a child is not showing the ability to distinguish words that rhyme, the teacher may need to skip ahead and provide instruction for some of the other skills.

Other than not spending too much time on the phonological awareness levels (Word, Syllable, and Onset-Rime), another aspect of pacing is moving to a more complex skill at the appropriate time. When children can easily complete the tasks, regardless of whether all the activities in a unit have been taught, it's time to move up to the next skill level. Moving as quickly as possible through the units, while at the same time assuring mastery of the underlying skills taught, is recommended.

Pacing also affects the way a single lesson is delivered. One of the most common errors made by teachers who are new to intervention instruction is that the pace of their instruction is too slow. Intervention instruction is fast-paced: children are given a task to respond to several times every minute. Children are not sitting and waiting for the teacher to ask the next question; they are continually thinking and responding. Therefore, it is critical for the teacher to keep the pace brisk and lively and eliminate downtime.

Monitoring Progress and Regrouping

Schools adopt different schedules for how often to assess children to monitor progress. This guide recommends that progress be monitored every three weeks using an alternate form of DIBELS. If the screening instrument used does not have alternate forms for progress monitoring, teachers will need to design some way of addressing the need for systematic evaluation of progress. Teachers can administer an informal literacy screening to track whether there is evidence that the intervention instruction is helping children improve in the skill area taught.

One of the most important features of intervention groups is that they are *flexible*. When a child is placed in a group, it is not expected that the child will continue to work with the exact same children for more than 10 weeks. Most likely at least one child will move in or out of a group within that period of time. Keeping the group composition flexible is necessary because some children will make more rapid progress than others. Even if they are appropriately grouped at the beginning, this will not be the case within a short time as their rate of progress varies.

Lesson Planning

Using a Two-Week Lesson Plan

Most curriculums that teach phonological awareness rely upon a series of activities to teach skills. A typical intervention lesson of 20–30 minutes will cover 2–3 activities in a day. Each activity takes about 5 minutes to explain, model, and provide guided practice. Then teachers typically allow additional time for children to practice independently. One child may be working on a word, while the teacher is working with another child. Rarely do children work independently without the teacher's input. This is because of the nature of phonological awareness instruction: it is oral and requires interaction with an instructor, especially for children who are struggling. Proper pronunciation of phonemes is important, so having a more advanced child help a struggling one is not recommended.

Although some teachers use a single page of paper to plan each lesson, this teacher's guide has made that unnecessary. It is easy to plan across a week or two by listing about 6–8 activities that teach the skill that is the focus for the group. Create columns for the days and use checkmarks to plan which 2–4 activities will be covered each day. The blank Two-Week Lesson Plan form provided on page 206 of this guide has been used successfully by many teachers.

In order to use the Two-Week Lesson Plan form, teachers need to pay careful attention to the instructional focus of the group. There is a place on the top of the form to write the focus for the group. Then the teacher lists the activities from the appropriate unit on the phonological awareness continuum that corresponds with the instructional needs of the group.

Using Sample Lesson Plans

A set of three sample lesson plans is provided on pages 203–205 of this guide. Each group of children is assumed to start at a different point in the continuum of phonological awareness. The purpose of these three sample lesson plans is to demonstrate how to plan. Intervention instruction should be developed based on the pace of instruction for each group rather than follow prescribed lesson plans. Fixed lesson plans to begin instruction at all the possible points are not provided. Planning instruction too far in advance for children in intervention groups is not recommended.

The varying rate of progress requires that teachers continually review where the group is and gauge how rapidly children are moving through the activities and units. Some groups will need lots of repetition, and the activities will be taught multiple times and varied slightly to offer additional practice. Other groups will learn the skills quite rapidly and will need only one or two repetitions of particular activities before mastery of the skill is evident. StarLIT provides a very carefully designed sequence of skills, from the simplest to the most complex level of phonological awareness. The sequential structure of the units provides an order for instruction. Teachers need to plan about two weeks at a time and should continually evaluate whether the pace of instruction is appropriate for each group.

Three sample lesson plans are provided in the StarLIT Literacy Intervention Toolkit. Each begins at a different entry point on the phonological awareness continuum. Sample A (p. 203) starts at the lowest point and is appropriate for children that have virtually no awareness at any level of the phonological awareness continuum. The pacing for Sample A is intentionally a bit slower than for Samples B and C because this group needs more repetition to master each skill.

Sample B (p. 204) is the middle group. It models what the teacher may use when the group is ready to start at a slightly higher point on the phonological awareness continuum. This lesson plan would be appropriate for children who can confidently recognize that words are separate speech units in a sentence, show awareness that words can be segmented into syllables, and demonstrate some rhyming ability. Since rhyming is not as important as learning to segment phonemes, only a little time is spent at the Onset-Rime Level before concentrating on developing Phoneme Isolation skills.

Sample C (p. 205) is an example of what a lesson plan might look like for a higher level group. This group not only demonstrates knowledge at the Word, Syllable, and Onset-Rime Levels, but also is competent at the Initial Sound Level. They are ready to focus on Phoneme Segmentation skills.

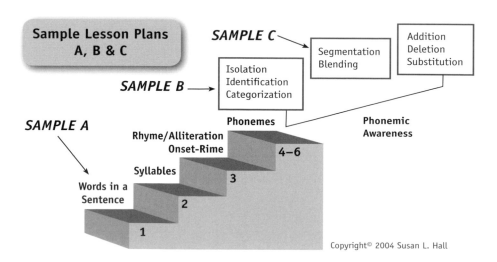

Copyright© 2004 Susan L. Hall

Record Keeping

Monitoring Child and Group Progress

It is important to assess the progress of the group and not just to evaluate individual progress. Therefore it is recommended that after assessing children individually, these scores be posted on a chart that includes scores for all three to five children in the group. This will enable the teacher to see when a single child is not progressing at the same rate as his/her peers and may need to be moved to another group. Additionally, it will enable the rate of progress of each group to be monitored to make sure that any changes in pacing or activities are appropriate for the group as a whole.

Keeping a Weekly Intervention Log

Teachers need to keep notes about the progress of children in order to assist when any group or child is not progressing rapidly enough. It is recommended that intervention teachers keep a weekly log to document which activities are taught to the group, whether every child attends each day, and how well each child is doing at the activity. This level of documentation is especially important given the new IDEA reauthorization and the Response to Intervention (RTI) model in which children will be referred for special education services only after they have received small group intervention in the general education classroom.

Keeping a log allows teachers to record their observations in one place and in a systematic way. It is difficult to write notes later, so this log provides the teacher with a convenient and simple way to write comments during the time between activities, or just after the group walks away. It is especially difficult for an intervention teacher who meets with up to eight groups in a day to remember her observations after seeing more than 25 children a day.

The weekly intervention log doesn't have to be lengthy or complicated. An effective log simply includes the following information:

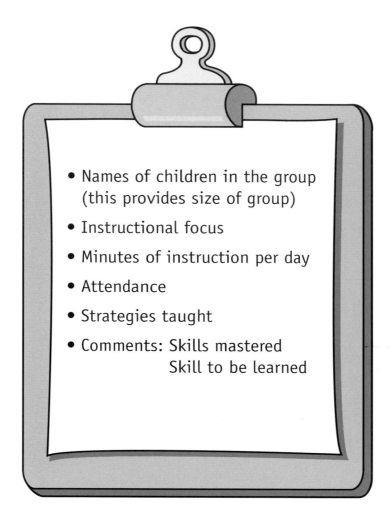

- Names of children in the group (this provides size of group)
- Instructional focus
- Minutes of instruction per day
- Attendance
- Strategies taught
- Comments: Skills mastered
  Skill to be learned

This information helps teachers make decisions about how to intensify instruction if a child is making unsatisfactory progress. If the instructional approach is working, but the rate of progress isn't adequate, maybe only more time is needed. If there is virtually no progress, the teacher must change the instructional approach. Comments on the log are helpful when changes in instruction must be made.

Two-Week Lesson Plan – Sample A

Children in Group: **Jeremy, Becky & Fernando**

Instructional Focus of Group: **Phonological awareness beginning at the level of words in a sentence. Instruction will continue up the levels of phonological awareness**

Week of: **9/15**   Week of: **9/22**

WORD LEVEL		M	T	W	Th	F	M	T	W	Th	F
1A	Bunny Hop	X	X	X				X	X	X	
1B	Frog on a Lily Pad				X	X	X				X
1C	How Long Is My Sentence?		X	X	X	X			X	X	X
1D	Take Away a Word										
1E	Word Cards	X	X	X	X	X	X				X
1F	Spin a Sentence							X	X	X	
SYLLABLE LEVEL											
2A	Compound Word Puzzles										
2B	Clapping Names & Puppet Talk										
2C	Syllable Pocket Chart										
2D	Fruit and Bugs										
2E	Syllable Spinner										
2F	Pass the Mystery Bag										
ONSET-RIME LEVEL											
3A	Complete My Sentence										
3B	Rhyming Picture Puzzles										
3C	Three in a Row										
3D	Erase/Draw a Rhyme!										
3E	Rhyming Bingo										
3F	*Eeny Meeny Miney Mouse*										
PHONEME ISOLATION LEVEL											
4A	Sound Bus										
4B	Picture Card Sound Match										
4C	Mystery Sound Bag										
4D	Feed the Animals										
4E	Sound Chart										
4F	Sound Concentration										
PHONEME SEGMENTATION AND BLENDING LEVEL											
5A	Puppet Talk										
5B	Move It & Say It										
5C	Chart a Sound										
5D	Counting Mat										
5E	Building Words										
5F	Guess That Object										
5G	Accent It!										
5H	Sound Bingo										
PHONEME MANIPULATION LEVEL											
6A	Changing Sounds Move It & Say It										
6B	Those Silly Bugs! Take Away a Sound										
6C	Stand Up and Change										
6D	Change That Word Mat										
6E	Substitute a Sound										
6F	*Fred Told Me*										

Two-Week Lesson Plan – Sample B

Children in Group: **Keisha, Juan, Armundo**

Instructional Focus of Group: **Start at the onset-rime level and briefly teach for several days. Then move to phonemic awareness at the initial sound level.**

Week of: **9/15**   Week of: **9/22**

		M	T	W	Th	F	M	T	W	Th	F
WORD LEVEL											
1A	Bunny Hop										
1B	Frog on a Lily Pad										
1C	How Long Is My Sentence?										
1D	Take Away a Word										
1E	Word Cards										
1F	Spin a Sentence										
SYLLABLE LEVEL											
2A	Compound Word Puzzles										
2B	Clapping Names & Puppet Talk										
2C	Syllable Pocket Chart										
2D	Fruit and Bugs										
2E	Syllable Spinner										
2F	Pass the Mystery Bag										
ONSET-RIME LEVEL											
3A	Complete My Sentence	X	X	X							
3B	Rhyming Picture Puzzles	X	X								
3C	Three in a Row			X	X	X					
3D	Erase/Draw a Rhyme!				X	X	X				
3E	Rhyming Bingo					X	X				
3F	*Eeny Meeny Miney Mouse*	X					X				
PHONEME ISOLATION LEVEL											
4A	Sound Bus						X	X	X		
4B	Picture Card Sound Match						X	X	X		
4C	Mystery Sound Bag							X	X	X	
4D	Feed the Animals									X	X
4E	Sound Chart									X	X
4F	Sound Concentration										X
PHONEME SEGMENTATION AND BLENDING LEVEL											
5A	Puppet Talk										
5B	Move It & Say It										
5C	Chart a Sound										
5D	Counting Mat										
5E	Building Words										
5F	Guess That Object										
5G	Accent It!										
5H	Sound Bingo										
PHONEME MANIPULATION LEVEL											
6A	Changing Sounds Move It & Say It										
6B	Those Silly Bugs! Take Away a Sound										
6C	Stand Up and Change										
6D	Change That Word Mat										
6E	Substitute a Sound										
6F	*Fred Told Me*										

Two-Week Lesson Plan – Sample C

Children in Group: __Brandon, Irene, José__

Instructional Focus of Group: __Quick review at the phoneme isolation level. Concentrate on__ __phoneme segmentation and blending.__

Week of: ___9/15___   Week of: ___9/22___

		M	T	W	Th	F	M	T	W	Th	F
WORD LEVEL											
1A	Bunny Hop										
1B	Frog on a Lily Pad										
1C	How Long Is My Sentence?										
1D	Take Away a Word										
1E	Word Cards										
1F	Spin a Sentence										
SYLLABLE LEVEL											
2A	Compound Word Puzzles										
2B	Clapping Names & Puppet Talk										
2C	Syllable Pocket Chart										
2D	Fruit and Bugs										
2E	Syllable Spinner										
2F	Pass the Mystery Bag										
ONSET-RIME LEVEL											
3A	Complete My Sentence										
3B	Rhyming Picture Puzzles										
3C	Three in a Row										
3D	Erase/Draw a Rhyme!										
3E	Rhyming Bingo										
3F	*Eeny Meeny Miney Mouse*										
PHONEME ISOLATION LEVEL											
4A	Sound Bus	X	X								
4B	Picture Card Sound Match										
4C	Mystery Sound Bag										
4D	Feed the Animals	X	X								
4E	Sound Chart	X	X								
4F	Sound Concentration										
PHONEME SEGMENTATION AND BLENDING LEVEL											
5A	Puppet Talk			X	X	X					
5B	Move It & Say It			X	X	X	X	X	X	X	X
5C	Chart a Sound			X	X						
5D	Counting Mat				X	X	X				
5E	Building Words					X	X	X			
5F	Guess That Object						X	X	X		
5G	Accent It!							X	X	X	
5H	Sound Bingo								X	X	X
PHONEME MANIPULATION LEVEL											
6A	Changing Sounds Move It & Say It										
6B	Those Silly Bugs! Take Away a Sound										
6C	Stand Up and Change										
6D	Change That Word Mat										
6E	Substitute a Sound										
6F	*Fred Told Me*										

Two-Week Lesson Plan – Blank

Children in Group: _____

Instructional Focus of Group: _____

_____

Week of: _____   Week of: _____

WORD LEVEL		M	T	W	Th	F	M	T	W	Th	F
1A	Bunny Hop										
1B	Frog on a Lily Pad										
1C	How Long Is My Sentence?										
1D	Take Away a Word										
1E	Word Cards										
1F	Spin a Sentence										
SYLLABLE LEVEL											
2A	Compound Word Puzzles										
2B	Clapping Names & Puppet Talk										
2C	Syllable Pocket Chart										
2D	Fruit and Bugs										
2E	Syllable Spinner										
2F	Pass the Mystery Bag										
ONSET-RIME LEVEL											
3A	Complete My Sentence										
3B	Rhyming Picture Puzzles										
3C	Three in a Row										
3D	Erase/Draw a Rhyme!										
3E	Rhyming Bingo										
3F	*Eeny Meeny Miney Mouse*										
PHONEME ISOLATION LEVEL											
4A	Sound Bus										
4B	Picture Card Sound Match										
4C	Mystery Sound Bag										
4D	Feed the Animals										
4E	Sound Chart										
4F	Sound Concentration										
PHONEME SEGMENTATION AND BLENDING LEVEL											
5A	Puppet Talk										
5B	Move It & Say It										
5C	Chart a Sound										
5D	Counting Mat										
5E	Building Words										
5F	Guess That Object										
5G	Accent It!										
5H	Sound Bingo										
PHONEME MANIPULATION LEVEL											
6A	Changing Sounds Move It & Say It										
6B	Those Silly Bugs! Take Away a Sound										
6C	Stand Up and Change										
6D	Change That Word Mat										
6E	Substitute a Sound										
6F	*Fred Told Me*										

StarLIT™ Literacy Intervention Toolkit for Phonological Awareness

Appendix I

Pronunciation of Phonemes

Consonant Sounds (25)	Key Words
/b/	bat
/d/	dot
/f/	fan, phone
/g/	gum
/h/	hat
/j/	jam, judge, gem
/k/	cat, kit, back
/l/	list
/m/	me
/n/	not, knit
/p/	pan
/r/	rod, wrote
/s/	see, cent
/t/	top
/v/	van
/w/	will
/y/	yes
/z/	zoom, rose
/sh/	shop, station, special
/hw/	when
/ch/	chill, hatch
/th/ or /th/	thin, that
/ng/	song
/zh/	treasure

Vowel Sounds (19)	Key Words
/ā/	table, bake, train, say
/ă/	apple
/au/	saw, caught, tall
/är/	car
/ē/	me, feet, leap, baby
/ĕ/	Ed, edge,
/ə/	about
/ī/	I, bite, light, sky
/ĭ/	itch, it
/ō/	okay, bone, soap, low
/ŏ/	octopus
/ôr/	for, quarter, pour
/o͞o/	boot, truth, rude, chew
/o͝o/	book, put
/oi/	soil, toy
/ou/	out, cow
/ū/	future, use, few
/ŭ/	umbrella
/ur/	fur, first, tiger

Appendix II

Minimal and Maximal Pairs
By Place and Manner of Articulation

Maximally Contrasting Pairs of Consonants:

<u>One from this column:</u>   <u>One from this column:</u>

Set 1:

/p/	/f/
/b/	/v/
/m/	/th/ (voiced or unvoiced)
	/s/
	/z/
	/sh/
	/zh/
	/l/
	/r/
	/w/
	/h/

Set 2:

/t/	/m/
/d/	/f/
	/th/
	/sh/
	/zh/
	/ch/
	/j/
	/w/
	/h/
	/l/
	/r/

Set 3:

/k/	/f/
/g/	/v/
/ng/	/th/ (voiced or unvoiced)
	/s/
	/z/
	/sh/
	/zh/
	/ch/
	/j/
	/l/
	/r/
	/w/
	/h/

Minimally Contrasting Pairs of Consonants

- /p/ and /b/ - both are stop sounds articulated at the lips
- /t/ and /d/ - both are stop sounds articulated at the ridge of the mouth
- /m/ , /n/, and /ng/ - both are nasal sounds
- /k/ and /g/ - both are stop sounds articulated at the back of the throat
- /f/ and /v/ - both are hissy sounds (fricatives) articulated at the teeth/lips
- /s/ and /z/ - both are hissy sounds (fricatives) articulated between the ridge and the teeth
- /sh/ and /zh/ - both are hissy sounds (fricatives) articulated at the roof of the mouth
- /ch/ and /j/ - both are affricates (hissy sounds that stop) articulated at the roof of the mouth

This analysis of the sounds of the consonant phonemes is based on the work of Dr. Louisa C. Moats, in *Language Essentials for Teachers of Reading and Spelling (LETRS)*, module 2, page 24.

Minimally Contrasting Pairs of Words

Minimal Pairs are words that differ in a single pair of sounds that occupy the same position in a word.

Examples:

Consonants	initial sound	end sound	blends	vowel sounds
/d/ and /k/	did/kid	lid/lick		
/k/ and /m/	cop/mop	trick/trim		click/clack
/p/ and /s/	pad/sad	sap/sass		pick/pack
/s/ and /b/	sow/bow	grass/grab		send/sand
/p/ and /l/	pane/lane	stoop/stool	play/pay	luck/lock
/k/ and /l/	came/lame	back/ball	clock/lock	load/lead

Minimally Contrasting Pairs of Words with Minimal Phonemes

Young children often experience difficulty distinguishing between these sounds.

/p/ and /b/	pat/bat	lop/lob
/t/ and /d/	tip/dip	let/led
/m/ and /n/	met/net	lime/line
/n/ and /ng/	tan/tang	din/ding
/m/ and /ng/	yum/young	climb/cling
/k/ and /g/	cane/gain	crack/crag
/f/ and /v/	fan/van	safe/save
/s/ and /z /	sink/zink	fleece/fleas
/ch/ and /j/	chunk/junk	rich/ridge
/f/ and /th/	fin/thin	reef/wreath
/l/ and /r/	lake/rake	belly/berry
/f/ and /th/	deaf/death	roofless/ruthless
/v/ and /w/	vet/wet	rover/rower
/d/ and /th/	dare/their	udder/other
/v/ and /th/	clove/clothe	loaves/loathes

Appendix III
Syllables and Phonemes Chart

READING RODS® PICTURE RODS AND PHONOLOGICAL AWARENESS POCKET CHART CARDS			
PICTURE WORD	PHONEMES	NO. OF PHONEMES	NO. OF SYLLABLES
ball	/b/ /a/ /l/	3	1
book	/b/ /o͞o/ /k/	3	1
cat	/k/ /ă/ /t/	3	1
cow	/k/ /ou/	2	1
cup	/k/ /ŭ/ /p/	3	1
dice	/d/ /ī/ /s/	3	1
dog	/d/ /ŏ/ /g/	3	1
duck	/d/ /ŭ/ /k/	3	1
feet	/f/ /ē/ /t/	3	1
fish	/f/ /ĭ/ /sh/	3	1
fox	/f/ /ŏ/ /k/ /s/	4	1
frog	/f/ /r/ /ŏ/ /g/	4	1
girl	/g/ /ûr/ /l/	3	1
goat	/g/ /ŏ/ /t/	3	1
grapes	/g/ /r/ /ā/ /p/ /s/	5	1
hand	/h/ /ă/ /n/ /d/	4	1
hat	/h/ /ă/ /t/	3	1
horse	/h/ /ôr/ /s/	3	1
house	/h/ /ou/ /s/	3	1
jar	/j/ /âr/	2	1
jeep	/j/ /ē/ /p/	3	1
jet	/j/ /ĕ/ /t/	3	1
key	/k/ /ē/	2	1
king	/k/ /ĭ/ /ng/	3	1
kite	/k/ /ĭ/ /t/	3	1
lamp	/l/ /ă/ /m/ /p/	4	1
leaf	/l/ /ē/ /f/	3	1
milk	/m/ /ĭ/ /l/ /k/	4	1
moon	/m/ /o͞o/ /n/	3	1
mouse	/m/ /ou/ /s/	3	1
nest	/n/ /ĕ/ /s/ /t/	4	1
nose	/n/ /ō/ /z/	3	1
pig	/p/ /ĭ/ /g/	3	1
queen	/k/ /w/ /ē/ /n/	4	1
quilt	/k/ /w/ /ĭ/ /l/ /t/	5	1
ring	/r/ /ĭ/ /ng/	3	1
rose	/r/ /ō/ /z/	3	1
saw	/s/ /ô/	2	1
seal	/s/ /ē/ /l/	3	1
sock	/s/ /ŏ/ /k/	3	1
sun	/s/ /ŭ/ /n/	3	1
van	/v/ /ă/ /n/	3	1
watch	/w/ /ă/ /tch/	3	1
well	/w/ /ĕ/ /l/	3	1

READING RODS® PICTURE RODS AND PHONOLOGICAL AWARENESS POCKET CHART CARDS (CONTINUED)			
PICTURE WORD	**PHONEMES**	**NO. OF PHONEMES**	**NO. OF SYLLABLES**
wig	/w/ /ĭ/ /g/	3	1
yarn	/y/ /är/ /n/	3	1
zoo	/z/ /o͞o/	2	1
camel	/k/ /ă/ /m/ /əl/	4	2
lion	/l/ /i/ /ən/	3	2
monkey	/m/ /ŭ/ /n/ /k/ /ē/	5	2
necklace	/n/ /ĕ/ /k/ /l/ /ĭ/ /s/	6	2
needle	/n/ /ē/ /d/ /əl/	4	2
pencil	/p/ /ĕ/ /n/ /s/ /əl/	5	2
pumpkin	/p/ /ŭ/ /m/ /p/ /k/ /ĭ/ /n/	7	2
quarter	/k/ /w/ /ôr/ /t/ /ər/	5	2
rabbit	/r/ /ă/ /b/ /ĭ/ /t/	5	2
rowboat	/r/ /ō/ /b/ /ō/ /t/	5	2
table	/t/ /ā/ /b/ /əl/	4	2
tiger	/t/ /ī/ /g/ /ər/	4	2
turtle	/t/ /ûr/ /t/ /l/	4	2
vacuum	/v/ /ă/ /k/ /yo͞o/ /əm/	5	2
wagon	/w/ /ă/ /g/ /ən/	4	2
x-ray	/ĕ/ /k/ /s/ /r/ /ā/	5	2
yo-yo	/y/ /ō/-/y/ /ō/	4	2
zebra	/z/ /ē/ /b/ /r/ /ə/	5	2
zipper	/z/ /ĭ/ /p/ /ər/	4	2
banana	/b/ /ə/ /n/ /â/ /n/ /ə/	6	3
bicycle	/b/ /ī/ /s/ /ĭ/ /k/ /əl/	6	3
gorilla	/gə/ /r/ /ĭ/ /l/ /ə/	5	3
valentine	/v/ /ă/ /l/ /ən/ /t/ /ī/ /n/	7	3
violin	/v/ /ī/ /ə/ /l/ /ĭ/ /n/	6	3
xylophone	/z/ /ī/ /l/ /ə/ /f/ /ō/ /n/	7	3
television	/t/ /ĕ/ /l/ /ə/ /v/ /ĭ/ /zh/ /ən/	8	4

INSECTS AND ARACHNIDS LEARNING PLACE® GAME CARDS			
PICTURE WORD	**PHONEMES**	**NO. OF PHONEMES**	**NO. OF SYLLABLES**
ant	/ă/ /n/ /t/	3	1
bee	/b/ /ē/	2	1
beetle	/b/ /ē/ /t/ /əl/	4	2
bumblebee	/b/ /ŭ/ /m/ /b/ /əl/ /b/ /ē/	7	3
butterfly	/b/ /ŭ/ /t/ /ər/ /f/ /l/ /ī/	7	3
dragonfly	/d/ /r/ /ă/ /g/ /ən/ /f/ /l/ /ī/	8	3
flea	/f/ /l/ /ē/	3	1
fly	/f/ /l/ /ī/	3	1
garden spider	/g/ /är/ /d/ /ən/ /s/ /p/ /ī/ /d/ /ər/	9	4
grasshopper	/g/ /r/ /ă/ /s/ /h/ /ŏ/ /p/ /ər/	8	3
ladybug	/l/ /ā/ /d/ /ē/ /b/ /ŭ/ /g/	7	3
lightning bug	/l/ /ī/ /t/ /n/ /ĭ/ /ng/ /b/ /ŭ/ /g/	9	3
monarch butterfly	/m/ /ŏ/ /n/ /är/ /k/ /b/ /ŭ/ /t/ /ər/ /f/ /l/ /ī/	12	5
mosquito	/m/ /ə/ /s/ /k/ /ē/ /t/ /ō/	7	3

Appendix III: Chart of Syllables and Phonemes for Picture Cards

INSECTS AND ARACHNIDS LEARNING PLACE® GAME CARDS (CONTINUED)

PICTURE WORD	PHONEMES	NO. OF PHONEMES	NO. OF SYLLABLES
moth	/m/ /ô/ /th/	3	1
rhino beetle	/r/ /ī/ /n/ /ō/ /b/ /ē/ /t/ /əl/	8	4
scorpion	/s/ /k/ /ôr/ /p/ /ē/ /ən/	6	3
tarantula	/tə/ /r/ /ă/ /n/ /ch/ /ə/ /l/ /ə/	8	4
termite	/t/ /ûr/ /m/ /ī/ /t/	5	2
wasp	/w/ /ô/ /s/ /p/	4	1

FRUITS AND VEGETABLES LEARNING PLACE® GAME CARDS

PICTURE WORD	PHONEMES	NO. OF PHONEMES	NO. OF SYLLABLES
apple	/ă/ /p/ /əl/	3	2
apricots	/ă/ /p/ /r/ /ĭ/ /c/ /ŏ/ /t/ /s/	8	3
artichokes	/är/ /t/ /ĭ/ /ch/ /ō/ /k/ /s/	7	3
bananas	/b/ /ə/ /n/ /â/ /n/ /ə/ /z/	7	3
broccoli	/b/ /r/ /ŏ/ /k/ /ə/ /l/ /ē/	7	3
cabbage	/k/ /ă/ /b/ /ĭ/ /j/	5	2
carrots	/k/ /ă/ /r/ /ət/ /s/	5	2
cauliflower	/k/ /ô/ /l/ /ĭ/ /f/ /l/ /ou/ /ər/	8	4
cherries	/ch/ /ĕ/ /r/ /ē/ /z/	4	2
grapes	/g/ /r/ /ā/ /p/ /s/	5	1
lemons	/l/ /e/ /m/ /ən/ /z/	5	2
watermelons	/w/ /a/ /t/ /er/ /m/ /el/ /ən/ /s/	8	4
oranges	/ôr/ /i/ /n/ /j/ /ə/ /z/	6	3
pineapple	/p/ /ī/ /n/ /a/ /p/ /əl/	6	3
potatoes	/p/ /ō/ /t/ /ā/ /t/ /ō/ /z/	7	3
radishes	/r/ /ă/ /d/ /ĭ/ /sh/ /ə/ /z/	7	3
spinach	/s/ /p/ /ĭ/ /n/ /ĭ/ /ch/	6	2
lettuce	/l/ /ĕ/ /t/ /ə/ /s/	5	2
onions	/ŭn/ /y/ /ən/ /s/	4	2
strawberries	/s/ /t/ /r/ /ô/ /b/ /ĕ/ /r/ /ē/ /z/	9	3

4- AND 5- SYLLABLE ANIMAL WORDS ON BLM 2-1 AND 2-2

PICTURE WORD	PHONEMES	NO. OF PHONEMES	NO. OF SYLLABLES
salamander	/s/ /ă/ /l/ /ə/ /m/ /ă/ /n/ /d/ /ər/	9	4
barracuda	/b/ /ă/ /r/ /ə/ /k/ /ōō/ /d/ /ə/	8	4
tarantula	/tə/ /r/ /ă/ /n/ /ch/ /ə/ /l/ /ə/	8	4
rhinoceros	/r/ /ī/ /n/ /ŏ/ /s/ /ər/ /ə/ /s/	8	4
alligator	/ă/ /l/ /ĭ/ /g/ /ā/ /t/ /ər/	7	4
armadillo	/är/ /m/ /ə/ /d/ /ĭ/ /l/ /ō/	7	4
hippopotamus	/h/ /ĭ/ /p/ /ə/ /p/ /ŏ/ /t/ /ə/ /m/ /ə/ /s/	11	5
bottlenose dolphin	/b/ /ŏ/ /t/ /əl/ /n/ /ō/ /z/ /d/ /ŏ/ /l/ /f/ /ĭ/ /n/	13	5

Appendix III: Chart of Syllables and Phonemes for Picture Cards

RHYME PICTURE CARDS			
PICTURE WORD	PHONEMES	NO. OF PHONEMES	NO. OF SYLLABLES
sack	/s/ /ă/ /k/	3	1
tack	/t/ /ă/ /k/	3	1
track	/t/ /r/ /ă/ /k/	4	1
map	/m/ /ă/ /p/	3	1
cap	/k/ /ă/ /p/	3	1
clap	/k/ /l/ /ă/ /p/	4	1
nest	/n/ /ĕ/ /s/ /t/	4	1
vest	/v/ /ĕ/ /s/ /t/	4	1
chest	/ch/ /ĕ/ /s/ /t/	4	1
nail	/n/ /ā/ /l/	3	1
pail	/p/ /ā/ /l/	3	1
mail	/m/ /ā/ /l/	3	1
bat	/b/ /ă/ /t/	3	1
rat	/r/ /ă/ /t/	3	1
cat	/k/ /ă/ /t/	3	1
net	/n/ /ĕ/ /t/	3	1
wet	/w/ /ĕ/ /t/	3	1
jet	/j/ /ĕ/ /t/	3	1
lake	/l/ /ā/ /k/	3	1
rake	/r/ /ā/ /k/	3	1
snake	/s/ /n/ /ā/ /k/	4	1
plate	/p/ /l/ /ā/ /t/	4	1
skate	/s/ /k/ /ā/ /t/	4	1
eight	/ā/ /t/	2	1
pin	/p/ /ĭ/ /n/	3	1
violin	/v/ /ī/ /ə/ /l/ /ĭ/ /n/	6	3
twin	/t/ /w/ /ĭ/ /n/	4	1
dice	/d/ /ī/ /s/	3	1
ice	/ī/ /s/	2	1
rice	/r/ /ī/ /s/	3	1
dog	/d/ /ŏ/ /g/	3	1
frog	/f/ /r/ /ŏ/ /g/	4	1
log	/l/ /ŏ/ /g/	3	1
run	/r/ /ŭ/ /n/	3	1
bun	/b/ /ŭ/ /n/	3	1
sun	/s/ /ŭ/ /n/	3	1
brick	/b/ /r/ /ĭ/ /k/	4	1
stick	/s/ /t/ /ĭ/ /k/	4	1
sick	/s/ /ĭ/ /k/	3	1
van	/v/ /ă/ /n/	3	1
fan	/f/ /ă/ /n/	3	1
pan	/p/ /ă/ /n/	3	1
dig	/d/ /ĭ/ /g/	3	1
pig	/p/ /ĭ/ /g/	3	1
wig	/w/ /ĭ/ /g/	3	1
jar	/j/ /är/	2	1

Appendix III: Chart of Syllables and Phonemes for Picture Cards

RHYME PICTURE CARDS (CONTINUED)			
PICTURE WORD	PHONEMES	NO. OF PHONEMES	NO. OF SYLLABLES
star	/s/ /t/ /är/	3	1
car	/k/ /är/	2	1
hill	/h/ /ĭ/ /l/	3	1
grill	/g/ /r/ /ĭ/ /l/	4	1
pill	/p/ /ĭ/ /l/	3	1
bell	/b/ /ĕ/ /l/	3	1
shell	/sh/ /ĕ/ /l/	3	1
well	/w/ /ĕ/ /l/	3	1
swing	/s/ /w/ /ĭ/ /ng/	4	1
sing	/s/ /ĭ/ /ng/	3	1
ring	/r/ /ĭ/ /ng/	3	1
boat	/b/ /ō/ /t/	3	1
coat	/k/ /ō/ /t/	3	1
goat	/g/ /ō/ /t/	3	1
mop	/m/ /ŏ/ /p/	3	1
stop	/s/ /t/ /ŏ/ /p/	4	1
pop	/p/ /ŏ/ /p/	3	1
lock	/l/ /ŏ/ /k/	3	1
clock	/k/ /l/ /ŏ/ /k/	4	1
sock	/s/ /ŏ/ /k/	3	1
bug	/b/ /ŭ/ /g/	3	1
rug	/r/ /ŭ/ /g/	3	1
hug	/h/ /ŭ/ /g/	3	1
nose	/n/ /ō/ /z/	3	1
rose	/r/ /ō/ /z/	3	1
toes	/t/ /ō/ /z/	3	1

FOOD PICTURE CARDS			
PICTURE WORD	PHONEMES	NO. OF PHONEMES	NO. OF SYLLABLES
popsicle	/p/ /ŏ/ /p/ /s/ /ĭ/ /k/ /əl/	7	3
pie	/p/ /ī/	2	1
peas	/p/ /ē/ /z/	3	1
pretzel	/p/ /r/ /ĕ/ /t/ /z/ /əl/	6	2
potato	/p/ /ō/ /t/ /ā/ /t/ /ō/	6	3
pizza	/p/ /ē/ /t/ /s/ /ə/	5	2
steak	/s/ /t/ /ā/ /k/	4	1
salt	/s/ /ô/ /l/ /t/	4	1
sandwich	/s/ /ă/ /n/ /d/ /w/ /ĭ/ /ch/	7	2
spaghetti	/s/ /p/ /ə/ /g/ /ĕ/ /t/ /ē/	7	3
soup	/s/ /ōō/ /p/	3	1
strawberry	/s/ /t/ /r/ /ô/ /b/ /ĕ/ /r/ /ē/	8	3
turkey	/t/ /ûr/ /k/ /ē/	4	2
toast	/t/ /ō/ /s/ /t/	4	1
tea	/t/ /ē/	2	1
tuna	/t/ /ōō/ /n/ /ə/	4	2
tomato	/t/ /ō/ /m/ /ā/ /t/ /ō/	6	3

FOOD PICTURE CARDS (CONTINUED)			
PICTURE WORD	PHONEMES	NO. OF PHONEMES	NO. OF SYLLABLES
taco	/t/ /ä/ /k/ /ō/	4	2
bacon	/b/ /ā/ /k/ /ən/	4	1
bread	/b/ /r/ /ĕ/ /d/	4	1
beet	/b/ /ē/ /t/	3	1
butter	/b/ /ŭ/ /t/ /ər/	4	2
broccoli	/b/ /r/ /ŏ/ /k/ /ə/ /l/ /ē/	7	3
banana	/b/ /ə/ /n/ /ă/ /n/ /ə/	6	3
candy	/k/ /ă/ /n/ //d/ /ē/	5	2
cookie	/k/ /o͞o/ /k/ /ē/	4	2
corn	/k/ /ôr/ /n/	3	1
carrots	/k/ /ă/ /r/ /ət/ /s/	5	2
cabbage	/k/ /ă/ /b/ /ĭ/ /j/	5	2
cake	/k/ /ā/ /k/	3	1
melon	/m/ /ĕ/ /l/ /ən/	4	2
milk	/m/ /ĭ/ /l/ /k/	4	1
mushroom	/m/ /ŭ/ /sh/ /r/ /o͞o/ /m/	6	2
marshmallow	/m/ /är/ /sh/ /m/ /ĕl/ /ō/	6	3
macaroni	/m/ /ă/ /k/ /ə/ /r/ /ō/ /n/ /ē/	8	4
muffin	/m/ /ŭ/ /f/ /ĭ/ /n/	5	2

Appendix III: Chart of Syllables and Phonemes for Picture Cards

Appendix IV
Unit 1 Teacher's Notes

Activity A Bunny Hop

1. I see a bunny.
2. I see a brown bunny.
3. I see a little brown bunny.
4. Stop, bunny, stop.
5. Sprinkle some salt.
6. Sprinkle some salt on his tail.
7. Will he stop?
8. He did not stop.
9. The bunny is hopping away.
10. Come back, bunny!

Activity B Frog on a Lily Pad

1. I live in a pond.
2. I can swim.
3. I sit on a lily pad.
4. I sit very still and wait.
5. Here comes a bug.
6. I like bugs.
7. Snap goes my tongue.
8. Down goes the bug.
9. I jump high.
10. I am a happy green frog.

Activity C How Long Is My Sentence?

1. Sam can build.
2. He builds a house.
3. Sam builds with wood.
4. There are tools in his truck.
5. Sam saws the lumber.
6. Sam hammers the nails.
7. He builds the walls.
8. He puts up the roof.
9. Sam covers the floor.
10. Sam is a good builder.

Activity D Take Away a Word

1. You can run.
   You can run fast.
   You can run very fast.
2. Help Emma.
   Help Emma read.
   Help Emma read this book.
3. We play.
   We play together.
   We play together on Fridays.
4. Dad mows.
   Dad mows the grass.
   Dad mows the green grass.
   Dad mows the long, green grass.

Activity E Word Cards

1. We are here.
2. Go through the gate.
3. We have our tickets.
4. I can see the animals.
5. Watch the monkeys.
6. The tiger is sleeping.
7. Look at the tall giraffe.
8. Where are the lions?
9. I found a feather.
10. I like the zoo.

Activity F Spin a Sentence

1. Apples are red.
2. Some apples are yellow.
3. We can pick apples.
4. We ride in a wagon.
5. We see the apples.
6. Can you find one?
7. Help me reach a red one.
8. Fill up the basket.
9. Apples taste sweet.
10. I like apples.

Unit 2 Teacher's Notes

Activity A Compound Word Puzzles

COMPOUND WORDS ON READING RODS® PHONOLOGICAL AWARENESS POCKET CHART CARDS

inchworm (on a single rod)
rowboat (on a single rod)
necklace (on a single rod)
dollhouse
doghouse
sunhat
catfish
cowgirl

COMPOUND WORD PUZZLE CARDS

	No. of Syllables
1. butterfly	3
2. cupcake	2
3. starfish	2
4. football	2
5. sunflower	3
6. mailbox	2
7. toothbrush	2
8. doorbell	2
9. snowman	2
10. matchbook	2
11. popcorn	2
12. horseshoe	2
13. ladybug	3
14. doghouse	2
15. cowboy	2
16. wheelchair	2
17. armchair	2
18. pinwheel	2
19. lighthouse	2
20. pinecone	2
21. pancake	2
22. rainbow	2
23. drumstick	2
24. clothespin	2

Activity C Syllable Pocket Chart Insects and Arachnids Learning Place® Game Cards

	No. of Syllables
beetle	2
flea	1
mosquito	3
dragonfly	3
lightning bug	3
bumblebee	3
tarantula	4
wasp	1
ladybug	3
rhino beetle	4
ant	1
bee	1
grasshopper	3
butterfly	3
fly	1
monarch butterfly	5
moth	1
garden spider	4
termite	2
scorpion	3

Activity D Fruit and Bugs

grasshopper	3
bumblebee	3
beetle	2
spider	2
dragonfly	3
caterpillar	4
banana	3
apple	2
grape	1
strawberry	3
lemon	2

FRUIT AND BUGS PICTURE CARDS IN READING RODS® PHONOLOGICAL AWARENESS POCKET CHART CARDS

grapes	1
pumpkin	2
apple	2
ant	1
inchworm	2

Activity E Syllable Spinner

NUMBER OF SYLLABLES IN FRUITS AND VEGETABLES LEARNING PLACE® GAME CARDS				
1	**2**	**3**	**4**	**5**
grapes	apple	apricots	cauliflower	
	cabbage	artichokes	watermelons	
	carrots	bananas		
	cherries	broccoli		
	lemons	oranges		
	spinach	potatoes		
	lettuce	radishes		
	onions	strawberries		

NUMBER OF SYLLABLES IN READING RODS® PHONOLOGICAL AWARENESS POCKET CHART CARDS				
1	**2**	**3**	**4**	**5**
	camel	kangaroo	television	
	monkey	valentine		
	necklace	violin		
	needle	xylophone		
	pumpkin	elephant		
	quarter	envelope		
	rabbit	octopus		
	rowboat	bicycle		
	wagon	umbrella		
	x-ray	gorilla		
	yo-yo	banana		
	zebra	Indian		
	zipper			
	apple			
	elbow			
	igloo			
	inchworm			
	ostrich			
	under			
	pencil			
	question			

ADDITIONAL 4- & 5- SYLLABLE WORD PICTURE CARDS ON BLM 2-1 AND 2-2				
			salamander	hippopotamus
			barracuda	bottlenose dolphin
			tarantula	
			rhinoceros	
			alligator	
			armadillo	

Unit 3 Teacher's Notes

Activity A Complete My Sentences

READING RODS® PHONOLOGICAL AWARENESS POCKET CHART CARDS WITH THE SAME INITIAL SOUNDS

ball	girl	lamp	quarter	vacuum	zebra
banana	goat	leaf	queen	valentine	zero
bicycle	gorilla	light bulb	question	van	zipper
book	grapes	lion	mark	violin	zoo
			quilt		
camel	hand	milk		wagon	**VOWEL**
cat	hat	monkey	rabbit	watch	**PICTURE**
cow	horse	moon	ring	well	**CARDS**
cup	house	mouse	rose	wig	ant
			rowboat		apple
dice	jar	necklace		exit sign	ax
dog	jeep	needle	saw	xylophone	
doll	jet	nest	seal	x-ray	elbow
duck	jump rope	nose	sock		elephant
			sun	yarn	envelope
feet	kangaroo	paper clip		yo-yo	
fish	key	pencil	table		igloo
fox	king	pig	television		Indian chief
frog	kite	pumpkin	tiger		inchworm
			turtle		

Activity B Rhyme Picture Cards

RHYME PICTURE CARDS

*track	tack	sack		*brick	stick	sick
*clap	cap	map		*van	fan	pan
*chest	vest	nest		*dig	pig	wig
*nail	pail	mail		*jar	star	car
*bat	rat	cat		*pill	hill	grill
*net	wet	jet		*well	bell	shell
*snake	rake	lake		*swing	sing	ring
*plate	skate	eight		*boat	coat	goat
*twin	violin	pin		*mop	stop	pop
*dice	ice	rice		*lock	clock	sock
*log	frog	dog		*rug	bug	hug
*run	bun	sun		*nose	rose	toes

* *target words*

220

Directions: Draw the picture on the dry erase board or chalkboard. Read the rhyming poem without the underlined words to the children. Have children complete the rhymes and supply the missing words. Ask them to erase those objects from the picture. (As an alternative, copy BLM 3-9: Color a Rhyme! and have children color the objects in the picture.)

Going to the Park

1. Come with us,
   Erase the <u>bus</u>.

2. It's not too late,
   Erase the <u>gate</u>.

3. The sidewalk is wet,
   Erase the <u>net</u>.

4. Now the sky is bright,
   Erase the <u>streetlight</u>.

5. Come down the block,
   Erase the <u>rock</u>.

6. Meet me by the wall,
   Erase the <u>ball</u>.

7. What should I bring?
   Erase the <u>swing</u>.

8. Bring your dog, Sable,
   Erase the <u>table</u>.

9. Bring your guitar,
   Erase the <u>car</u>.

10. We'll take a hike,
    Erase the <u>bike</u>.

11. We'll run and glide,
    Erase the <u>slide</u>.

12. We'll jump over the log,
    Erase the <u>dog</u>.

13. We'll spin and twirl,
    Erase the <u>girl</u>.

14. Jump for joy,
    Erase the <u>boy</u>.

15. Let's have a snack,
    Erase the <u>backpack</u>.

16. We can walk and talk,
    Erase the <u>sidewalk</u>.

17. We're happy and glad,
    Erase the <u>dad</u>.

18. The park is so much fun!
    Erase the <u>sun</u>.

Activity D Draw a Rhyme!

Directions:
- Draw the background on the board or use copies of BLM 3-10: Draw a Rhyme!
- Ask children to help you draw the alien in the story.
- Remind children to listen to the rhymes for hints about how the alien looks.
- Read each rhyme aloud, omitting the underlined word.
- Have children fill in the missing word aloud.
- Invite volunteers to draw the alien or have each child draw it independently.

The Alien Landed

1. An alien landed from outer space
   With a puzzled look on his alien <u>face</u>.

2. The little man stared up at the sky,
   With one big green and purple <u>eye</u>.

3. His planet home was just a tiny speck,
   He stretched out his long and skinny <u>neck</u>.

4. The creature decided to stay a while,
   His rubbery red lips began to <u>smile</u>.

5. "I'm hungry and need something
         really yummy.
   There are grumbles down in my fat,
         round <u>tummy</u>."

6. The little man called out,
   "Is anyone here?"
   He place a hand by his polka-dotted <u>ear</u>.

7. "Where are the animals,
         where are the farms?"
   He cried as he waved his big furry <u>arms</u>.

8. "Where are the people?
         Where's all the rest?"
   His big heart thumped in his
         freckled <u>chest</u>.

9. "There's no one here. There's no one there."
   He shook his head of long blue <u>hair</u>.

10. "Isn't this where we planned to meet?"
    He tapped three toes on all three <u>feet</u>.

11. "Oh, what a mess! What a mess I am in!"
    He muttered as he rubbed his
          whiskery <u>chin</u>.

12. "I made a wrong turn.
          Well, that's how it goes.
    Never follow a crooked <u>nose</u>!"

Activity E Rhyming Bingo

RHYMES WITH READING RODS® PHONOLOGICAL AWARENESS POCKET CHART CARDS

ox/fox	pig/wig
cup/up	ring/king
dog/frog	nose/rose
house/mouse	hat/cat

RHYMING BINGO
24 TARGET RHYME PICTURE CARDS
(Denoted by shaded corners)

track	van
clap	dig
chest	pill
nail	jar
bat	well
net	twin
snake	swing
plate	boat
dice	mop
log	lock
run	rug
brick	nose

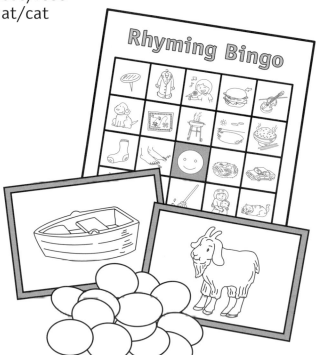

IMAGES SHOWN ON CHILDREN'S RHYMING BINGO CARDS

tack	sack	cap	map
stop	pop	vest	nest
pail	mail	sing	ring
rat	cat	shell	bell
wet	jet	star	car
rake	lake	grill	hill
skate	eight	pig	wig
ice	rice	fan	pan
frog	dog	stick	sick
bun	sun	rose	toes
clock	sock	bug	hug
violin	pin	coat	goat

Unit 4 Teacher's Notes

Activity A Sound Bus

MINIMAL PAIRS OF PHONEMES

/s/ and /z/	/t/ and /k/
/m/ and /n/	/r/ and /l/
/f/ and /v/	/t/ and /d/
/b/ and /p/	/p/ and /d/
/g/ and /j/	/r/ and /w/

Activity B Picture Card Sound Match

MAXIMAL PAIRS PICTURE CARDS

cat/hat	rose/hose	dice/rice	bug/rug
king/ring	jar/car	net/wet	bat/cat
pig/wig	house/mouse	bell/well	map/cap
van/pan	sun/bun	sock/clock	coat/goat

MINIMAL PAIRS PICTURE CARDS

pig/dig	van/fan	lake/rake	nail/mail
mop/pop	vest/nest	ox/fox	up/cup
tack/track	clock/lock	sick/stick	ice/rice

Activity D Feed the Animals

ANIMAL HEADS	FOOD CARDS					
Pedro the Pony	popsicle	pie	peas	pretzel	potato	pizza
Sasha the Seal	salt	steak	soup	sandwich	spaghetti	strawberry
Carla the Cat	candy	cookie	corn	carrots	cake	cabbage
Toby the Toucan	turkey	toast	tea	tuna	tomato	taco
Benny the Bear	bread	beet	bagel	butter	broccoli	banana
Mandy the Monkey	melon	milk	macaroni	muffin	mushroom	marshmallow

Activity E Sound Chart

Picture Cards with the Same Initial Sound

FRUITS AND VEGETABLES LEARNING PLACE® GAME CARDS

/a/   apple   apricots   artichokes
/b/   bananas   broccoli
/c/   cabbage   carrots   cauliflower   cherries
/g/   grapes
/l/   lemons   lettuce
/w/ watermelons
/o/   oranges
/p/   pineapple   potatoes
/r/   radishes
/s/   spinach   strawberries
/o/   onions

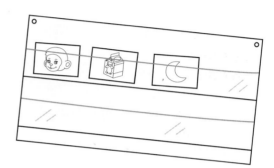

INSECTS AND ARACHNIDS LEARNING PLACE GAME CARDS

/b/   beetle   bumblebee butterfly   bee
/f/   flea   fly
/m/ mosquito   moth   monarch butterfly
/s/   spider   scorpion
/t/   tarantula   termite
/l/   lightning bug   ladybug
/g/   grasshopper   garden spider

RHYME PICTURE CARDS WITH THE SAME INITIAL SOUND (INITIAL BLENDS OR DIGRAPHS EXCLUDED)

/b/   boat bug   bat   bell bun   /p/   pin   pill pan   pail pig   pop
/c/   cap   cat   car   coat   /r/   rice rat   rake ring rug   rose run
/d/   dig   dice dog   /s/   sack sing sock sick sun
/g/   game goat   /t/   tack toes
/h/   hill hug   /v/   vest violin van
/j/   jet   jar   /w/   wet   well wig
/l/   lake lock log
/m/ map   mop mail
/n/   net   nest nose nail

Activity F Sound Concentration

Combine Rhyme Picture Cards, Reading Rods® Pocket Chart Cards, and Food Cards to create pairs of picture cards with the same initial sounds.

B	boat beet	bug broccoli	bat butter	ball bagel	banana bell	book bun	bicycle brick	bread
C	cat cauliflower	cap carrots	camel car	cow coat	cup candy	cupcake clap	cookie clock	corn
D	dice	dog	doll	duck	dig			
F	feet	fish	fox	frog	fan			
G	game	gate	goat	girl	gorilla	grapes	grill	
H	hay	hill	hand	hat	horse	house	hug	
J	jet	jar	jump rope	jeep				
K	kangaroo	key	king	kite	king			
L	lake	lock	lamp	leaf	light bulb	lion	log	
M	map melon	mop mushroom	mail macaroni	moon marshmallow	muffin	milk	monkey	mouse
N	net	nail	nest	nose	necklace	needle		
P	pin popsicle	pill pie	pan peas	pop pretzel	pail potato	pig pizza	pumpkin paper clip	pencil plate
Q	quarter	queen	question					
R	rice run	rat	rake	ring	rug	rose	rabbit	rowboat
S	sack salt shell	saw soup star	sing sandwich stop	sick steak swing	sock strawberry	sun snake	seal skate	spaghetti stick
T	tack turkey	toes toast	table tea	taco tuna	tomato	television track	tiger twin	turtle
V	vest	violin	van	valentine	vacuum			
W	wet	well	wig	watch	wagon			
X	xylophone	exit sign						
Y	yo-yo	yarn						
Z	zoo	zipper	zero					

Unit 5 Teacher's Notes

Activity A Puppet Talk-Animal Picture Cards

PICTURE WORD	PHONEMES	NO. OF PHONEMES	NO. OF SYLLABLES
INSECTS AND ARACHNIDS LEARNING PLACE® GAME CARDS			
ant	/ă/ /n/ /t/	3	1
bee	/b/ /ē/	2	1
beetle	/b/ /ē/ /t/ /el/	4	2
bumblebee	/b/ /ŭ/ /m/ /b/ /əl/ /b/ /ē/	7	3
butterfly	/b/ /ŭ/ /t/ /ər/ /f/ /l/ /ī/	7	3
dragonfly	/d/ /r/ /ă/ /g/ /ən/ /f/ /l/ /ī/	8	3
flea	/f/ /l/ /ē/	3	1
fly	/f/ /l/ /ī/	3	1
garden spider	/g/ /är/ /d/ /ən/ /s/ /p/ /ī/ /d/ /ər/	9	4
grasshopper	/g/ /r/ /ă/ /s/ /h/ /ŏ/ /p/ /ər/	8	3
ladybug	/l/ /ā/ /d/ /ē/ /b/ /ŭ/ /g/	7	3
lightning bug	/l/ /ī/ /t/ /n/ /ĭ/ /ng/ /b/ /ŭ/ /g/	9	3
monarch butterfly	/m/ /ŏ/ /n/ /är/ /k/ /b/ /ŭ/ /t/ /ər/ /f/ /l/ /ī/	12	5
mosquito	/m/ /ə/ /s/ /k/ /ē/ /t/ /ō/	7	3
moth	/m/ /ô/ /th/	3	1
rhino beetle	/r/ /ī/ /n/ /ō/ /b/ /ē/ t/ /əl/	8	4
scorpion	/s/ /k/ /ôr/ /p/ /ē/ /ən/	6	3
tarantula	/tə/ /r/ /ă/ /n/ /ch/ /ə/ /l/ /ə/	8	4
termite	/t/ /ûr/ /m/ /ī/ /t/	5	2
wasp	/w/ /ô/ /s/ /p/	4	1
4- & 5- SYLLABLE ANIMAL CARDS ON BLM 2-1 AND 2-2			
salamander	/s/ /ă/ /l/ /ə/ /m/ /ă/ /n/ /d/ /ər/	9	4
barracuda	/b/ /ă/ /r/ /ə/ /k/ /ōō/ /d/ /ə/	8	4
tarantula	/tə/ /r/ /ă/ /n/ /ch/ /ə/ /l/ /ə/	8	4
rhinoceros	/r/ /ī/ /n/ /ŏ/ /s/ /ər/ /ə/ /s/	8	4
alligator	/ă/ /l/ /ĭ/ /g/ /ā/ /t/ /ər/	7	4
armadillo	/är/ /m/ /ĭ/ /d/ /ĭ/ /l/ /ō/	7	4
hippopotamus	/h/ /ĭ/ /p/ /ə/ /p/ /ŏ/ /t/ /ə/ /m/ /ə/ /s/	11	5
bottlenose dolphin	/b/ /ŏ/ /t/ /l/ /n/ /ō/ /z/ /d/ /ŏ/ /l/ /f/ /ĭ/ /n/	13	5
RHYME PICTURE CARDS			
bat	/b/ /ă/ /t/	3	1
rat	/r/ /ă/ /t/	3	1
cat	/k/ /ă/ /t/	3	1
snake	/s/ /n/ /ā/ /k/	4	1
dog	/d/ /ŏ/ /g/	3	1
frog	/f/ /r/ /ŏ/ /g/	4	1
goat	/g/ /ō/ /t/	3	1
bug	/b/ /ŭ/ /g/	3	1

Activity B Move It & Say It

LIST OF WORDS WITH NUMBER OF PHONEMES

1. car	2	/k/ /är/
2. door	2	/d/ /ôr/
3. bag	3	/b/ /ă/ /g/
4. mat	3	/m/ /ă/ /t/
5. pan	3	/p/ /ă/ /n/
6. lid	3	/l/ /ĭ/ /d/
7. sun	3	/s/ /ŭ/ /n/
8. kit	3	/k/ /ĭ/ /t/
9. top	3	/t/ /ŏ/ /p/
10. bug	3	/b/ /ŭ/ /g/
11. cake	3	/k/ /ā/ /k/
12. bell	3	/b/ /ĕ/ /l/
13. drum	4	/d/ /r/ /ŭ/ /m/
14. hand	4	/h/ /ă/ /n/ /d/
15. girl	4	/g/ /ûr/ /l/
16. wind	4	/w/ /ĭ/ /n/ /d/
17. brush	4	/b/ /r/ /ŭ/ /sh/
18. lady	4	/l/ /ā/ /d/ /ē/
19. pink	4	/p/ /ĭ/ /n/ /k/
20. lamp	4	/l/ /ă/ /m/ /p/

Activity H Sound Bingo Cards

COVER THE PICTURE NAME...

1. with three sounds that ends with /p/	jeep	/j/ /ē/ /p/
2. with two sounds that begins with /k/	cow	/k/ /ou/
3. with three sounds that rhymes with *fun*	sun	/s/ /ŭ/ /n/
4. with four sounds that rhymes with *camp*	lamp	/l/ /ă/ /m/ /p/
5. with two sounds that begins with /k/	key	/k/ /ē/
6. with three sounds that ends with /t/	goat	/g/ /ō/ /t/
7. with four sounds that ends with /l/	camel	/c/ /ă/ /m/ /əl/
8. with two sounds that begins with /j/	jar	/j/ /är/
9. with three sounds that rhymes with *silk*	milk	/m/ /ĭ/ /l/ /k/
10. with three sounds that rhymes with *rock*	sock	/s/ /ŏ/ /k/
11. with three sounds that rhymes with *barn*	yarn	/y/ /är/ /n/
12. with two sounds that begins with /s/	saw	/s/ /ô/
13. with three sounds that begins with /w/	well	/w/ /ĕ/ /l/
14. with six sounds that ends with /a/	banana	/b/ /ə/ /n/ /ă/ /n/ /ə/
15. with three sounds that begin with /k/	kite	/k/ /ī/ /t/
16. with three sounds that rhymes with *met*	jet	/j/ /ĕ/ /t/
17. with four sounds that rhymes with *too*	igloo	/i/ /g/ /l/ /o͞o/
18. with four sounds that rhymes with *flipper*	zipper	/z/ /ĭ/ /p/ /ər/
19. with seven sounds that begins with /v/	valentine	/v/ /ă/ /l/ /ən/ /t/ /ī/ /n/
20. with four sounds that ends with /d/	hand	/h/ /ă/ /n/ /d/
21. with three sounds that rhymes with *house*	mouse	/m/ /ou/ /s/
22. with three sounds that ends with /f/	leaf	/l/ /ē/ /f/
23. with five sounds that rhymes with *habit*	rabbit	/r/ /ă/ /b/ /ĭ/ /t/
24. with three sounds that begins with /v/	van	/v/ /ă/ /n/
25. with five sounds that end with /a/	gorilla	/gə/ /r/ /ĭ/ /l/ /ə/

Unit 6 Teacher's Notes

Phoneme Manipulation

The focus of these activities is on phoneme or sound manipulation, not on letters or correct spellings. These activities increase recognition of the sounds of words and how the sounds of words change when phonemes are added or deleted.

Activity A Phoneme Addition

ADDING INITIAL SOUNDS

1. ace – add /b/ or /r/   base or race
2. age – add /p/ or /c/   page or cage
3. an – add /v/ or /m/   van or man
4. ap – add /n/ or /s/   nap or sap
5. art – add /p/ or /t/   part or tart
6. at – add /b/ or /r/   bat or rat
7. ate – add /d/ or /m/   date or mate
8. ay – add /d/ or /p/   day or pay
9. ice – add /m/ or /r/   mice or rice
10. ink – add /p/ or /w/   pink or wink
11. ing – add /r/ or /w/   ring or wing
12. lip – add /s/   slip

13. it – add /b/ or /h/   bit or hit
14. mall – add /s/   small
15. now – add /s/   snow
16. pit – add /s/   spit
17. pot – add /s/   spot
18. rack – add /t/   track
19. rap – add /t/   trap
20. ray – add /t/   tray
21. rip – add /t/   trip
22. room – add /b/   broom
23. way – add /s/   sway
24. well – add /s/   swell

ADDING FINAL SOUNDS

	Sounds like:		Sounds like:
25. bell – add /t/	belt	38. pain – add /t/	paint
26. day – add /t/	date	39. pan – add /t/	pant
27. den – add /t/	dent	40. pay – add /j/	page
28. grew – add /p/	group	41. plan – add /t/	plant
29. he – add /t/	heat	42. play – add /s/	place
30. her – add /t/	hurt	43. row – add /z/	rose
31. hi – add /t/	height	44. sell – add /f/	self
32. I – add /s/	ice	45. she – add /p/	sheep
33. me – add /n/	mean	46. toe – add /st/	toast
34. men – add /d/	mend	47. tree – add /t/	treat
35. miss – add /t/	mist	48. tray – add /d/	trade
36. my – add /t/	might	49. way – add /t/	weight
37. knee – add /d/	need	50. will – add /t/	wilt

Activity B Phoneme Deletion

DELETING INITIAL SOUNDS

1. blend – without /bl/   end
2. brand – without /br/   and
3. bring – without /b/   ring
4. broom – without /b/   room
5. chat – without /ch/   at
6. chin – without /ch/   in
7. crash – without /cr/   ash
8. crow – without /c/   row
9. land – without /l/   and
10. lend – without /l/   end
11. play – without /p/   lay
12. pout – without /p/   out
13. shout – without /sh/   out

14. skit – without /s/   kit
15. slip – without /s/   lip
16. small – without /s/   mall
17. spit – without /s/   pit
18. stop – without /s/   top
19. sway – without /s/   way
20. swell - without /s/   well
21. switch – without /s/   witch
22. that – without /th/   at
23. trace – without /t/   race
24. trap – without /t/   rap
25. tray – without /t/   ray

DELETING FINAL SOUNDS

Sounds like:

1. bald – without /d/   ball
2. belt – without /t/   bell
3. beetle – without /l/   beat
4. butter – without /r/   but
5. date – without /t/   day
6. group – without /p/   grew
7. heat – without /t/   he
8. hurt – without /t/   her
9. ice – without /s/   I
10. mean – without /n/   me
11. might – without /t/   my
12. mist – without /t/   miss
13. page – without /j/   pay

Sounds like:

14. paint – without /t/   pain
15. pant – without /t/   pan
16. place – without /s/   play
17. plant – without /t/   plan
18. race – without /r/   ace
19. self – without /f/   sell
20. sheep – without /s/   heap
21. start – without /t/   star
22. treat – without /t/   tree
23. trade – without /t/   raid
24. warn – without /n/   war
25. wilt – without /t/   will

Activity C Phoneme Substitution

CHANGING INITIAL PHONEMES

1. back – change /b/ to /tr/   track
2. band – change /b/ to /l/   land
3. big – change /b/ to /f/   fig
4. boss – change /b/ to /m/   moss
5. fast – change /f/ to /l/   last
6. fell – change /f/ to /b/   bell
7. fog – change /f/ to /d/   dog
8. frog – change /fr/ to /l/   log
9. go – change /g/ to /sn/   snow
10. had – change /h/ to /s/   sad
11. hat – change /h/ to /m/   mat
12. hid – change /h/ to /k/   kid
13. hit – change /h/ to /s/   sit
14. hot – change /h/ to /n/   not
15. jog – change /j/ to /f/   fog
16. kit – change /k/ to /p/   pit
17. lad – change /l/ to /b/   bad
18. led – change /l/ to /b/   bed
19. lip – change /l/ to /s/   sip
20. list – change /l/ to /m/   mist
21. lot – change /l/ to /p/   pot
22. mad – change /m/ to /b/   bad
23. man – change /m/ to /t/   tan
24. mass – change /m/ to /p/   pass
25. mat – change /m/ to /b/   bat

26. may – change /m/ to /st/   stay
27. melt – change /m/ to /b/   belt
28. mess – change /m/ to /dr/   dress
29. mint – change /m/ to /h/   hint
30. mist – change /m/ to /f/   fist
31. no – change /n/ to /g/   go
32. pond – change /p/ to /f/   fond
33. pot – change /p/ to /l/   lot
34. rag – change /r/ to /b/   bag
35. ring – change /r/ to /s/   sing
36. ripe – change /r/ to /p/   pipe
37. sand – change /s/ to /h/   hand
38. send – change /s/ to /m/   mend
39. say – change /s/ to /tr/   tray
40. sift – change /s/ to /l/   lift
41. silk – change /s/ to /m/   milk
42. sill – change /s/ to /st/   still
43. sing – change /s/ to /br/   bring
44. tan – change /t/ to /f/   fan
45. tap – change /t/ to /n/   nap
46. tell – change /t/ to /s/   sell
47. tent – change /t/ to /d/   dent
48. till – change /t/ to /h/   hill
49. top – change /t/ to /st/   stop
50. wing- change /w/ to /th/   thing

Activities D–E Phoneme Substitution

CHANGING FINAL PHONEMES

1. beam – change /m/ to /t/   beat
2. bend – change /d/ to /ch/   bench
3. bet – change /b/ to /l/   let
4. bus – change /s/ to /g/   bug
5. dot – change /t/ to /g/   dog
6. got – change /t/ to /b/   gob
7. ham – change /m/ to /t/   hot
8. hip – change /p/ to /t/   hit
9. led – change /d/ to /g/   leg
10. lip – change /p/ to /t/   lit
11. less – change /s/ to /t/   let
12. mat – change /t/ to /d/   mad
13. men – change /n/ to /t/   met
14. mitt – change /t/ to /s/   miss
15. pen – change /n/ to /t/   pet
16. pet – change /t/ to /p/   pep
17. rag – change /g/ to /t/   rat
18. rat – change /t/ to /n/   ran
19. rim – change /m/ to /p/   rip
20. sell – change /l/ to /t/   set
21. sent – change /t/ to /d/   send
22. sat – change /t/ to /p/   sap
23. sip – change /p/ to /t/   sit
24. tap – change /t/ to /n/   nap
25. top – change /p/ to /t/   tot

CHANGING MEDIAL PHONEMES

1. barn – change /är/ to /ur/   burn
2. bed – change /ĕ/ to /ă/   bad
3. beg – change /ĕ/ to /ă/   bag
4. cap – change /ă/ to /ŭ/   cup
5. cat – change /ă/ to /ŭ/   cut
6. cot – change /ŏ/ to /ă/   cat
7. dart – change /är/ to /ûr/   dirt
8. dish – change /ĭ/ to /ă/   dash
9. drop – change /ŏ/ to /ĭ/   drip
10. far – change /är/ to /ûr/   fur
11. fin – change /ĭ/ to /ă/   fan
12. fun – change /ŭ/ to /ĭ/   fin
13. firm – change /ûr/ to /är/   farm
14. heart – change /är/ to /ûr/   hurt
15. hop – change /ŏ/ to /ĭ/   hip
16. hot – change /ŏ/ to/ĭ/   hit
17. lad – change /ă/ to /ĭ/   lid
18. last – change /ă/ to /ĭ/   list
19. let – change /ĕ/ to /ŏ/   lot
20. lick – change /ĭ/ to /ŏ/   lock
21. lip – change /ĭ/ to /ă/   lap
22. note – change /ō/ to /ŏ/   not
23. pack – change /ă/ to /ĭ/   pick
24. pan – change /ă/ to /ĭ/   pin
25. pet – change /ĕ/ to /ŏ/   pot
26. pick – change /ĭ/ to /ă/   pack
27. port – change /ôr/ to /är/   part
28. stick – change /ĭ/ to /ă/   stack
29. stir – change /ûr/ to /är/   star
30. stop – change /ŏ/ to /ĕ/   step
31. tack – change /ă/ to /ĭ/   tick
32. trip – change /ĭ/ to /ă/   trap

Bibliography

Armbruster, B., F. Lehr, and J. Osborn. 2001. *Put Reading First: The Research Building Blocks for Teaching Children to Read*. Washington, D.C.: The National Institute for Literacy.

Gillon, Gail. 2004. *Phonological Awareness: From Research to Practice*. New York, N.Y.: The Guilford Press.

Lyons, C.A. 1994. Reading Recovery and learning disability: Issues, challenges, and implications. *Literacy Teaching and Learning: An International Journal of Early Literacy* 1(1).

Moats, Louisa C. 2004. *Language Essentials for Teachers of Reading and Spelling (LETRS)*, Longmont, CO: Sopris West, Inc.

Nagy, W.E., and J. A. Scott. 2000. Vocabulary processes. In M. L. Kamil, P. Mosenthal, P.D. Pearson & R. Barr (Eds.), *Handbook of Reading Research* (Vol. 3, pp. 269–284). Mahwah, NJ: Erlbaum.

Snow, C., M. S. Burns, and P. Griffin. 1998. *Preventing Reading Difficulties in Young Children*. Washington, DC: National Academy Press.

Snow, C., M. S. Burns, and P. Griffin. 1999. *Starting Out Right: A Guide to Promoting Children's Reading Success*. Washington, DC: National Academy Press.

Report of the National Reading Panel: Teaching Children to Read, 2001. Washington, DC: US Department of Education.

Torgesen, J.K. 2004. Preventing Early Reading Failure—and Its Devastating Downward Spiral: The Evidence for Early Intervention. *American Educator,* Fall 2004.

University of Texas at Austin, Vaughn Gross Center for Reading and Language Arts. *Preventing Reading Difficulties: A Three-Tiered Intervention Model. http://www. texasreading.org/3tier (accessed May 17, 2005).*

Reproducible Materials

	Unit 1	Unit 2	Unit 3	Unit 4	Unit 5	Unit 6
	Word Level	**Syllable Level**	**Onset-Rime Level**	**Phoneme Isolation Level**	**Phoneme Segmentation and Blending Level**	**Phoneme Manipulation Level**
BLM 1-1 Bunny Cutouts	Activity A					
BLM 1-2, 1-3 Lily Pad Pathway	Activity B					
BLM 2-1, 2-2, 2-3 Compound Word Puzzle Cards		Activity A				
BLM 2-4 4- and 5- Syllable Animal Cards		Activity E				
BLM 2-5 Elkonin Boxes		Activity F				
BLM 3-1 thru 3-8 Rhyme Picture Cards			Activity B			
BLM 3-9 Color a Rhyme! Going to the Park			Activity D			
BLM 3-10 Draw a Rhyme! The Alien Landed			Activity D			
BLM 3-11, 3-12, 3-13 Rhyming Bingo			Activity E			
BLM 4-1, 4-2 Sound Bus				Activity A		
BLM 4-3 Two Sounds Chart				Activity B		
BLM 4-4 Animal Head Cutouts				Activity C		
BLM 4-5 thru 4-10 Food Picture Cards				Activity C		
BLM 5-1 Fruit Bowl					Activity B	
BLM 5-2 Bears' Den					Activity B	
BLM 5-3 Frog Pond					Activity B	
BLM 5-4 Sound Train					Activity G	
BLM 5-5 Train Car Cards					Activity G	
BLM 5-6, 5-7, 5-8 Sound Bingo Cards					Activity H	
BLM 6-1 Insect Net						Activity B
BLM 5-1 Fruit Bowl						Activity C
BLM 5-2 Bears' Den						Activity E

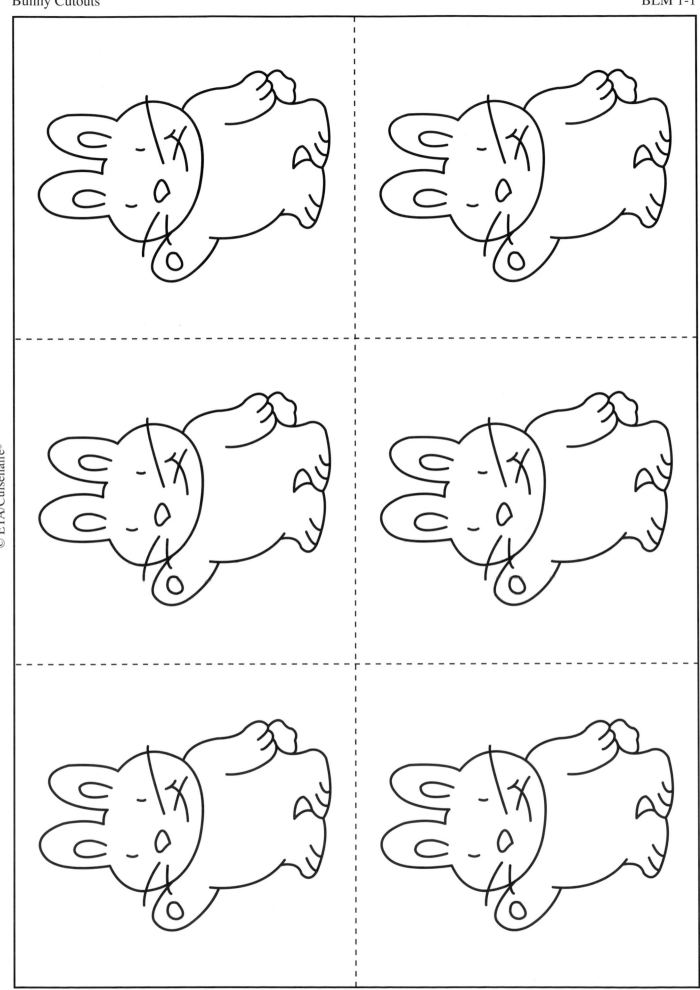

Lily Pad

Start

Pathway

Home

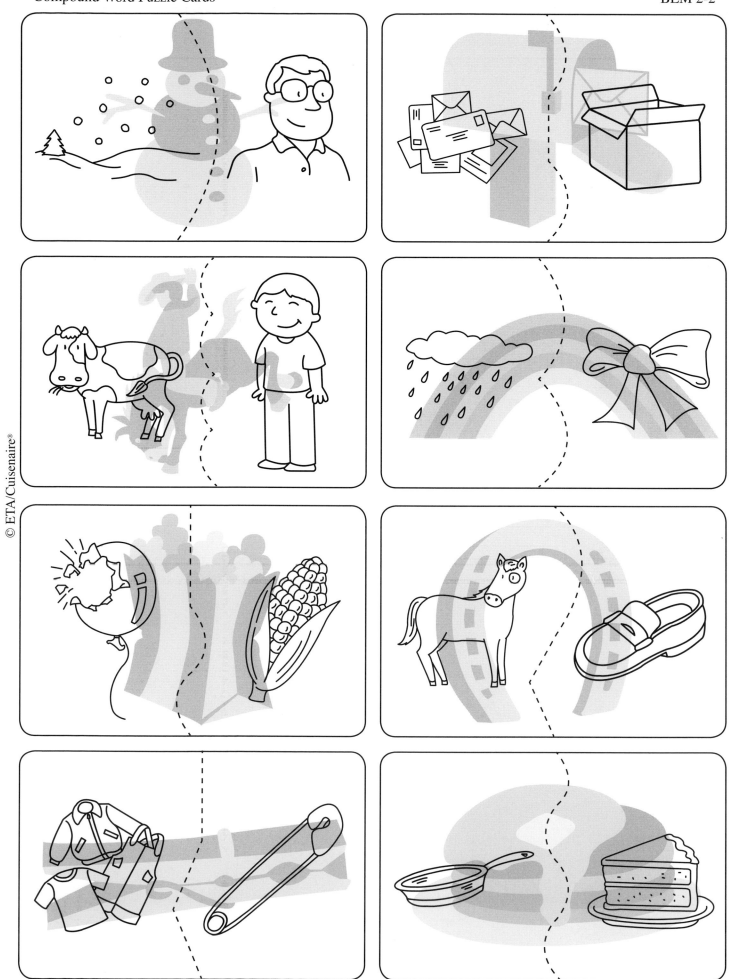

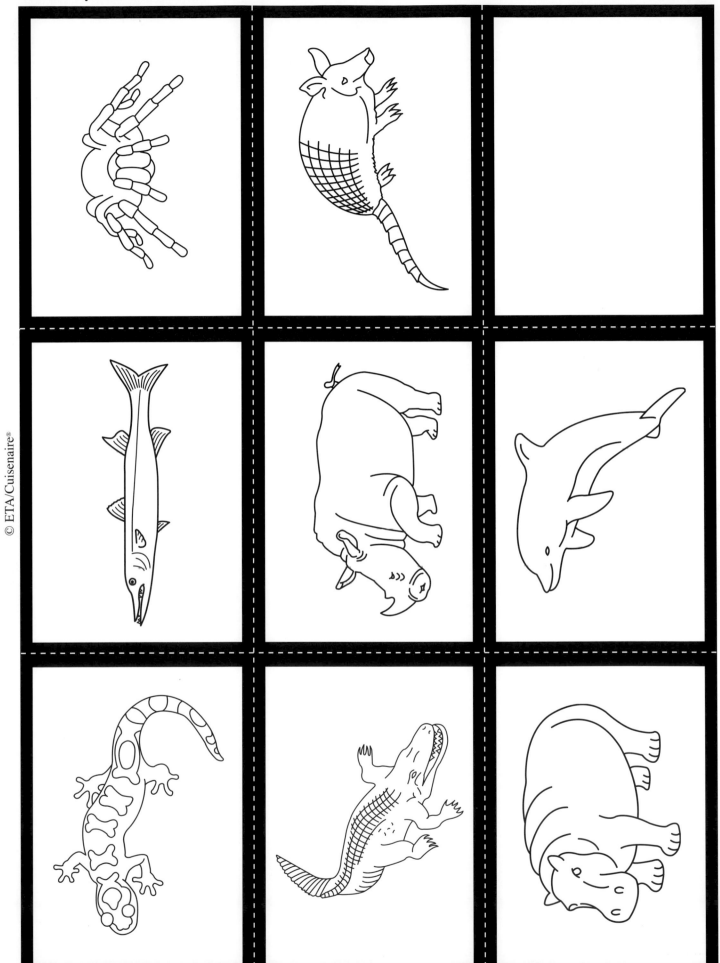

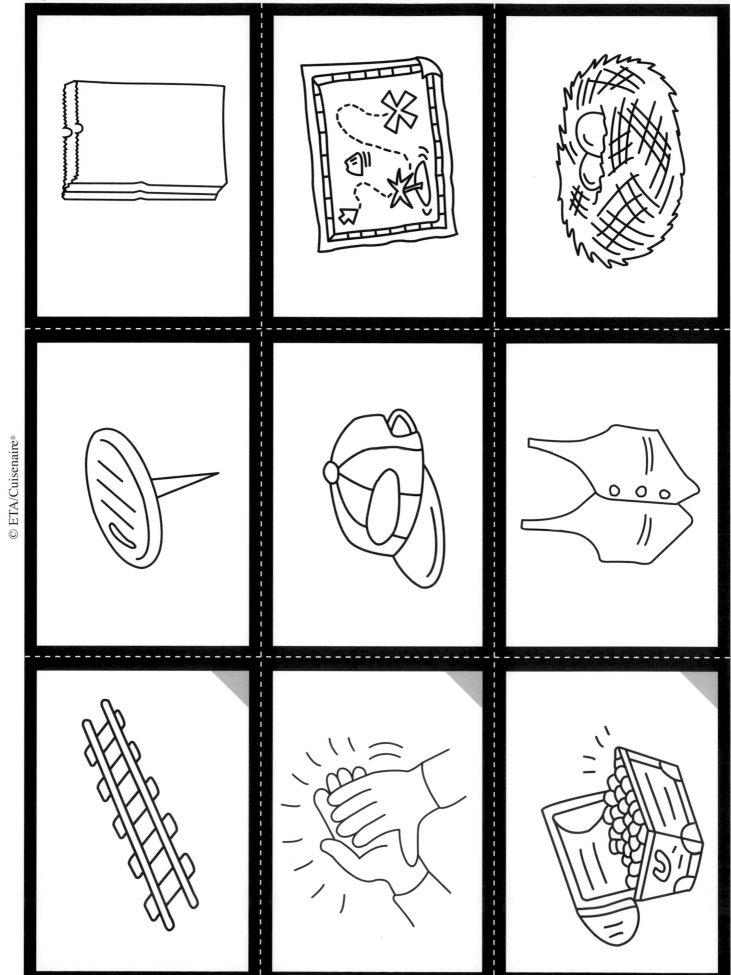

© ETA/Cuisenaire®

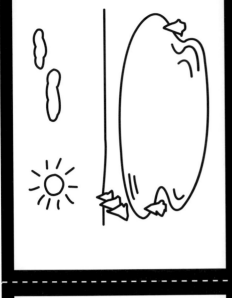

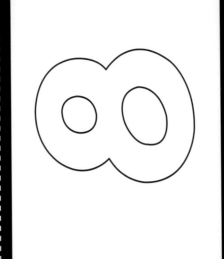

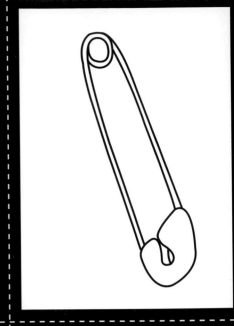

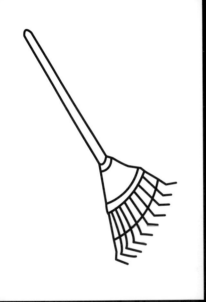

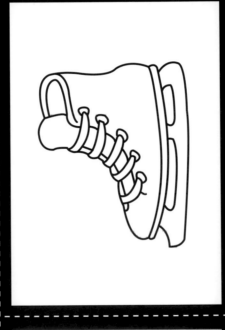

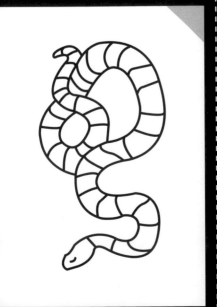

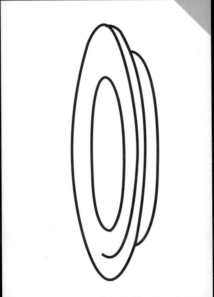

© ETA/Cuisenaire®

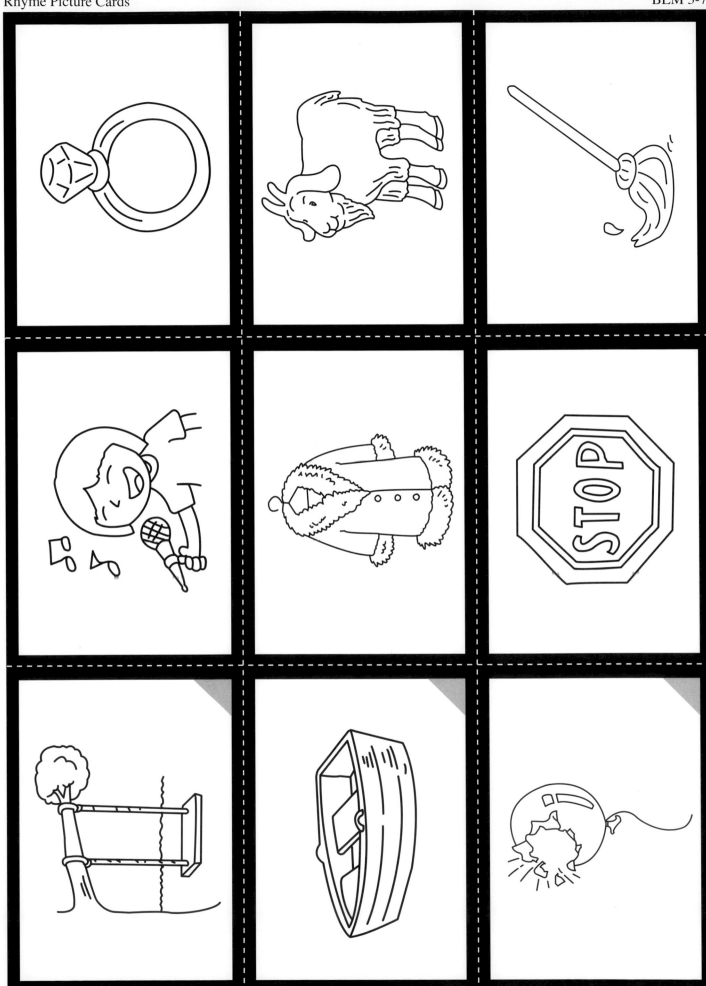

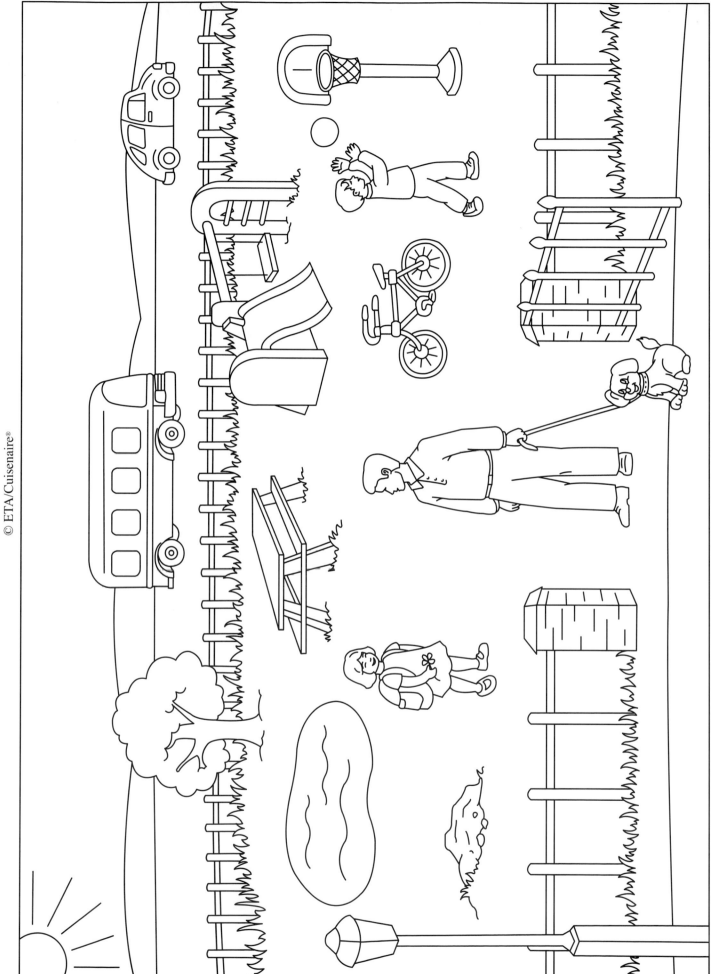

Rhyming Bingo

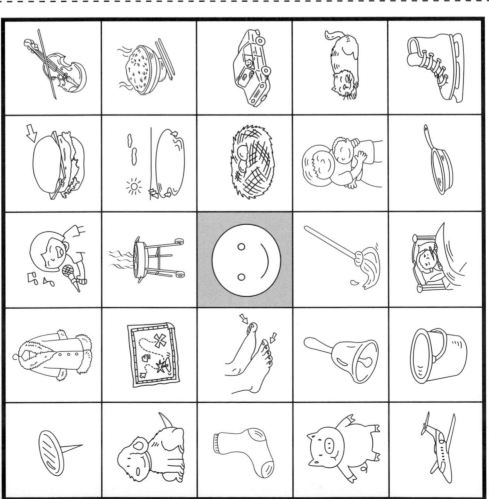

Rhyming Bingo

Rhyming Bingo

Rhyming Bingo

Rhyming Bingo

© ETA/Cuisenaire®

Rhyming Bingo

© ETA/Cuisenaire®

© ETA/Cuisenaire®

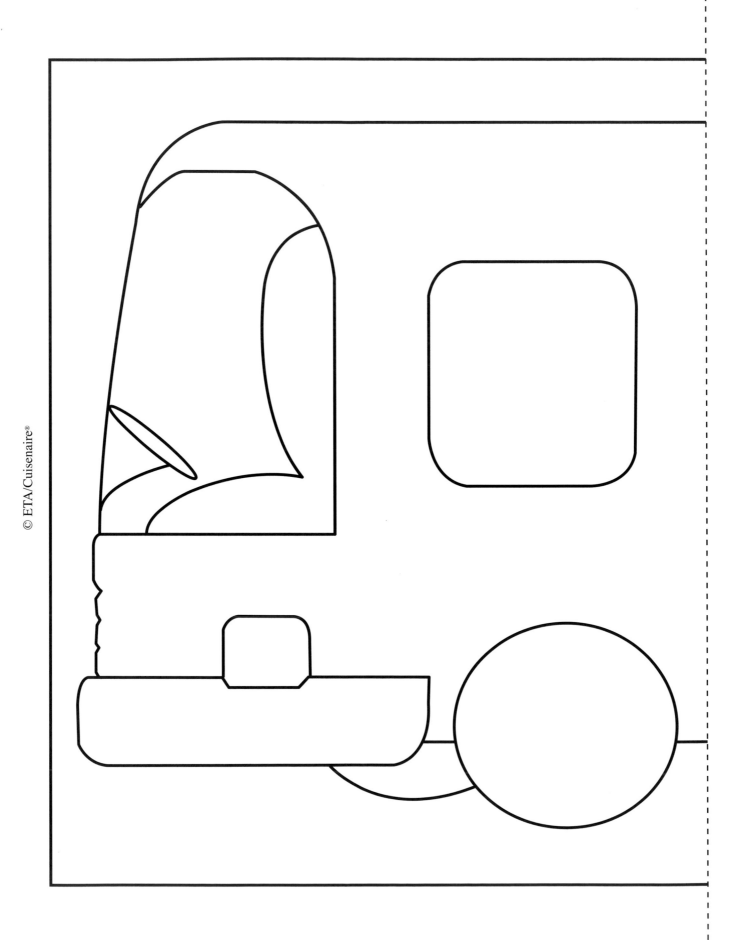

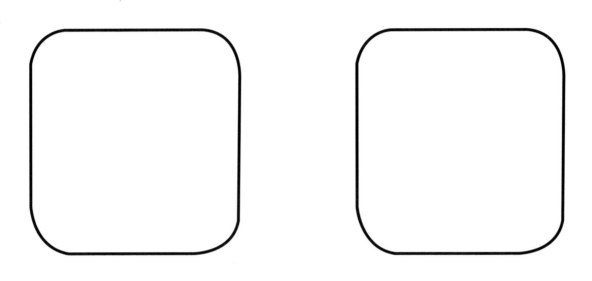

© ETA/Cuisenaire®

Toby the Toucan

Mandy the Monkey

Sasha the Seal

Carla the Cat

Pedro the Pony

Benny the Bear

© ETA/Cuisenaire®

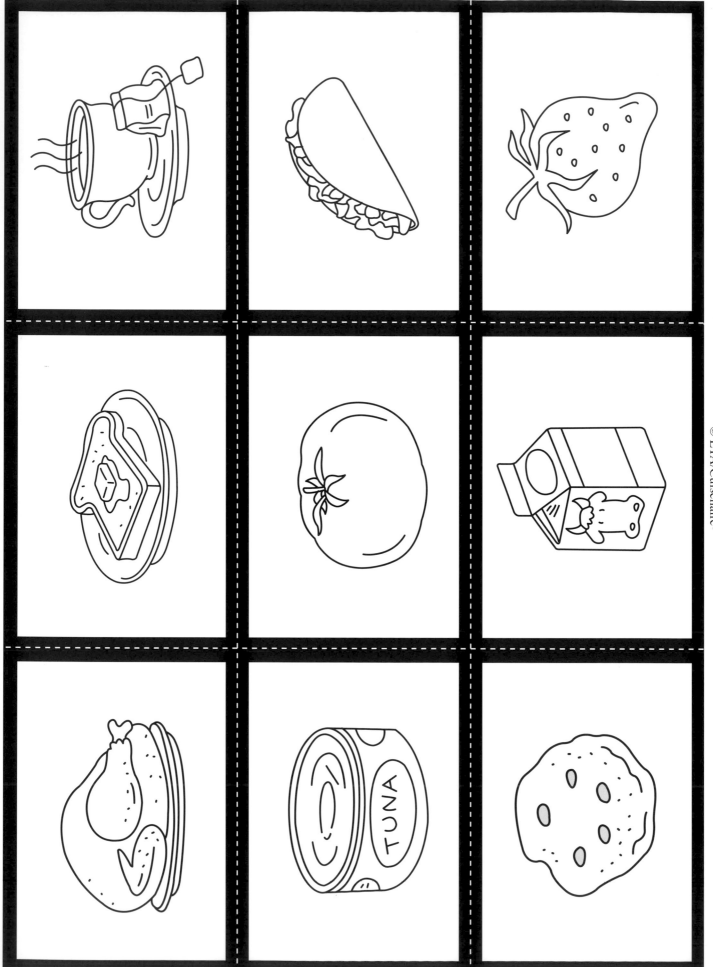

© ETA/Cuisenaire®

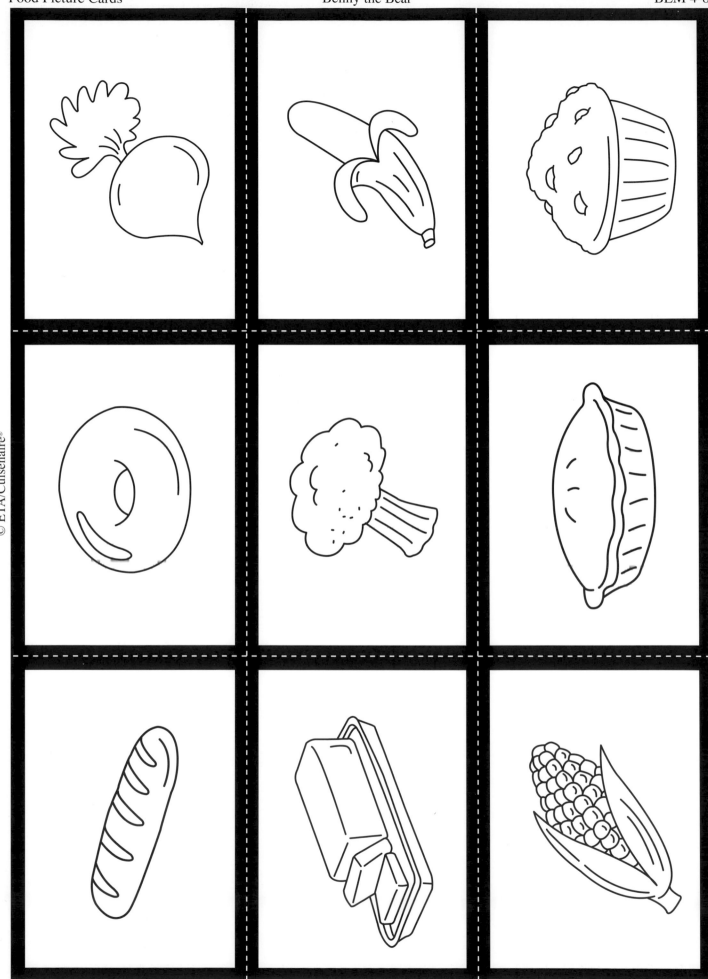

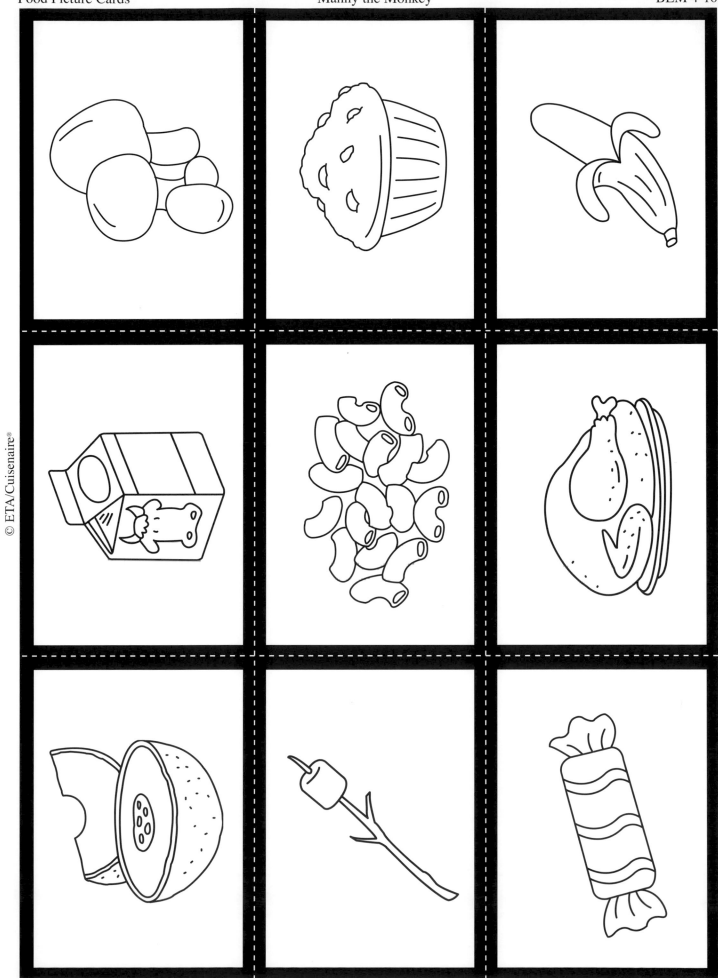

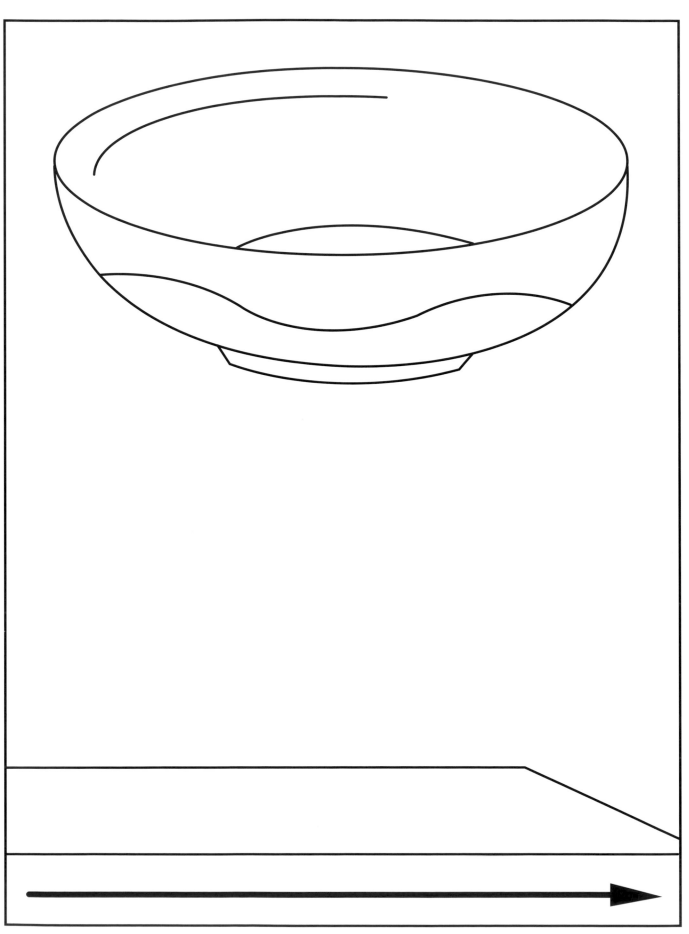

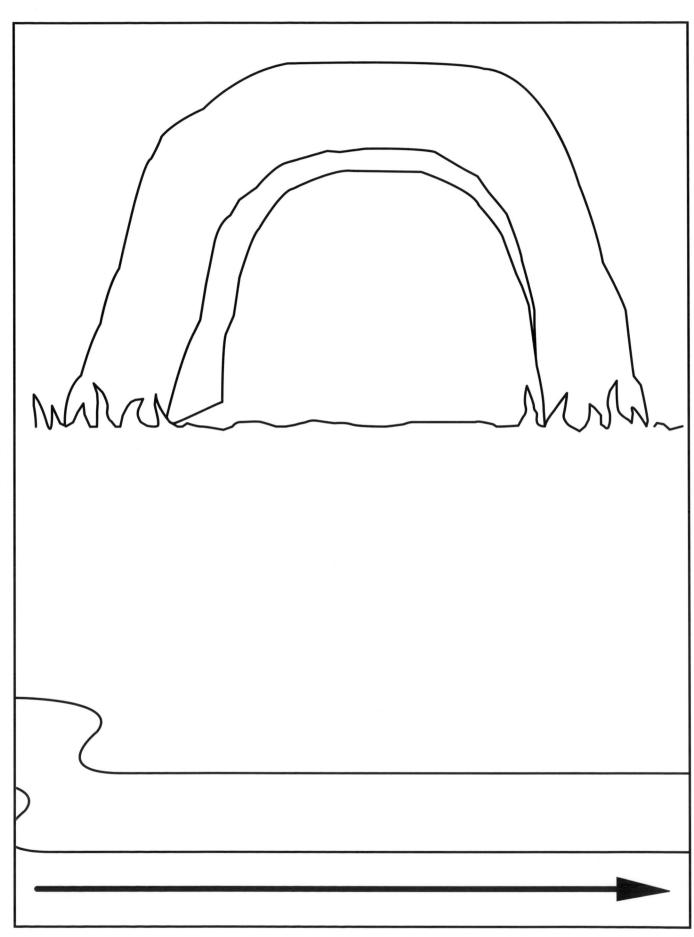

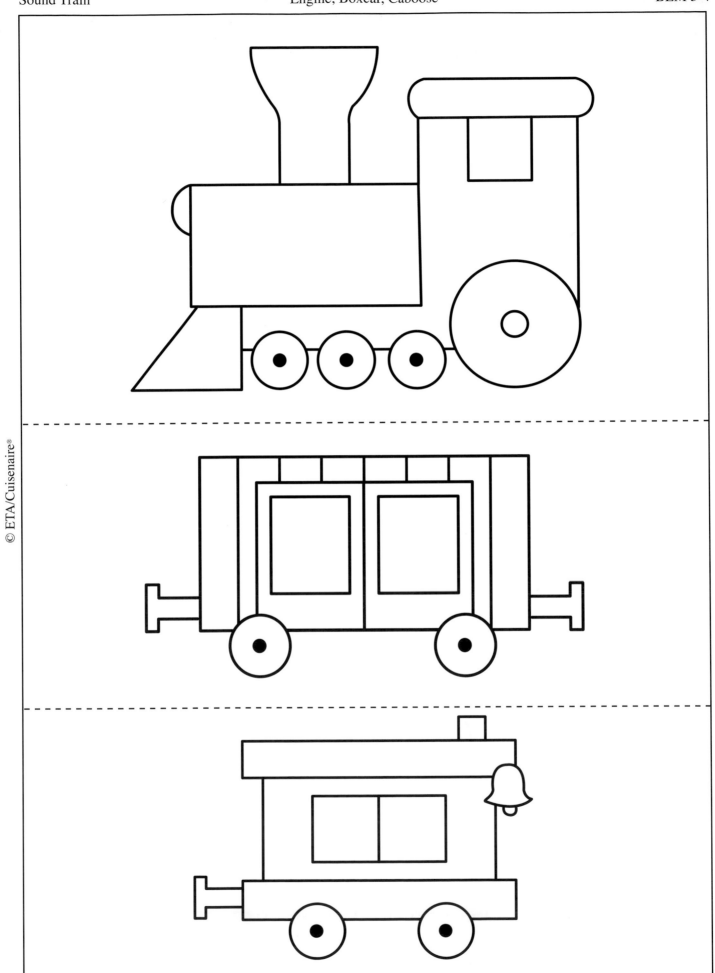

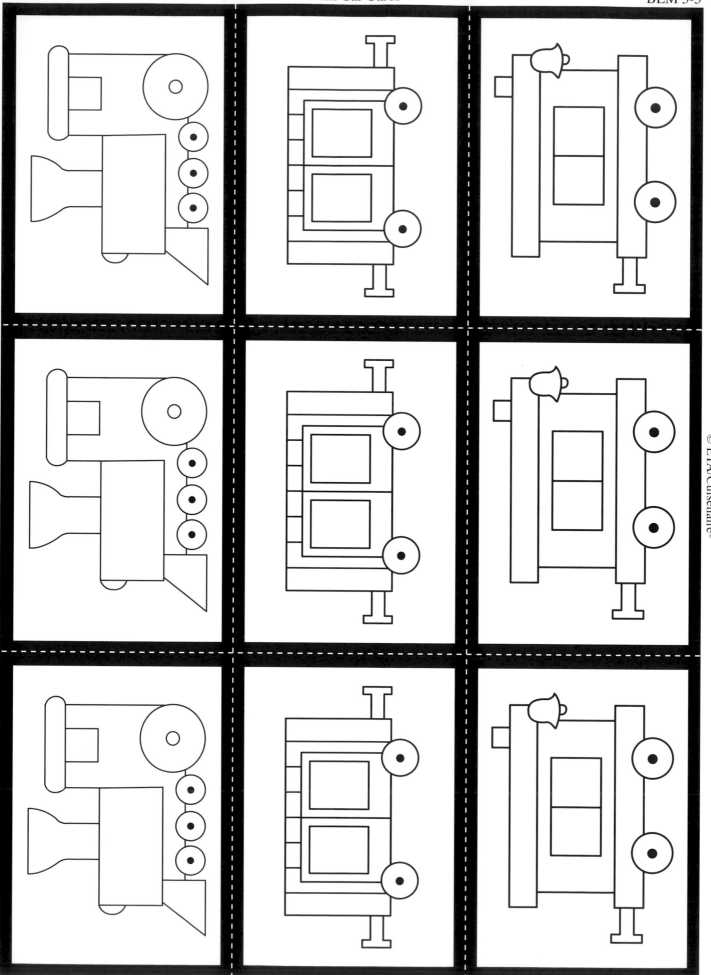

Sound Bingo

© ETA/Cuisenaire®

Sound Bingo

© ETA/Cuisenaire®

Sound Bingo

© ETA/Cuisenaire®

Sound Bingo

Sound Bingo

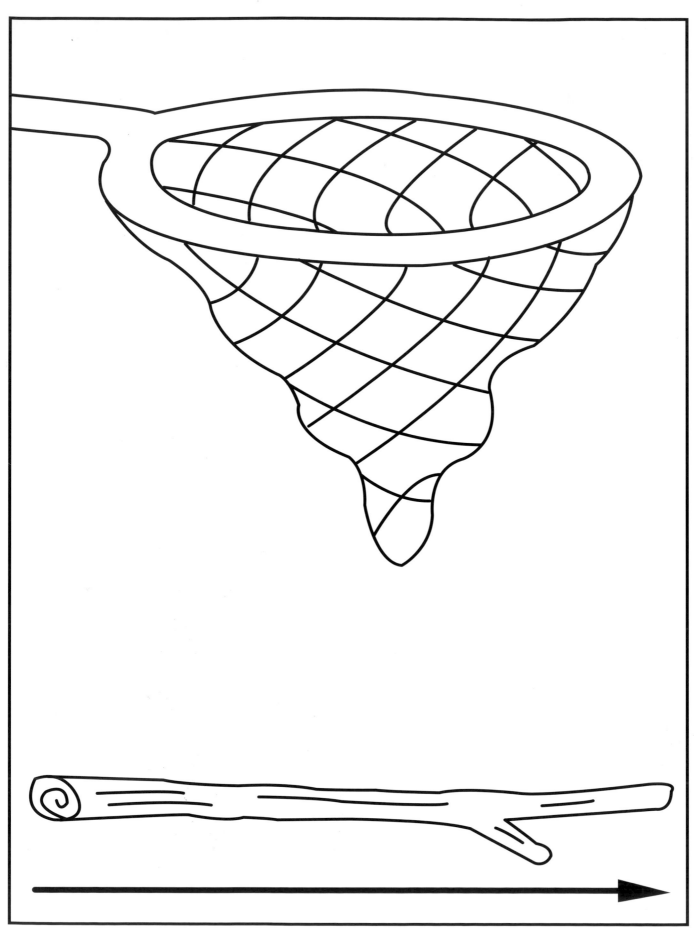